The Culture of
The Babylonian Talmud

THE JOHNS HOPKINS UNIVERSITY PRESS

Also by the Author

Talmudic Stories:
Narrative Art, Composition, and Culture

The Culture of
The Babylonian Talmud

Jeffrey L. Rubenstein

The Johns Hopkins University Press
Baltimore & London

This book has been brought to publication with the generous assistance
of the Boone Estate Endowment.

Johns Hopkins Paperbacks edition, 2005
2 4 6 8 9 7 5 3 1

The Johns Hopkins University Press
2715 North Charles Street
Baltimore, Maryland 21218-4363
www.press.jhu.edu

The Library of Congress has cataloged the hardcover edition of this book as follows:
Rubenstein, Jeffrey L.
The culture of the Babylonian Talmud / Jeffrey L. Rubenstein.
p.   cm.
Includes bibliographical references and index.
ISBN 0-8018-7388-6 (hardcover: alk. paper)
1. Talmudic academies.   2. Talmud—Criticism, Redaction.   3. Rabbis—
Iraq—Babylonia—Intellectual life.   4. Aggada—History and criticism.
5. Talmud—Language, style.   6. Logic—Iraq—Babylonia.   7. Narration
in rabbinical literature.   I. Title.
BM502.R93 2003
296.1'25067—DC21   2002156775

ISBN 0-8018-8265-6 (pbk.: alk. paper)

A catalog record for this book is available from the British Library.

Contents

Chapter 7

Elitism: The Sages and the Amei ha'arets 123

Chapter 8

Conclusion: The Legacy of the Stammaim 143

Preface and Acknowledgments

T*he Culture of the Babylonian Talmud* builds on some lines of thought explored in my previous book, *Talmudic Stories: Narrative Art, Composition, and Culture*. I argued there that the redactors of the Babylonian Talmud (the Bavli), the Stammaim, made a significant contribution to Talmudic narratives, often revising the Palestinian versions they received in profound ways. In detailed studies of six narratives I pointed out the evidence of the intervention by the Stammaim and illustrated the compositional techniques with which they reworked their sources. Many narrative traditions, especially the lengthy, highly developed stories, therefore shed light on the cultural situation of the Stammaim, who should be considered the storytellers or authors. The concluding chapter included a brief section on the themes that cut across these stories, themes largely absent from the parallel Palestinian accounts, that I believe point to leading concerns of Stammaitic culture. This book offers expanded discussion of those themes, analysis of other issues found in Stammaitic sources, and comprehensive documentation for those claims that draws on sources throughout the Bavli. It differs from previous scholarly treatments by focussing on these narratives as sources that shed light on late Babylonian rabbinic culture.

Earlier versions of several chapters appeared in the following journals, and I thank the editors for permission to reprint and revise them: "The Thematization of Dialectics in Bavli Aggadah," *Journal of Jewish Studies* (forthcoming, 2003) (=Chapter 2); "The Bavli's Ethic of Shame," *Conservative Judaism* 53:3 (2001), 27-39 (=Chapter 4). Some of the translations and analysis draw on my previous books *Talmudic Stories: Narrative Art, Composition, and Culture* (Baltimore, MD: Johns Hopkins University Press, 1999) and *Rabbinic Stories* (Classics of Western Spirituality; Mahwah, NJ: Paulist Press, 2002), and I am grateful for permission to reprint them here.

Much of this book was written during a Sabbatical leave generously granted by New York University. The Skirball Department of Hebrew and Judaic Studies has been a fertile environment to study and teach, and I have been blessed with outstanding colleagues and students, all of whom have provided encouragement while I worked on this project. I would like to thank Matthew Santirocco, Dean of the College of Arts and Sciences, and Lawrence Schiffman, chairman of the department, for their constant support. I am most indebted to Michael Satlow, who reviewed the manuscript for the press and made detailed comments and suggestions that improved the book considerably. I am extremely grateful to friends and colleagues who read and commented on drafts of chapters and who assisted me with particular questions: Adam Becker, Robert Chazan, Yaakov Elman, Charlotte Fonrobert, David Weiss Halivni, Catherine Hezser, Jonathan Klawans, Aaron Mate, Leib Moskowitz, James Robinson, Jay Rovner, Seth Schwartz, Lawrence Schiffman, Elliot Wolfson.

I warmly thank all of my family, relatives and friends for their support. My mother, father, brother and extended family have given me unconditional encouragement and love: Denise, Arthur, Errol, Evelyn, Milton, Ronald, Miriam, Shulie, Dan, Rena, Talia, Sarah, Gili, Chaya, Dani, Raquel, Tracey, Ivor, Maureen, and Ezra too.

My daughter Ayelet was born as I began work on this book, and my daughter Maya as I completed it. They are responsible for slowing down the rate of progress, but making the endeavor so much more enjoyable.

This book is dedicated to my wife Dr. Mishaela Ruth Rubin. Her unusual capacity to love—as wife, daughter, sister, mother, and friend—continually enriches my life and the lives of all her friends and relatives.

~∴~

Abbreviations and Conventions

Full bibliographic information for the editions listed below appears in the Selected Bibliography.

In parentheses following references to rabbinic texts I provide the page numbers of the editions used in the citation. Thus, *LevR* 5:1 (123) = *Leviticus Rabbah, parasha* 5, section 1, p. 123 in Margulies's edition.

All translations of rabbinic texts are my own unless otherwise indicated. Square brackets in the translations indicate words and phrases that do not appear explicitly in the original but are needed to understand the source. This information is essentially entailed in the wording and would have been understood by the audience. Parentheses in the translations enclose explanations that most likely underpin the source, though they are not as strongly implied by the actual language. Translations of biblical verses are from the New Jewish Publication Society translation, although I have freely modified them when needed.

Hebrew transliteration is phonetic: q = ק, kh = כ, ts = צ, h – ח. I have not differentiated א from ע, ח from ה, or ס from ש except when a philological point is at issue. The *dagesh* is generally not represented.

AJSR	*Association for Jewish Studies Review*
ARNA	'*Avot derabbi natan,* version A (ed. S. Schechter)
ARNB	'*Avot derabbi natan,* version B (ed. S. Schechter)
b	Bavli (Babylonian Talmud)
b.	ben, bar (= son of)
BT	Babylonian Talmud
DQS	*Diqduqei sofrim,* ed. Rabbinovicz. For *Seder Nashim,* ed. Hershler and Liss

GenR	*Genesis Rabba* (*Midrash bereshit rabba,* ed. J. Theodor and H. Albeck)
HUCA	*Hebrew Union College Annual*
JJS	*Journal of Jewish Studies*
JQR	*Jewish Quarterly Review*
LamR	*Lamentations Rabba* (ed. S. Buber)
LevR	*Leviticus Rabba* (*Midrash vayiqra rabba,* ed. Margulies)
m	Mishna
ms, mss	manuscript, manuscripts
OG	*Otsar hageonim* (ed. B. Lewin)
PRK	*Pesiqta derav kahana* (ed. Mandelbaum)
QohR	*Qohelet Rabba* (Vilna printing)
R.	Rabbi (Palestinian sages are usually designated as "Rabbi"; Babylonians as "Rav")
SifDeut	*Sifre* to Deuteronomy (ed. L. Finkelstein)
t	Tosefta (ed. S. Lieberman or M. Zuckermandel)
y	Yerushalmi. First printing, Venice, 1523 (facsimile: Leipzig, 1925).

.:.~

Tractates

References to tractates are preceded by b (Babylonian Talmud), y (Yerushalmi or Palestinian Talmud), t (Tosefta) or m (Mishna). Thus, bNaz 35a refers to Babylonian Talmud, Tractate Nazir, folio 35a; and tBer 6:5 refers to Tosefta, Tractate Berakhot, chapter 6, paragraph 5.

Ah	Ahilot	Makh	Makhshirin
A	Arakhin	Me	Meila
AZ	Avoda Zara	Meg	Megilla
BB	Bava Batra	Men	Menahot
Bekh	Bekhorot	Mid	Middot
Ber	Berakhot	MQ	Moed Qatan
Bes	Besa	MS	Ma'aser Sheni
Bik	Bikkurim	Naz	Nazir
BM	Bava Metsia	Ned	Nedarim
BQ	Bava Qama	Nid	Nidda
De	Demai	Par	Para
Ed	Eduyot	Pe	Pe'a
Eruv	Eruvin	Pes	Pesahim
Git	Gittin	Qid	Qiddushin
Hag	Hagiga	RH	Rosh Hashana
Hal	Halla	Sanh	Sanhedrin
Hul	Hullin	Shab	Shabbat
Kel	Kelim	Sheq	Sheqalim
Ket	Ketubot	Shev	Sheviit
Kil	Kilayim	Shevu	Shevuot
Ma	Ma'aserot	Sot	Sota
Mak	Makkot	Suk	Sukka

Ta	Ta'anit	Yad	Yadayim
Tam	Tamid	Yev	Yevamot
Ter	Terumot	Yom	Yoma
Toh	Tohorot	Zev	Zevahim

The Culture of
The Babylonian Talmud

Introduction

The Babylonian Talmud or Bavli, the great compilation of rabbinic tradition edited in Sasanid Mesopotamia in the fifth through seventh centuries C.E., is arguably the most important Jewish text. While Judaism frequently is designated "the religion of the book"—and by "book" the Bible is meant—the Bavli occupied pride of place in rabbinic tradition.[1] Medieval and modern rabbinic academies based their curriculum almost exclusively upon the Bavli and its derivitive literature of commentaries, legal codes, and responsa. Not every Jew, of course, received the education and training necessary for Talmud study. Yet, from their rabbis, generations of Jews were schooled upon the laws, traditions, ethics, scriptural interpretations, and ideals of the Bavli. The culture of the Bavli is therefore crucial to understanding both the primary influence on the culture of rabbinic academies throughout medieval and modern times as well as important forces that impacted many general Jewish beliefs and practices.

This book argues that the Bavli's dominant culture is the product of its anonymous redactors (editors), known as "Stammaim," who lived 450–650 C.E. Their culture differed in significant respects from the culture of their predecessors, the sages named in the Talmud and known as Amoraim (200–450 C.E.), due to the development of a new form of social organization: the rabbinic academy. In Amoraic times small groups of sages studied with an individual master in disciple circles. By the fifth and sixth centuries C.E. permanent academic institutions had been organized, the precursors of the great rabbinic academies of the Islamic era. Bavli sources, especially stories about sages and other aggadic traditions, often tell of the issues and tensions of academic life and thereby provide a crucial window into the world of the academy.

The picture presented by Bavli traditions looks something like this: The rabbinic academy is an insular space. Sages leave their wives and homes for many years, take up residence at the academy, and spend all disposable time in passionate study of the beloved Torah. Their esteem for Torah as the ultimate good is accompanied by a contempt for outsiders and a devaluation of all other pursuits — sometimes even ostensibly praiseworthy spiritual activities such as prayer and the commandments — as inferior undertakings. A rigid hierarchy, perhaps even a tendency to dynastic succession, characterizes the organization of the academy. Leading positions are reserved for outstanding scholars who boast noble lineage, although whether knowledge or pedigree provides the primary claim to leadership is contested.

A highly competitive, even combative ethos prevails within the academy. The sages attempt to excel in dialectic argumentation, in the constant probing of traditions by propounding objections and providing solutions. Through such debates — many of which are hypothetical and artificial — the sages explore every aspect of Torah, creating new lines of analysis and expanding the ever-growing body of tradition. Debate is simultaneously the means to greater status and even rank. A sage gains respect and a higher position within the academic hierarchy by raising unimpeachable objections against his disputant's claims while successfully parrying objections against his opinions. This verbal sparring sometimes takes an unfortunate turn from healthy, competitive debate to insults and hostility, which can make the academy feel like a violent arena. A sage's constant fear is that he will be unable to answer attacks upon his position and suffer public humiliation. This is a grave danger, for the sages experience shame as a type of social death, and the failure to perform may also jeopardize their positions within the hierarchy. Yet, inasmuch as the victim suffers from being shamed, so the perpetrator risks divine punishment for shaming a fellow sage. To achieve academic success is therefore an extremely delicate task. Sages try to demonstrate their prowess in debate through brilliant arguments while simultaneously neither opening themselves to refutation nor offending their colleagues. This new emphasis on dialectical argumentation was critical to the process of redaction of earlier traditions and creation of the Babylonian Talmud as we know it.

The Stammaitic Innovation

To understand how and why Bavli culture differs from the previous rabbinic cultures it is helpful to compare the corresponding Talmud compiled in the Land of Israel, the Palestinian Talmud or Yerushalmi. Anyone who has studied even a small amount of Talmud is well aware of the striking differences between the Bavli and the Yerushalmi. The legal discussions of the Bavli are typically intricate, highly developed, and multitiered; those of the Yerushalmi tend to be brief and elliptical. The Bavli's argumentation is frequently sustained, an entire folio or more devoted to one topic; that of the Yerushalmi is generally terse, rarely continuing for more than a paragraph or two. Bavli *sugyot* (literary units; singular: *sugya*) often evince well-defined, precise structures; Yerushalmi *sugyot* are usually crude and unstructured.

Bavli argumentation, far more than that of the Yerushalmi, focuses on minority opinions, which have no bearing on practical law. Extended dialectical discussions probe different Amoraic opinions, testing, hypothesizing, and investigating various possibilities, and then conclude much where they start, often failing to arrive at any resolution whatsoever. The Bavli features contrived arguments that satisfy the structural needs of the *sugya* but add little substance to the discussion. We find spurious questions and forced answers as literary devices to emphasize aspects of the debate. Sections of the give-and-take may be repeated verbatim for rhetorical or pedagogical purposes. In many cases rhetoric and style, more than substantive law or final conclusions, motivated the construction of argumentation. Rarely are these phenomena found in the Yerushalmi.

It is tempting to attribute these differences between the Bavli and the Yerushalmi to chronological disparity. The last sages named in the Yerushalmi lived in the mid fourth century C.E., and most scholars assume that the redaction took place shortly thereafter (360–370 C.E.).[2] The last sages of the Bavli are usually identified with the sixth generation of Amoraim, who lived from about 380–420 C.E. However, sages of the seventh and eighth generations (c. 420–480) are mentioned sporadically, as are occasionally even later sages. Perhaps the latest authority named is Rav Revai of Rov, who died about 550, according to Geonic traditions.[3] The redaction of the Bavli therefore continued well into the sixth century C.E., and probably into the seventh. This puts at least two centuries (400–600), perhaps as many as three (350–650), between the completion of the two Talmuds. Such a vast time span clearly would allow for material to accrete and the complexity to increase as generation after generation made their contribution.[4]

Yet chronological disparity can provide but a partial explanation. The differences between the Bavli and Yerushalmi are as much qualitative as quantitative. The Bavli is not simply a lengthier version of the Yerushalmi containing more traditions and additional voices in the discussions. The texture of the Bavli's argumentation, the style of its discourse, the character of its literary units, the flow of the text — all differ markedly from its Palestinian counterpart. A span of 200–300 years, however, is ample time for styles,

interests, and values to change along with shifting social, political, economic, and cultural circumstances. To the extent that we look to the relative
chronology as an explanation, it is that the intervening centuries gave rise to
new intellectual trends. Innovation, more than accretion, gave the Bavli its
distinct character. The question then becomes, When did that innovation
take place?

A closer look at the two Talmuds reveals that the major differences are
concentrated in one of the Bavli's layers. The Bavli contains two distinct literary strata: traditions attributed to named sages, that is, statements of the
Amoraim (*memrot*), on the one hand, and unattributed or anonymous material (*stam*), on the other. Attributed statements in the Bavli and Yerushalmi
are very similar in style. Most are brief, apodictic statements of law or comments to the Mishna. It is in the anonymous material of the two Talmuds,
which generally provides analysis of, and context for, the Amoraic traditions, where the major disparity is found. That of the Bavli exhibits the complex argumentation and rhetorical features described above. That of the Yerushalmi does not differ much from the terse style of the Amoraic stratum.
The anonymous stratum comprises about half the text of the Bavli. That of
the Yerushalmi is extremely thin, amounting to about one-tenth of the text.[5]
If one removes the anonymous stratum of the Bavli and compares the Amoraic material with the Yerushalmi, the styles of the texts are quite similar.[6]

Talmudic scholars have determined that the anonymous layer of the Bavli
postdates the Amoraic stratum.[7] This layer is the legacy of a later group of
sages, whom David Weiss Halivni called "Stammaim," after the term for
the "anonymous Talmud" (*stam hatalmud*). The Stammaim were redactors
insofar as they created *sugyot* that included the Amoraic traditions they
inherited. But they can simultaneously be considered the "authors" of the
Bavli (to the extent that the concept of authorship applies) in that they
placed those Amoraic traditions in a sustained superstructure of their own
composition.

From the fact that the Stammaitic stratum contains most of the Talmud's
argumentation, Halivni concluded that a shift in values took place between
the Amoraic and Stammaitic periods. Whereas the Amoraim valued practical law and the conclusions of legal discussions, the Stammaim placed
higher value on the argumentation itself. The Amoraim preserved only conclusions of their debates, which they formulated as brief traditions to be
memorized and passed on to succeeding generations. Because Talmudic tradition was oral and had to be committed to memory, verbal economy was
necessary. The essential tradition, the conclusion alone, was preserved and
transmitted during Amoraic times. The Stammaim, however, attempted to

reconstruct the argumentation that produced the conclusions and to preserve it for posterity.[8]

Fundamental differences between the Bavli and the Yerushalmi therefore should be attributed to the Stammaim. The innovative argumentation of the Bavli and the intellectual shift it represents likewise should be identified with the transition from the Amoraic to Stammaitic periods. The Stammaim subjected Amoraic traditions to an extended and heavy-handed redactional process that created a *talmud* substantially different from that which had existed before, a process to which Palestinian traditions were not subjected. The Bavli's distinct character, its sequences of logical argumentation, its highly structured literary units, its style and rhetoric — all are products of this group of author-redactors. Around the beginning of the fifth century C.E. there was a significant break with the past and the beginning of an independent cultural period characterized by new values and expressive styles.

Choosing to express themselves anonymously, the Stammaim left no overt testimony to this intellectual shift, to their penchant for debate and love of argumentation, much less to their identities or existence. But they did leave one acknowledgement of historical change in the Talmud. A brief anecdote relates that Shmuel found a tradition recorded in the "Book of Primordial Adam," apparently a compendium of esoteric lore, that "Ravina and Rav Ashi are the end of instruction" (*sof horaa;* bBM 86a). Ravina and Rav Ashi were the leading sages of the sixth and seventh generations of Babylonian Amoraim, and "instruction" (*horaa*) is a technical term for Amoraic rulings.[9] The "end of instruction" means that these sages, representing other sages of their time, were the last to have the authority to legislate in this way. In other words, they were the last to possess the status of Amoraim. Now, major intellectual and cultural changes, even abrupt ones, do not happen over night, and the breaks are rarely as neat as presented by schematic periodization; so we find a few traditions attributed to sages of later generations, as mentioned above. Nevertheless, from the retrospective view of the Stammaim, a watershed took place after the sixth and seventh Amoraic generations. The Amoraic period ended then, and a new, postclassical age began. Unfortunately, beyond this vague allusion to the "end of instruction," the Stammaim tell us nothing explicit of their values, ideas, conflicts, and cultural situation.

There is one available window into the culture of the Stammaim. Recent Talmudic research has shown that the Stammaim made a parallel contribution to the aggadic portions of the Talmud.[10] Their influence was not confined to *halakha,* to the explanation and justification of legal debates, but extended to exegetical and narrative traditions. Many Bavli stories, especially the longer and more literarily developed ones, evince marked disparities when compared to the parallel versions preserved in the Yerushalmi and in Palestinian midrashim. Detailed comparison reveals that the earlier versions were reworked with techniques similar to those with which legal traditions were revised to form the complex Bavli *sugyot*.[11] Often these stories contain motifs, issues, and language unprecedented in the Yerushalmi but found in late Bavli legal passages. Certain descriptions and details cohere with those found in post-Talmudic Geonic traditions, pointing again to a late provenance. In other words, the Bavli storytellers and homilists, in many cases, were the Stammaim.[12]

That stories and other aggadic traditions should bear evidence of Stammaitic concerns is plausible also because of the nature of the genre. In antiquity biographical anecdotes, historical accounts, and other narratives were not preserved out of a dispassionate interest in history or biography. By modern standards these ancient narrative types should be classified as didactic fiction.[13] Authors wrote, and storytellers told, stories in order to instruct their audience, to teach morals, to stake claims, and to provide positive and negative models. Stories accordingly had to be relevant to the audience and the audience's situation, values, conflicts, and struggles or they would not be transmitted or preserved. Oral narrative, in particular, is generally far more malleable than stories transmitted in writing. As storytellers retell stories they update them so as to make them comprehensible and pertinent to their audience. They tend to jettison older terms that would be poorly understood, transform anachronistic situations, and replace obsolete issues with contemporary concerns. Moreover, in an oral milieu a storyteller typically receives, memorizes, and transmits only the skeletal outline of the story. When he performs it in front of an audience, however, he embellishes the core plot with vivid descriptions, additional twists and turns, character development, and other improvised details in order to spark the audience's interest. Those enhancements typically are taken from his or her experience.

As the Stammaim retold the stories they received from Palestinian sources and the Babylonian Amoraim, they refracted them through the prism of their experience. Many changes occurred unintentionally or subconsciously as transmitters replaced outmoded ideas with those more familiar to them. However, recent studies have shown that numerous changes resulted from a process of deliberate, intentional reworking.[14] We must keep in mind that aggadic traditions carried much less authority than halakhic dicta.[15] The Stammaim were reluctant to meddle with the legal statements of the Amoraim but had less compunction about "modifying" exegetical or narrative elements. In my opinion the reworking of stories also provided the

Stammaim with an indispensable way to address leading tensions of their times. Because they chose to function anonymously and no longer to formulate authoritative dicta, they had little opportunity to grapple with contemporary concerns in an explicit manner. To retell stories of earlier sages, casting them in their own image and reworking the plots, provided the Stammaim a means to express themselves while preserving the veneer of anonymity. In all these ways stories and homiletical traditions absorbed elements of Stammaitic culture. By carefully attending to these traditions and the differences from Palestinian sources, we catch glimpses of the culture of the Stammaim.

This book attempts to describe aspects of Stammaitic culture by studying the motifs, themes and issues that repeatedly appear in late narrative and midrashic traditions. The window to that culture, to be sure, is narrow, and methodological problems impede the view. But the reward is proportionately great. For the culture of the Stammaim pervades the Bavli. By studying the origins and dynamics of fundamental elements of Bavli culture, we can understand the forces that shaped important streams of Jewish intellectual history and influenced the culture of rabbinic academies until the present day.

Methodological Considerations

The main methodological challenge for this type of study is that of distinguishing Stammaitic from Amoraic material.[16] Unfortunately, not every tradition can be definitively assigned to one of the two strata. The different formal and stylistic characteristics of the Amoraic and Stammaitic strata outlined above are found frequently in halakhic material but less often in aggadic traditions. While recent studies have identified characteristics of the processes of Stammaitic reworking of aggadic traditions, in some cases the extent of that reworking is difficult to establish. As a consequence, while some aggadic traditions can be assigned to the Stammaim based on defined characteristics and other considerations, in other cases it is difficult to determine whether the tradition has been reworked and now reflects Stammaitic concerns or was not reworked and expresses authentic Amoraic ideas.

What can be shown with more confidence is that a particular motif is Babylonian, not Palestinian, despite the fact that the Bavli attributes statements containing the motif to Palestinian sages. The optimal evidence of a distinctly Babylonian issue derives from comparisons between parallel versions of sources found in the Bavli and in Palestinian works such as the Yerushalmi. Because the Palestinian versions generally predate those of the Bavli, and in many cases were the sources of those Bavli versions, the differences most likely result from the different interests of the Babylonian sages.[17] This obtains even if the tradition is attributed to a Palestinian sage in the Bavli or appears in a source that resembles a *baraita*.[18] It is extremely implausible that a second Palestinian version, though not preserved in Palestinian works, made its way to Babylonia and was transmitted in pristine condition. Let us briefly look at one example to illustrate this strategy. A tradition found in both the Yerushalmi and the Bavli relates R. Eleazar's response to a difficult question posed to him:

yBik 1:8, 64d	*bBB 81a–b*
R. Eleazar said to him: "You ask about a matter which the sages of the assembly-house still need [to explain]."	He [R. Eleazar] said to him, "Do you ask me in the study-house about a matter which former scholars did not explain in order to shame me?"

In the Yerushalmi R. Eleazar simply explains why he does not know the answer: it is a very difficult issue that the sages as a group have not resolved. In the Bavli, however, R. Eleazar responds with annoyance, protesting that the inquirer is liable to embarrass him by exposing his inability to answer before the other sages present in the study-house. I take this difference as evidence that shame, especially the danger of being shamed in the study-house or academy, is a Babylonian concern. As we shall see in chapter 4, the theme of public humiliation appears in many other Babylonian sources.

Second, some themes consistently appear in numerous traditions in the Bavli, including many attributed to Palestinians, but are never found in Palestinian compilations. Yet we lack parallel Palestinian versions with which we can directly compare the traditions to pinpoint the Babylonian coloring. In such cases too it is most likely that Babylonian tradents have reworked earlier Palestinian traditions. That a theme is authentically Palestinian but somehow escaped all mention in the Palestinian works themselves is very unlikely. The Bavli, for example, contains a number of extremely negative traditions concerning the *am ha'arets*, the nonlearned or nonrabbinic Jew, including the dispensation to tear him apart "like a fish."[19] These traditions are attributed to Palestinian sages, and some appear in purported *baraitot*, yet not one of these traditions has a parallel in the Yerushalmi or in other Palestinian documents. Genuine Palestinian sources describe the *am ha'arets* in a different way and have a much more benign view. In all likelihood the negative traditions reflect an elitist Babylonian attitude and have been retrojected to earlier Palestinian sages.

These two types of evidence of Babylonian provenance will be combined with documentation of characteristic signs of Stammaitic reworking wherever possible. The evidence includes the formal and stylistic markers of the Stammaitic halakhic stratum, linguistic peculiarities, parallels in other late texts, syntactic difficulties that point to a gloss, dependence on earlier traditions, lack of attestation among the dicta of Babylonian Amoraim, manuscript variants, and content.

Thus, I present a hypothesis and data, and argue that the data are best explained by the hypothesis. The data are that certain motifs and themes appear exclusively in the Bavli, sometimes attributed to Palestinian sages, but never in Palestinian sources themselves. The hypothesis is that these concerns result from Stammaitic redaction, from the reworking of Amoraic traditions, and hence shed light on Stammaitic culture. The alternative hypothesis, that Babylonian Amoraim revised the Palestinian material, is less likely. First, there is little evidence that Amoraim reworked traditions in the same way as did the Stammaim.[20] That is, we know that the Stammaim substantially revised earlier traditions, hence the presumption should be that they, not the Amoraim, are responsible for these reworkings too. Second, in many cases the motifs do not appear in any Babylonian Amoraic dicta but only in narratives and traditions attributed to Palestinians.[21] If the Babylonian Amoraim revised the Palestinian sources we would expect to find the motifs occasionally attested in their legal dicta too. Third, the shift from the Amoraic to Stammaitic periods constitutes a break with the past. As suggested above, it was probably the rise of rabbinic academies that was responsible for the cultural shift. Uniquely Babylonian concerns that cannot be connected to the direct influence of the ambient cultures are best explained as products of the new culture of the Stammaitic academy.[22] Finally, since some traditions can be assigned with confidence to the Stammaitic stratum based on specific considerations, it stands to reason that similar traditions that cannot be dated with certainty should be assigned a similar provenance.

Let me emphasize that I am not arguing for a radical discontinuity between Amoraic and Stammaitic times, despite speaking of a break with the past. The later generations of Babylonian Amoraim had more in common with the Stammaim than earlier generations did. Where differences between the Bavli and Yerushalmi can be coordinated with known differences between Greco-Roman and Sasanian cultures, we should consider the cultural element to be Amoraic, not specifically Stammaitic. Chapter 5, for example, assesses an issue of this type. In most other cases discussed here, however, I see little evidence of the direct influence of the ambient cultures.[23] These cases tend to deal with the internal concerns, institutions, and relationships of the rabbis, and the differences more profitably can be attributed to a new social setting and self-conception.

In taking an approach that neither ignores attributions nor accepts them completely I am trying to avoid the pitfalls of two methods that enjoy some currency among scholars today. The first, associated primarily with Jacob Neusner and known as the "documentary approach," focuses almost exclusively on the final form of the Bavli.[24] Neusner holds that the final redactors exercised complete control over antecedent sources, reworking them at will, such that the attempt to discern earlier layers is futile and misguided. Everything within the Bavli represents the Bavli at its final stage of redaction. This method treats attributions and early traditions skeptically, arguing that there is no way to verify that particular sages made the statements — or anything remotely like them — which the Bavli places in their mouths. It also rejects the possibilities of distinguishing Babylonian from Palestinian traditions within the Bavli and of separating Amoraic from Stammaitic sources.

The second approach accepts attributions as reliable indicators of earlier traditions.[25] While proponents of this method do not necessarily believe that the sage articulated the exact words attributed to him, they claim that the tradition probably represents his basic views. Some errors such as the interchange of two similar names or the confusion of a student's statement with that of his master occasionally occur, but these exceptions do not impugn the overall presumptive reliability of attributions. This method considers traditions attributed to Palestinian sages in the Bavli as accurately representing Palestinian views. Similarly, *baraitot* are considered authentic Palestinian sources even if they are found only in the Bavli and not in the Tosefta and other Palestinian compilations.

Neither approach is completely satisfactory, as both are contradicted by empirical evidence. If one compares Amoraic statements in the Yerushalmi with their parallels in the Bavli, one finds considerable variation in the accuracy of transmission. In some cases the Bavli transmits exactly the same words, in some cases the Bavli version expresses an equivalent idea in a paraphrase, and in other cases the Bavli's version differs markedly or completely contradicts the Palestinian original.[26] Similar variations appear when *baraitot* are compared.[27] Some appear in almost exactly the same form in the Bavli; others have been changed substantially. Still others are completely fabricated.[28] Although the cases of exact duplication still do not prove that sages actually articulated the words attributed to them, they demonstrate that in some cases the Bavli redactors preserved traditions exactly as they received them.[29] While there is no external repository of Babylonian Amoraic traditions with which to compare those found in the Bavli, we can expect that these traditions received similar treatment. Thus, one can neither accept all attributions as reliable indicators of Amoraic tradition nor reject them *in toto*.

Both approaches, moreover, are based on false assumptions concerning the powers and policies of tradents and redactors. The first assumes that transmitters and redactors exercised complete control over antecedent traditions, reworking them without constraint to suit their own needs and purposes. Later sages, however, considered earlier traditions holy and saw themselves primarily as conduits.[30] A widely known and authoritative tradition could not be easily changed, no matter how distressing to later sensibilities. Such traditions were reinterpreted, recontextualized, and glossed, but in most cases they were not totally fabricated. The second assumes that transmitters and redactors possessed almost photographic memories and never made mistakes. But unintentional errors in transmission inevitably occur, as do subconscious changes. Traditions received in corrupted or confused form would be reconstructed to the best of the redactors' abilities but might not accurately represent the original form. And as we have said, aggadic traditions and stories were not vested with the same authority as legal sources; here later tradents sometimes intentionally modified traditions in light of their situations.[31] This odd blend of pious conservatism and innovation is difficult for us moderns to understand. As with so many other cases, it is a puzzling, but characteristic, aspect of the ancient mentality.

If these methodological considerations seem messy, it is because the nature of the evidence — the attribution, transmission, and redaction of rabbinic traditions — is indeed messy. For those who reject my methodology, this study still has value in demonstrating general differences between the rabbinic cultures of Babylonia and Palestine, although not specifically Stammaitic culture. They will have to find other explanations for the differences — another hypothesis to explain the data. As noted above, some of these differences indeed have roots in the Amoraic period. In other cases, when we look at consistent tendencies found in numerous sources, distinctions between the Stammaim and their Amoraic predecessors appear. Those differences comprise the essence of the Stammaitic contribution to rabbinic culture.

Finally, a brief word on my use of the term "culture" is apposite. I am clearly not using the term to refer to anthropological field work or ethnography, but in the more general sense of a society and its way of life. Neither the material culture of the Talmudic rabbis nor other documentary evidence survives. Yet the Talmud is itself a literary artifact of significant proportion, and one that contains a variety of genres — law, narrative, exegesis, homily, maxims, and so forth. Reading and interpretation of these genres therefore provide some access to elements of the web of rabbinic beliefs and practices. Clifford Geertz compares the approach of the ethnographer analyzing culture to that of a literary critic analyzing a text, "sorting out the structures of signification . . . and determining their social ground and import. . . . Doing ethnography is like trying to read (in the sense of 'construct a reading of') a manuscript."[32] For the study of rabbinic culture, we might say that doing ethnography *is exactly* analyzing a text to uncover those structures of signification. The diversity of sources, the different literary strata, and the voices of sages over the course of four hundred years render the Bavli an excellent candidate for a type of literary ethnographic study.

My choice of the term "culture" also indicates an attempt to go beyond a straightforward enterprise of literary criticism to achieve a broader vision of the nature of rabbinic society. To some extent I am trying to explicate the ideology of the Stammaim, and certain chapters are oriented towards describing attitudes and dispositions.[33] Yet my main goal is to understand the institutional framework in which the sages operated and how this contributed to their beliefs and practices. In other words, I mean to "observe" the sages and their way of life within the rabbinic academy, that is, observe the traces that the academy and academic life left within the Bavli.

This difficulty of reconstructing culture from literary texts confronts scholars of paganism and Christianity in late antiquity, not only scholars of rabbinic Judaism. To take a comparable example, consider the copious work spawned by Peter Brown's seminal research, on the late antique Christian "Holy Man," a social type some scholars suggest was analogous to the rabbinic sage.[34] Besides the hagiographical lives, the scholar enjoys all the sources available to classicists: historical writings; ecclesiastical records; inscriptions; archaeological remains of churches, monasteries, and mosaics; and so forth. Yet when it comes to understanding the Holy Man's actual role in Byzantine culture — his social function, relations with Church officials and peasants, religious practices — the only substantive resource is those accounts of the individual men's lives. Here the scholar encounters the same obstacle as the scholar of rabbinics, the problem of interpreting literature. Claims about culture based on texts are interpretative judgments open to question.[35]

Granted that literary texts are not transparent reflections of the rabbinic culture that produced them, they nevertheless both express and help create the wider set of ideas and patterns of behavior that constitute culture. Moreover, since the Bavli is largely dialogical in structure, presenting opinions and arguing them back and forth, significant cultural tensions are rarely suppressed.[36] They tend to be exaggerated, as two opposing sides contest issues as if conducting a heated debate. In this way study of Bavli traditions, their literary strata, internal tensions, and differences from Palestinian versions, illuminate aspects of Stammaitic culture.

Outline

The first part of the book describes aspects of the academic life represented in late Bavli stories, which I believe reflect the situation of the Stammaim. Chapter 1 discusses a number of sources that portray a highly structured and densely populated rabbinic academy. These depictions differ from both Palestinian sources and accounts of the Babylonian Amoraim, which describe gatherings of a much smaller scale. It appears that rabbinic institutions of higher learning (*yeshivot*) first developed in the Stammaitic period. This organizational innovation helps explain both the different concerns and values found in the Stammaitic stratum as well as the general shift from the Amoraic to Stammaitic eras. The formation of large-scale rabbinic academies created a sense of discontinuity with the past and a new self-conception. When we study the culture of the Bavli we study the culture of the Stammaitic academy.

Chapters 2–4 focus on prominent narrative motifs that point to the leading concerns of Stammaitic academic life. The same complex of stories that describes the rabbinic academy contains illustrations of the extensive dialectical abilities of the protagonists (Chap. 2). Leading sages engage successfully in the "give-and-take" of debate, propounding objections and solutions at will. In contrast to Palestinian sources, late Bavli traditions consider dialectical skill to be the acme of academic ability. Now, the bulk of the Stammaitic stratum of halakhic material is devoted precisely to dialectical argumentation. Thus, we see a close correlation between the halakhic literary production of the Stammaim and the aggadic descriptions of academic excellence. This correspondence provides further support for assigning these stories to the Stammaim.

Chapter 3 analyzes the thematization of violence. Many stories and midrashic traditions portray the academy as a hostile and dangerous place. Military imagery is frequently employed: sages battle for their opinions to prevail, attack opposing claims, and defend their rulings from verbal assaults. It seems that in the heat of debate some sages assailed their colleagues, rather than their colleagues' rulings, so that insults and verbal jabs were not uncommon. The violent character is probably a product of the emphasis on dialectical argumentation. If sages displayed their acumen and even gained status by propounding irrefutable objections against their peers, then the academy would have been experienced as an intensely competitive and combative arena. Portrayals of the academy or school-house as a violent forum are rare in Palestinian sources.

Chapter 4 takes up the motif of shame. While all rabbinic compilations warn that humiliating another person is a particularly serious sin, only the Bavli tells stories about sages who shamed others or experienced shame within the academy. The presence of numerous sages, which rendered the academy a public place, together with the importance of debate created the potential for humiliation. A sage who could not respond to an objection directed against his opinion experienced a loss of face and felt ashamed. That sages constantly risked public humiliation, and perhaps experienced it periodically, contributed to the conception of the academy as a dangerous place. We see here the close connections among the themes addressed in the first four chapters: the large-scale academy, the emphasis on argumentation, verbal violence, and the danger of shame.

The second part of the book turns to issues at the intersection of the academy and the world beyond. Chapter 5 explores the Bavli's surprising preoccupation with matters of lineage and kinship. Judaism had always esteemed lineage (*yihus*), especially priestly and Davidic descent. This historical legacy combined with the significance of pure pedigree in the ambient Persian culture to exert a powerful influence on the sages. Bavli stories present lineage as an important factor in contracting desirable marriages. Most importantly, it appears that noble lineage influenced academic status and even constituted a prerequisite to attaining the leading positions in the academic hierarchy. This influence, however, was contested by other sages, who evidently believed that authority should be vested in those most proficient in Torah. Stories that express this tension shed some light on the structure of the Stammaitic academy.

Chapter 6 examines tensions between Torah study and marital obligations. Both important rabbinic values, the conflict between the two is an inherent systemic tension of rabbinic Judaism, and we find it expressed from time to time in Palestinian sources. The tension seems to have been experienced more acutely, however, by the Stammaim, perhaps because the practice of leaving home for extended periods of study became more common among them. Bavli stories also describe Torah in erotic terms and as in competition with the wife for a sage's passions.

Attitudes of contempt for the *amei ha'arets,* Jews ignorant of Torah and who may have rejected rabbinic authority, are the subject of Chapter 7. The hostility depicted in Stammaitic traditions goes far beyond anything found in Palestinian sources. This elitist mentality probably resulted from a sense of distance or alienation from nonrabbis produced by the scholastic pursuits and academic life of the Stammaim.

The concluding chapter discusses the legacy of the Stammaim. Here I trace in subsequent Jewish history the main topics covered in the seven chapters of the book, charting lines of continuity and change. Through their contribution to the Bavli, the Stammaim played a formative role in many aspects of post-Talmudic rabbinic cultures.

Chapter 1

⌣∶⌢

The Rabbinic Academy

The Talmuds transmit a great many rabbinic conversations but provide comparatively little description of the settings in which those discussions took place. Various forums are mentioned — private house, study-house (*bet midrash, be midrasha*), assembly-house (*bet vaad*), academy (*yeshiva*), school (*be rav*), upper-story (*aliya*) — but few details are preserved about their structures. How large were these frameworks? How many sages and students gathered together? What protocol governed the discussions and study-sessions? Were the sages arrayed in a particular order? How were ranks and honors distributed?

In a comprehensive study of this topic, David Goodblatt concluded that the Babylonian Amoraim actually congregated on a smaller scale than had been thought previously.[1] The Bavli typically introduces an Amoraic discussion by stating that several sages "sat before" another rabbi. Such limited assemblies amounted to no more than "disciple circles" in Goodblatt's view, small groups of students who studied with a rabbinic master in a loose and informal association. These aspiring sages probably met at their master's residence or in a quiet, shady spot in the public domain to carry out their studies. Students would leave one teacher and proceed to another when their master died or when they felt the urge to seek other instruction. After a number of years they might try to strike out independently and attract a group of students of their own. "Disciple circles" were the common form of organization of Greco-Roman philosophers and characterize much of the higher learning in antiquity. The crucial point here is not the precise size of the group but the absence of institutions — permanent organizations with corporate identities that transcend the individuals present at any given time.[2]

Yet there are some Bavli traditions that paint a considerably different picture of rabbinic gatherings, hinting that large groups of sages assembled in a more established institutional arrangement:

> When the rabbis departed from the school of Rav, twelve hundred rabbis still remained.

> [When the rabbis departed] from the school of Rav Huna, eight hundred rabbis remained. Rav Huna expounded with thirteen speakers. When the rabbis would rise up [to depart] from the study-sessions (*metivata*) with Rav Huna and shake out their clothes, the dust would rise and cover the sun, and they would say in the West [Palestine], "They arose from the study-session of Rav Huna the Babylonian."

> When the rabbis rose [to depart] from the schools of Rabbah and Rav Yosef, four hundred rabbis remained, and they called themselves "orphans."

> When the rabbis departed from the school of Abaye — some say from the school of Rav Papa, and some say from the school of Rav Ashi — two hundred rabbis remained, and they called themselves "orphans among orphans" (bKet 106a).[3]

Although this tradition tells us much less than we would like to know, it gives the unmistakable impression that the sages congregated, at least periodically, in large assemblies. The "departing rabbis" apparently traveled to attend intermittent lectures of the leading sages, after which they returned to their places of residence. The remaining rabbis, on the other hand, seem to have been full-time students who remained with the master throughout the year.[4] Even controlling for the hyperbole, we have a vision that differs substantially from the small-scale disciple circle reflected in the vast majority of Bavli sources. A cadre of two hundred rabbis in residence still considers themselves "orphans of orphans," expressing a sense of isolation and of abandonment by their numerous colleagues. So populous was the assembly in Rav Huna's time that he required thirteen human loudspeakers to broadcast his words to the multitude. In an age before microphones, the large crowd depended on middlemen to shout out Rav Huna's words. The figure of the dust storm stirred up as the rabbis rise up and depart en masse indicates a population of prodigious size.

This tradition is clearly schematic.[5] The numbers incrementally decrease from 1,200 to 800 to 400 to 200 while the leading Babylonian Amora of each generation is mentioned: Rav, one of the founders of rabbinic Judaism in Babylonia (1st generation), his student and successor Rav Huna (2nd generation), Huna's student Rabbah together with Rav Yosef (3rd generation), their student Abaye (4th generation), his student Rav Papa (5th generation), and finally Rav Ashi, among the last of the Amoraim (6th generation). Post-Talmudic tradition anachronistically considered each of these sages to have been the head of the academy in his time: Rav and Rav Huna are associated with Sura; Rabbah, Rav Yosef, and Abaye with Pumbedita; Rav Papa with Neres; and Rav Ashi again with Sura. Indeed, the term *metivata,* which I have translated "study-sessions," also refers to rabbinic academies (*yeshivot*). Mention of the Palestinian perception and of Rav Huna as "the Babylonian" highlights the contrast between the two centers and focuses on the distinct Babylonian situation. The tradition essentially offers an exaggerated and nostalgic vision, romanticizing the halcyon days when study of Torah took place on a colossal scale. And while the numbers taper over the course of the Amoraic period, consistent with the generally pessimistic rabbinic historical view,[6] they nevertheless assume an institution of significant proportions.

Several Bavli traditions that point to large rabbinic gatherings purportedly depict Palestinian conditions, often those of the Tannaitic period. According to bBer 27b–28a, after the rabbis depose Rabban Gamaliel from his position as head of the academy and end his policy of restricting entry, they add either four hundred or seven hundred benches of students. The story does not tell us how many benches were initially there, but the increase itself is formidable. Reference to Gamaliel's title as "head of the academy" (*resh metivta*) points to a hierarchically structured institution. Another story about Rabbi's academy (*metivta*) relates that when Rabbi entered all the students scrambled to sit down: "Those who were nimble sat in their places; R. Ishmael b. R. Yose, because he was heavy, continued to stride [to his place]. Avdan said to him, 'Who is this who presumes to stride upon the heads of the holy people' (bYev 105b)?" In the continuation of the story the tables are turned when Avdan comes back after a brief exit from the academy: "Avdan was striding and going [to his place]. R. Ishmael b. R. Yose said to him, 'He whom the holy people needs may stride over the heads of the holy people; but how does he whom the holy people does not need stride over the heads of the holy people?'" Here the sages seem to be sitting on the floor (since those walking among them almost tread upon their heads) and to occupy designated positions. No numbers are given, but the fact that slowpokes have trouble getting to their places hints at a sizable and crowded assembly.

A comparable depiction of the academy appears in the story of Rav Kahana's travels to Palestine to attend the lectures of R. Yohanan (bBQ 117a–b). The Palestinian sages initially seat Rav Kahana in the first row of students, believing him to be a great sage, but subsequently move him back row by row until the seventh and final row. R. Yohanan sits atop seven cushions facing the rows of students. This description portrays a precise hierarchical arrangement with students positioned according to their scholarly abilities. Similarly, the famous story of God transporting Moses to the school of R. Akiba relates that Moses "went and sat at the back of eighteen rows of students, but he did not understand what they were saying" (bMen 29b).[7] Seated towards the rear with the most inferior students, Moses cannot follow the complicated discussions of Torah. Another story relates a conversation between R. Yohanan and a Babylonian sage named Isi b. Hini who had traveled to Palestine:

> He [R. Yohanan] asked him, "Who is the Head Teacher[8] in Babylonia?" He said to him, "Abba Arikha." He said to him, "You call him simply Abba Arikha? I remember that when I sat before Rabbi, seventeen rows behind Rav, sparks of fire flew from the mouth of Rabbi to the mouth of Rav, and from the mouth of Rav into the mouth of Rabbi, and I could not understand what they were saying! And you simply call him Abba Arikha?!" (bHul 137b)

R. Yohanan expresses surprise that Isi b. Hini neglects the honorific sobriquet "Rav," literally "Master," and calls the famous sage by his real name "Abba Arikha." He illustrates Rav's prowess by the imagery of flying sparks, probably symbolizing fast-paced debate, and by locating Rav many rows forward, evidently with the most proficient students. Here too the depiction of rabbinic study assumes a collection of numerous sages arranged according to ability. And again a sage in the rear cannot follow the heated interchanges of the leader with the top students. Yet another tradition relates that Resh Laqish eulogized a sage "who used to repeat halakhot before twenty-four rows of students" by calling him a "great man" (bMeg 28b).[9]

Can these traditions of large assemblies of rabbis be reconciled with Goodblatt's compelling evidence that the Babylonian Amoraim gathered in small disciple circles? One is tempted to suggest that large-scale academies were found only in Palestine, as most of the traditions surveyed above are set there. But this position cannot be defended. First, with one exception, none of these traditions has a parallel in Palestinian sources.[10] Nor are there comparable depictions of crowded academies full of students in Palestinian documents. Our knowledge of the nature of Palestinian rabbinic institutions is sparse, but no evidence suggests that large academies existed. In a recent study of rabbinic social organization in Palestine, Catherine Hezser concluded that "[t]here is no reason to assume that study houses, houses of meeting, or halls were 'rabbinic academies.' . . . Those study houses which were associated with a particular rabbi would have ceased to exist with that rabbi's death."[11] Second, as explained in the Introduction, to view these depictions as accurate historical memories of the Palestinian rabbis, their conflicts, and their academies ignores the consensus of recent scholarship on the rabbinic narrative.[12] Rabbinic stories are didactic fictions, not reliable historical accounts, and tell us more about the values, culture, and situation of the storytellers than of the characters. We are dealing with Babylonian (mis)representations of the Palestinian reality, not historical accounts of the Palestinian rabbinate. Third, almost all of these sources seem to be late Babylonian traditions, that is, they can be dated to the Stammaitic stratum.[13] For example, Daniel Sperber noted that the story of Rav Kahana contains Persian words and motifs attested in medieval Iranian sources and that the content—a polemic insisting on the superiority of the Babylonian sages—points to a post-Amoraic setting.[14] Significant descriptive elements do not appear in one of the manuscript traditions, which suggests that they were added at a considerably late stage.[15] Israel Ben-Shalom has argued that the Bavli portrayals of Avdan and R. Ishmael b. R. Yose in this story bear no resemblance to the way these characters appear in Palestinian sources and that their nasty interchange resembles the coloring found in other Bavli versions of Palestinian narratives.[16] The story of the deposition of Rabban Gamaliel contains post-Amoraic terminology and has been reworked with Stammaitic techniques.[17]

The most plausible explanation for the contradictory evidence is that the "aberrant" Bavli traditions depicting large assemblies of rabbis in a structured framework derive from the Stammaitic period.[18] The Amoraim, as Goodblatt argued, congregated in small disciple circles. Early in the Stammaitic period, in the late fifth or early sixth century, the sages formed large and enduring academic institutions, including the *yeshivot* of Sura and Pumbedita, that would continue to flourish in the Geonic era. As the Stammaim reworked earlier narratives and occasionally constructed new fictional stories, they introduced elements that reflected their own situation. The result: the vast majority of traditions of Amoraic interactions suggest that the sages gathered in small disciple circles, while a handful of sources, most of them lengthy and highly developed narratives bearing signs of late composition, point to the existence of academic institutions.

The depiction of the rabbinic academy in these traditions coheres with descriptions found in Geonic sources. Our most detailed picture of the structure of the Geonic academy (*yeshiva*) comes from the "Epistle of R. Nathan the Babylonian," a brief account of a visit to the Suran academy at Baghdad in the late tenth century.[19] Nathan arrived in Baghdad during one of the two *kallah* months during which disciples traveled to the academies for periods of intensive instruction:

> And this is the order in which they sit. The Head of the Academy stands [var.: sits] at the head, and before him are ten men [comprising] what is called the "first row," all facing the Head of the Academy. Of the ten who sit before him, seven of them are "Heads of the Kallah" and three are associates. . . .
>
> . . . And the seventy [comprising] the Sanhedrin are the seven rows. The first row sits as we mentioned. In back of them are [another] ten [and so on] until [there are] seven rows, all of them facing the Head of the Academy. All the disciples sit behind them without any fixed place. But in the seven rows each one has a fixed place, and no one sits in the place of his colleague. . . .
>
> When the Head of the Academy wants to test them in their studies, they all meet with him during the four Sabbaths of Adar. He sits and the first row recite before him while the remaining rows listen in silence. When they reach a section requiring comment, they discuss it among themselves while the Head of the Academy listens and considers their words. Then he reads[20] and they are silent, for they know that he has already discerned the matter of their disagreement. When he finishes reading, he expounds the tractate which they studied during the winter, each one at home, and in the process he explains what the disciples had disagreed over. Sometimes he asks them the interpretation of laws. They defer to one another and then to the Head of the Academy, asking him the answer. And no one can speak to him until he gives permission. And [then] each one of them speaks according to his wisdom. . . .[21]

The core of the academy, called the "Sanhedrin" after the ancient Jewish court, consists of seven rows of ten students each, consistent with the seven rows of R. Yohanan's academy in the story of Rav Kahana. Like R. Yohanan, the head of the academy sits before the rows and questions various students. Each member of the seven rows has a "set place" or rank, as is implied in the story of Avdan, and in the continuation of the passage R. Nathan explains how that place was determined.[22] Other "disciples" sit behind the seven rows without any set place. These may be the students who traveled to the academies for the two months of intensive study (the *kallah* months) as opposed to the seventy rabbis "in residence." The Bavli traditions that mention sitting behind numerous rows and not understanding the "sparks" flying from the brilliant rabbis seated up front seem to reflect the perspective of the disciples. The two-tiered organization of a permanent nucleus of rabbis and others who visit coheres with the tradition of the departing rabbis cited above. Later R. Nathan mentions that the number of disciples with no set place is about four hundred.[23] If so, we can well imagine that the core group felt like "orphans" when their colleagues went home at the end of the month.

These strong connections between the Talmudic traditions and Geonic sources suggest that academies similar to those of the Islamic era (7th–10th centuries) arose during Stammaitic times (5th–7th centuries). Because the Stammaim, for the most part, transmitted Amoraic halakhic traditions faithfully (except for unintentional changes and errors), the vast majority of Talmudic sources reflect the small disciple circles of the Amoraic period. But, because the Stammaim occasionally functioned as creative authors or active editors, especially with aggadic and narrative traditions, a few sources reflect the academies of post-Amoraic times.

To locate the rise of the rabbinic academy in the Stammaitic period may also help to account for one of the puzzles of Talmudic history. What explains the shift from the Amoraic to Stammaitic periods? Why did the sages stop functioning as Amoraim and attaching their (or their masters') names to sayings? What accounts for the "end of *horaah* (instruction)," the cessation of authoritative dicta, that the Bavli associates with the final Amoraim (bBM 86a)?[24] Shifts in periodization are notoriously difficult to explain, and few are as clean and neat as books of history suggest. Yet in this case the Talmud itself recognizes the end of one era and the beginning of another: at issue is the self-perception of the Bavli itself, not simply the conventions of modern scholars. Earlier Talmudic historians tended to adopt the "lachrymose conception of Jewish history," suggesting that persecutions at the end of the Amoraic period forced the closing of rabbinical schools and resulted in a new historical epoch.[25] Recent scholars, however, have generally abandoned this historiographical perspective and its propensity to attribute many significant historical changes to persecutions.[26] Moreover, in a detailed study, Richard Kalmin has argued that Sasanian persecutions do not satisfactorily account for the conclusion of the Amoraic era.[27]

It may be more profitable, then, to attribute this change to the rise of a new form of social organization, that is, the rabbinic academy. In other words, I am suggesting that the shift in styles from the short, apodictic utterances of the Amoraim to the expansive comments of the Stammaim, as well as the sense of the closing of a previous era (the end of *horaah*), are related to a shift in the institutional framework in which the rabbis operated. The production of a new literary stratum and a different set of values may reflect this larger structural change in the form of rabbinic association.[28] And the scholastic values of the Stammaim — dialectical argumentation, "objections and solutions," and hypothetical problems — suit the academic setting where numerous students study, train, and compete together.[29]

To engage in some speculation, one wonders whether the academic institutional framework is also responsible in part for the anonymous voice of the Stammaim, namely, the decision no longer to assign attributions. A disciple circle emphasizes individuality: one particular master teaches a few students. An academy, on the other hand, has a corporate identity: numerous students study under the tutelage of many masters simultaneously, as sages of varying degrees of ability are present. Whatever official policies or pronouncements an academy disseminates tend to be issued in the name of the academy rather than that of an individual sage. To compare the Geonic situation once again, it is striking that we know the names of only a handful of sages apart from the Geonim who were the heads of the academies. Robert Brody points out that while the Gaon alone had the prerogative to issue responsa, he spoke in the name of the sages of his academy as well.[30] Geonic responsa invariably make "use of the first-person plural, even when reference is made to the 'author' as an individual."[31] The sages of the academies debated the questions during their assemblies, hence the answers could be delayed until they had the opportunity to congregate.[32] In this way the Geonic academies functioned primarily as a collective body that cloaked the identities of the individual sages. If the Stammaim operated in comparable academies, or at least in institutions larger than disciple circles, they too may have experienced a type of corporate identity and therefore terminated the practice of preserving individual attributions. This may also explain why we find an occasional attribution to sages who lived between 450 and 550, whom Rav Sherira calls Saboraim, such as Rav Eina, Rav Revai of Rov, and Rav Ahai of Be Hatim.[33] They may have been the heads of the Stammaitic academies who spoke for all the sages of the academy, as did the Geonim. This theory, I emphasize, is speculative, as there is no direct evidence for the existence of Stammaitic academies, much less their operation. I offer it as a hypothesis to tie together some of the evidence cited above until a more satisfactory explanation is proposed.

The Academic Setting

In his monumental work, "Introduction to the Text of the Mishna," Jacob Nahum Epstein noted that where Palestinian sources mention the "assembly-house" (*bet vaad, be vaada*), the Bavli parallels tend to substitute "study-house" (*bet midrash, be midrasha*).[34] This phenomenon occurs in both halakhic and narrative sources. In the stories of the Oven of Akhnai, for example, the Yerushalmi relates that "the columns of the assembly-house were trembling" (yMQ 3:1, 81c–d), while the Bavli reports, "the walls of the study-house inclined to fall, " (bBM 59b). Similarly, a brief anecdote in the Yerushalmi tells that "the people" in the assembly-house wished to cease rising before R. Meir (yBik 3:3, 65c). The Bavli's considerably expanded story takes place in the study-house (bHor 13b–14a). Now, one could argue that the difference is simply terminological: that the Yerushalmi calls the rabbinic school-house the "assembly-house" while the Bavli calls it the "study-house," but both refer to the same institution. On the other hand, the Yerushalmi often mentions the "study-house," sometimes even juxtaposing it with the "assembly-house," which suggests these were different structures.[35] The "assembly-house" seems to be closer to, or even synonymous with, the "synagogue" (*bet keneset*), which literally translates "assembly-house." If so, then the Bavli may transform mentions of the assembly-house / synagogue, a community-oriented institution, into the study-house, a rabbinic institution. That is, while the Yerushalmi typically locates sages among nonsages in a community building, the Bavli storytellers assume the sages would be found in their own academic institution. This in turn may support our hypothesis that the Bavli redactors were located in an academic institution and imposed that situation on earlier sources.

Support for this conjecture can be found in the two versions of the story of the controversy provoked when a Babylonian sage intercalated the calendar, arrogating a traditional Palestinian prerogative. Both Talmuds relate that the Palestinian sages sent two scholars to Babylonia to deter the sage, Hananiah the nephew of R. Yehoshua, from proclaiming that an extra month should be added to the year. The emissaries, however, adopt different strategies:

ySanh 1:2, 19a	*bBer 63a*
R. Yizhaq rose and read [in the Torah], "These are the set times of Hananiah the son of R. Yehoshua's brother." They [the people] said to him, "[No! It says,] *The set times of the Lord (Lev 23:4).*" He said to them, "(That is the reading) with us (but apparently not with you.)"[36]	He began to rule impure and they [the emissaries] ruled pure. He forbade and they permitted. He announced concerning them, "These men are fraudulent. [These men] are vacuous." They said to him, "You have already built and you cannot destroy. You have already fenced in and you cannot break apart."[37]

R. Natan rose and read the *haftarah* [from the Prophets], "For Torah shall come forth from Babylonia and the word of God from Nehar Pekod."[38] They said to him, "[No! It says,] *For Torah shall come forth from Zion, the word of God from Jerusalem (Isa 2:3).*" He said to him, "(That is the reading) with us (but apparently not with you.)"

He said to them, "Why do I rule impure and you rule pure, I forbid and you permit?" They said to him, "Because you intercalate years and fix new moons outside of the Land [of Israel]."

. . . Why all this? Because it says, *For Torah shall come forth from Zion, the word of God from Jerusalem (Isa 2:3).*

The Yerushalmi describes the emissaries encountering Hananiah in what appears to be a synagogue. By misreading the Torah and *haftarah,* apparently in the course of the regular prayer service, they attempt to show the Babylonians the errors of their ways. The assembly who cry out upon hearing the phony verses are not identified but seem to be people congregated for prayer. In the Bavli, the encounter takes place in an academic setting. The emissaries do not read Scripture; they state phony rulings in the course of legal discussions in order to protest Hananiah's actions. The Bavli storytellers retain Isa 2:3, which contains the crucial datum that Torah should emanate from the Holy Land, the basis of the Palestinians' claim. But since they have replaced the synagogual scriptural reading with a legal debate, they utilize the verse as a general prooftext to conclude their account. Although the story takes place in Babylonia, the Yerushalmi storytellers set the affair where they expect rabbis to be found—the synagogue or community center. The Babylonian storytellers place the encounter in the study-house or academy, the institution with which they are familiar.[39]

A more telling sign of institutional developments in Babylonian rabbinic culture is the appearance of the study-house (*bet midrash*) as the setting for Bavli stories when no comparable location is given in the Palestinian versions. The Tosefta, for example, reports that a scorpion once bit R. Hanina b. Dosa while he was praying, but Hanina's disciples found the scorpion dead at the entrance of its hole (tBer 3:20). This story appears in the Yerushalmi with minor variants (yBer 5:1, 9a). In the Bavli, however, R. Hanina goes to the hole of the scorpion, lets it bite him, puts the dead scorpion on his shoulder and then goes to the study-house where he teaches a lesson about the cause of death (bBer 33a). Thus the Bavli locates an encounter between a master and his disciples specifically in the study-house. Similarly, the Yerushalmi relates: "Once R. Hiyya, R. Yasa and R. Ami went up to make the bridal canopy for R. Eleazar. They heard the voice of R. Yohanan. [They said], 'If he should speak a new word [of Torah], who will go down and hear it from him?' They said, 'Let R. Eleazar go down for he is very diligent. He went down and came back up'" (yBer 2:3, 5a). The Bavli, however, tells us: "Once R. Ami and R. Asi were decorating the bridal canopy of R. Eleazar. He said to them, 'Meanwhile I will go and hear a word in the study-house, and I will come back and bring it to you.' He went and heard a *tanna* reciting before R. Yohanan. . . . He returned and told them" (bBer 16a). In the Yerushalmi the sages overhear the voice of R. Yohanan and send R. Eleazar to listen to his teaching. No location is specified; that they overhear R. Yohanan's voice suggests that neither party was inside a study-house.[40] In the Bavli R. Eleazar goes to the study-house explicitly for the purpose of hearing Torah from R. Yohanan.

In some cases the Bavli goes an additional step, changing the location provided by the Palestinian source into the study-house. A story found in both Talmuds describes the tremendous honor that R. Tarfon showed his mother. In the Yerushalmi the story takes place in a private home: "Once the sages came to visit him [R. Tarfon] . . . and she told them his deed" (yQid 1:7, 61b). The Bavli parallel relates instead, "He [R. Tarfon] went and praised himself in the study-house," that is, that he (not his mother) told the other sages of his deeds in the study-house, not in his home (bQid 31b). The Bavli seems to have assumed that R. Tarfon would encounter his colleagues in a study-house, not a private home. The appropriate location for a discussion about the commandment of parental honor, in the view of the Bavli storytellers, is the study-house. Because his mother would have had no business there, the Bavli has R. Tarfon report his deed to his colleagues rather than have his mother speak directly to the sages. Similarly, the famous Mishna recounting the day when the sages of the House of Shammai outnumbered those of the House of Hillel and instituted eighteen decrees of Shammaite halakha locates the gathering in the "upper-story of Hananiah b. Hizqia b. Goren" (mShab 1:4). Numerous Tannaitic sources in fact place rabbinic meetings in the upper-stories of various private homes, presumably those of aristocratic families. Consistent with this Mishna, the Yerushalmi cites two *baraitot:* "R. Yehoshua Onaya taught: Students of the House of Shammai stood below and were killing those of the House of Hillel. It was taught: Six of them went up and the rest stood upon them with swords and spears" (yShab 1:4, 3c). Thus, the Yerushalmi traditions follow the Mishna, portraying the sages in a bilevel dwelling in which some stay below while others sit above. The Bavli, in contrast, recounts: "They stuck a sword in the study-house. They said: Let he who would enter, enter. But let he who would depart, not depart" (bShab 17a). The upper-story has been replaced by a study-house, which creates a certain degree of tension between the Bavli's tradition and the Mishnaic version. Unlike the previous examples, where the Yerushalmi gave no specific location and the Bavli set the event in the study-house, in these two cases the Bavli transforms the location given by Palestinian sources into a study-house. This relatively minor yet consistent alteration of Palestinian accounts suggests that the Bavli storytellers were located in a study-house or similar institution and imposed this aspect of their reality on the characters. They evidently considered it unusual that sages would congregate in a private home or undefined location where scorpions would be found and therefore shifted the action to an academic setting.

At the risk of belaboring the point, let me mention an example where Bavli storytellers could not locate the encounter between sages in the study-house but nevertheless felt compelled to address this consideration. Both Talmuds tell a story of a longstanding controversy between the House of Shammai and House of Hillel concerning the laws of levirate marriage.[41] In both Talmuds the rabbis hear that Dosa b. Harkinas, a great sage,[42] ruled like the House of Shammai, and they set out to investigate whether the report is accurate. The Yerushalmi states simply, "The sages went to Dosa to ask him . . ." The Bavli storytellers seem to have been puzzled by this datum. Why wasn't Dosa in the study-house / academy where the sages discuss such issues? The Bavli therefore relates, "His [Dosa's] *eyes were too dim for him to come to the study-house.* They [sages] said, 'Who will go and inform him?'" Now, the end of the Yerushalmi's version also alludes to Dosa's poor vision. Dosa says, "Lift up my eyes so that I can see the sages of Israel." The Bavli has transformed Dosa's blindness into the reason he was not in the study-house, which explains why the sages went to his residence to ask the question. In this case the story cannot be set in the study-house. The plot requires the sages to investigate whether Dosa b. Harkinas in fact rules against them, and it turns out that it is not Dosa but his brother, Yonatan b. Harkinas, to whom the sages then journey. In contrast to the previous cases, where the Bavli storytellers change the setting of their source from a private home to the study-house, here they take pains to clarify why an encounter between sages does not take place there but in a private home.

A more profound transformation occurs in the stories of Honi the Circle Drawer. Here the Bavli revises a story that has nothing to do with the study-house into a narrative that features the study-house and its dealings in a substantive way. In the Mishna Honi appears as a miracle worker who stands outside the orbit of the sages but successfully brings rain (mTa 3:8). Both Talmuds tell additional stories about Honi, portraying him as a Rip Van Winkle figure who falls asleep for seventy years. The Yerushalmi relates that when he awoke, "[t]hey said to him (Honi), 'We have heard that when he (= you, Honi) would go into the courtyard [of the temple] it would light up.' He entered, and it lit up" (yTa 3:10, 66d). In the Bavli version when Honi awakes he enters the study-house and hears the students say, "Our traditions are as light today as they were in the days of Honi, for when he entered the study-house, he would solve all the sages' difficulties" (bTa 23a). The physical light that shone when Honi entered the temple courtyard is transformed into intellectual light that shone when Honi entered the study-house. The change in setting from the temple to the rabbinic study-house is consistent with the general shift in Jewish piety from the temple and priestly cult to Torah and the rabbinic tradition. Together with the change in setting comes an interesting metaphorization of light into clarity of tradition. Once again, in the background we can sense the storytellers working in some kind of institutional environment akin to the rabbinic academy.

Heavenly Visions and Dreams

Two interesting reflexes of this phenomenon can be seen in depictions of rabbinic activities in the heavenly realm and in the interpretations of dreams. Both of these imaginative domains, though considered much more "real" in antiquity than today, allowed for greater creative expression than did stories of the past. To begin with the heavenly realm: Tannaitic sources mention the "heavenly court" (*bet din shel maala*) and occasionally the "heavenly session" (*yeshiva shel maala*), where the "session" refers to a session of the court. This image derives from a long tradition, dating back to the second temple and even biblical periods, which pictures God presiding in a heavenly court, surrounded by angels and righteous humans. Palestinian Amoraic literature provides similar allusions to the heavenly court. The Yerushalmi, for example, observes that, "The earthly court decreed three things and the heavenly court assented" (yBer 9:5, 14c). According to R. Hiyya bar Abba, "When Israel goes out to battle, the heavenly court judges them, whether they will defeat or be defeated" (yShab 2:6, 5b). In all of these traditions the heavenly court / session carries out judicial activities: judging, punishing, enacting decrees.[43] In Bavli traditions, however, the "heavenly session" begins to change its character into that of a study-house or academy, not a court. And eventually the word for session (*yeshiva, metivta*) came to designate the rabbinic academy, thereby complicating the translation. It is difficult to determine whether the term refers to a heavenly study-session or a heavenly academy. A fantastic legend about the demon king Asmodeus relates that "every day he goes up to heaven and learns the (or 'from the') heavenly session (*metivta*), and he goes down to the earth and learns the (or 'from the') earthly session" (bGit 68a).[44] While we do not exactly know where he studies—a heavenly court, study-house, or academy—the activity is Torah study, not court business. A tradition about Judah's posthumous fate that we will discuss in detail in the following chapter mentions a heavenly session / academy (*metivta deraqiyya*) that involves "debate with the sages" and solving objections.[45] Here the essential practices of the study-house / academy are projected onto the heavenly realm. Perhaps the most interesting such tradition concerns the summoning of Rabbah bar Nahmani.

> They were debating in the heavenly academy / session: If the leprous affection precedes the white hair—he is impure. If the white hair precedes the leprous affection—he is pure.[46] If it is in doubt [which precedes which]—the Holy One, blessed be he, says "Pure" and the whole heavenly session / academy says "impure." They said, "Who will decide? Let Rabbah bar Nahmani decide." For Rabbah bar Nahmani said, "I am unrivalled in [knowledge] of leprous impurity, I am unrivalled in [knowledge] of tent-impurity." They sent a messenger after him. (bBM 86a)

Rabbah bar Nahmani, as he dies, utters, "Pure, pure," apparently resolving the debate. In heaven the sages argue over a point of law with the Holy One himself. This is clearly not a trial or a judicial case, but a matter of theoretical law, a marginal detail of the rules of leprous impurity not explicitly specified in the Torah. God is portrayed not as the indomitable judge upon his heavenly throne but as a sage engaging in quintessential academic activity: debate over law.

Finally, the Bavli contains a long section about dreams and interpretations spanning almost three full folios, sometimes referred to as the "tractate on dreams" (bBer 55a–57b).[47] This section, like many other lengthy Bavli narratives, is a late source: textual variants are numerous, later rabbis are portrayed in a highly fictionalized manner, and the discrepancies from the Yerushalmi version are considerable.[48] Consistent with almost all late antique thought, rabbinic sources generally consider dreams to be "true" in many respects, providing the dreamer with hints at a hidden or potential reality.[49] Among the dream interpretations offered are several that concern matters related to the academy and its control: He who sees a goose in his dream should expect to achieve greatness . . . and he who has sex with it will become the Head of an Academy (*rosh yeshiva*). Rav Ashi said, 'I saw it and had sex with it and rose to greatness.'" "He who dreams that he enters a marsh will become Head of an Academy; [he that enters] a forest will become the Head of a Study-session" (bBer 57a).[50] How exactly avian intercourse portends academic leadership is fortunately beyond the scope of this study, but that these interpretations of apparently standard rabbinic dreams express anxiety about achieving academic status seems evident. The passage itself observes that, "a man is shown in the dream only what is suggested by his own thoughts,"[51] and such thoughts were naturally in the mind of aspiring pupils in the academy.

Similar anxiety is expressed in a bizarre story of Abaye and Rava, who consulted a professional dream-interpreter named Bar Hedaya. The story assumes that "all dreams follow the mouth," that is, that the interpretation determines the meaning of the dream. Because Abaye pays Bar Hedaya while Rava does not, Abaye receives an auspicious interpretation and Rava an inauspicious one, though they recount the same dream. Due to Bar Hedaya's interpretations, Abaye enjoys good fortune, such as commercial success, flourishing crops, and healthy children, while Rava suffers the death of his wife and children, pestilence, false arrest, impoverishment, and beating. Finally Rava compensates Bar Hedaya and receives propitious predictions. Several of the interpretations relate to academic affairs:

> [Rava and Abaye] said to Bar Hedaya, "We were made to read [in our dreams], *And all the peoples of the earth shall see that the Lord's name is proclaimed over you (Deut 28:10)*." He said to Abaye, "Your name will become great, for you will become the Head of an Academy, and you will be held in awe by the people."

> They said, "We saw a young ass standing beside our cushion and braying." To Abaye he said, "You will rule (*malakh;* = become head of the academy) and a speaker will stand beside you."

> [Rava] said to Bar Hedaya, "I saw Abaye's mansion collapse and its dust cover me." He said to him, "Abaye will die and his academy[52] will pass to you." (bBer 56a)

Projected upon a strange account of two of the Talmud's leading sages, these dream-interpretations probably express the collective concerns of the Stammaim. As in several of the stories discussed above, jockeying for status and competition for leadership positions appear to have been important matters of institutional life.

Esteem of Torah

All expressions of rabbinic Judaism deemed Torah study to be the greatest commandment, the most noble practice, and a universe-maintaining activity.[53] Study of Torah replaced sacrifices as the ritual that sustained the cosmos. According to a tradition cited several times in the Bavli — "R. Eleazar said, 'Were it not for the Torah, heaven and earth would not exist, as it says, *If I had not established my eternal covenant, I would not have fashioned heaven and earth' (Jer 33:25)"* — God would not have created the cosmos ("fashioned heaven and earth") were it not for Torah ("the eternal covenant").[54] Similar mythic conceptions present the Torah as the blueprint of creation or the instrument with which God constructed the universe.[55]

This view of Torah and Torah study is also found in Palestinian sources. Tractate Avot of the Mishna is essentially a collection of paeans in praise of Torah. The Bavli, however, offers some of the most extreme formulations of the significance of Torah:

> R. Alexandri said, "Whoever busies himself with Torah for its own sake creates peace in the celestial family and in the earthly family. . . ."
> Rav said, "It as if he built the heavenly and earthly temples. . . ."
> Resh Laqish said, "He even protects the entire world (from punishment for sin). . . ."
> And Levi said, "He even hastens the redemption." (bSanh 99b)

> The Holy One said . . . "Better to me is one day that you engage in Torah before me than one thousand sacrifices." (bMak 10a)

> "Torah study is superior to the saving of life. . . ."
> "Torah study is superior to building the temple. . . ."
> "Torah study is superior to the honor of father and mother." (bMeg 16b)

I would attribute such exaggerated expressions, which are essentially unparalleled in Palestinian sources, to the scholastic mentality and academic preoccupations of the Bavli.[56] For the Stammaim, the "world of the academy" was coextensive with the world, and the central activity of the academy played a critical role in the structure of the universe.

The Stammaitic view of the importance of Torah can be appreciated by examining narratives that contain the maxim "they forsake eternal life and busy themselves with temporal life." This maxim expresses in a concise manner the fundamental difference between rabbis and others, the opposition between a life of Torah (= eternal life) and secular pursuits. A story found at bTa 21a recounts that two sages, Ilfa and R. Yohanan, decide to quit their studies because they suffer unbearable poverty. After they set out R. Yohanan hears an angel propose killing the two sages because "they forsake eternal life and busy themselves with temporal life," but his fellow angel objects. R. Yohanan resolves to return to his studies, remarking that he will exemplify the verse, "The poor shall never cease out of the land" (Deut 15:11). He attains a position of leadership, while the sages eventually inform Ilfa that had he remained and studied, he would have achieved even higher honor.

The notion that one who desists from full time study of Torah even for purposes of survival deserves death, albeit opposed by another voice in the text, comprises a rather uncompromising perspective. Yet that is essentially the text's message: better to starve and study than cease and risk death. That this standard was not applied exclusively to sages can be seen in the Bavli's version of the story of R. Shimon bar Yohai and the cave (bShab 33b–34a). At the outset of the story, R. Shimon expresses a negative view of the Romans and their accomplishments, complaining that they built markets, bathhouses, and bridges for their own selfish purposes, not to benefact humanity as his colleague R. Yehuda suggests. The Romans sentence R. Shimon to death, so he flees to a cave, where he and his son R. Eleazar study Torah in splendid isolation for thirteen years. When they emerge they see Jewish peasants plowing and tilling the soil. Appalled that the men "forsake eternal life and busy themselves with temporal life," they look at them and "everywhere they turn their eyes was immediately burned." A heavenly voice thereupon orders them back into the cave, displeased with the destruction. After twelve months they reemerge and see a man running with two myrtles on Friday afternoon. When the man explains that the myrtles will be used to honor the Sabbath, "their minds were set at ease." R. Shimon subsequently moderates his extreme views and attempts to benefact the residents of a city, although the story continues to struggle with the tension between Torah study and worldly occupations.[57]

It is no accident that the story begins with denunciation of gentiles and gentile institutions but quickly shifts to attacks on ordinary Jews. The two groups share a fundamental defect in Stammaitic eyes, namely, lack of engagement with Torah. Because the Jewish peasants "forsake eternal life and busy themselves with temporal life," even for the ostensibly legitimate task of earning a living, they are destroyed by the sages. To be sure this story rejects that radical perspective. The heavenly voice directs the sages back to the cave to learn precisely this lesson, and the sages subsequently recognize the merit of simple Jews who use the fruits of their "temporal life" to fulfill the commandments. Nevertheless, both the mere expression of the radical view and the failure of the story to resolve the tension completely indicate that such ideas circulated in Stammaitic circles. A current of Stammaitic thought considered the lives of those who did not study Torah to be worthless. In Chapter 7 we will see other chilling expressions of such views.

The two other appearances of the maxim illustrate the radical nature of the Bavli's perspective along slightly different lines. In a brief report found in bShab 10a, Rava reacts to his colleague Rav Hamnuna's lengthy prayers by saying, "[H]e forsakes eternal life and busies himself with temporal life!" Although prayer fulfills a commandment and comprises a noble spiritual activity, lengthy petitions entreat God for worldly needs. Even this limited concern for "temporal life" offends Rava because it detracts precious time from the study of Torah. Finally, another story tells that on an unspecified festival R. Eliezer sits and studies with his disciples (bBes 15b). As time passes groups of students depart to enjoy their festival meals, and as each group withdraws R. Eliezer makes a derogatory remark about their character. Eventually he reassures the remaining students that he was not speaking of them but about the others, "who forsake eternal life and busy themselves with temporal life." Here again the text pits Torah study against an important religious value, the celebration of a festival. In this way the Stammaim almost categorize the commandments and other valued aspects of rabbinic piety as "temporal life" and valence them negatively against Torah study.

The Palestinian versions of the story of R. Shimon bar Yohai lack the maxim and the entire scene where the sages encounter the peasants.[58] The other sources have no parallels in Palestinian sources, nor does the maxim appear elsewhere. While Palestinian sages and Babylonian Amoraim of course esteemed Torah study as the most laudable activity, its value never reached the same level as in Stammaitic culture where it trumped other pietistic practices to the point of becoming almost the only spiritual path of any worth, and perhaps the only reason for living. In earlier rabbinic cultures, performing the commandments, devotion to prayer, and pursuit of moral perfection were also highly valued spiritual activities.

Another significant aspect of the Bavli's conception of Torah is a consciousness of its expansion. Several traditions are keenly aware that the Torah produced in the contemporary academy far exceeded that of previous generations. One manifestation of this sensibility is the story mentioned above of Moses's visit to R. Akiba's academy. Moses feels distress when he did not "understand what they were saying" but feels comforted when R. Akiba explains that the source of his claim is a law given to Moses on Sinai. Moses cannot understand the discussions because new Torah has been generated in the intervening years, even if it all, paradoxically, inheres in the original revelation.[59] The storytellers admit how alien the complex argumentation produced in their time would be to earlier sages.

A more explicit testimony of this gap appears in the following tradition:

(A) Rav Papa said to Abaye: What is the difference between the early sages, for whom miracles happened, and us, for whom no miracles happen?

(B) If it is on account of learning — in the years of Rav Yehuda their studies were limited to [the Order of] Damages. But we study all six Orders [of the Mishna]. And when Rav Yehuda came to [the Mishna in Tractate] Uqtsin, *A woman who pickles a vegetable in a pot (= mToh 2:1)*, and some say to [the law] *Olives pressed with their leaves are pure (= mUq 2:1)*, he would say, "I see (difficulties) here (in this one Mishna equal to) the disputations of Rav and Shmuel," whereas we teach thirteen sessions on [Tractate] Uqtsin!

(C) Yet when Rav Yehuda [merely] took off his shoe, rain would fall. Whereas we afflict ourselves and cry out, and no one pays attention to us.

(D) He said to him: The early sages were willing to give up their lives to sanctify [God's] name. We are unwilling to give up our lives to sanctify [God's] name. (bBer 20a)

The interchange asserts that later generations of sages are simultaneously more learned and less pious than their predecessors. Their superiority in Torah is explained in two ways. Former sages only studied one division of the Mishna, whereas contemporary rabbis study all six.[60] Moreover, former sages found laws in Tractate Uqtsin, the last tractate in the Mishna, as difficult to understand as the complicated discussions of Rav and Shmuel, the leading sages of the first generation of Amoraim.[61] These same laws, however, present no difficulties to Rav Papa and his associates, who can expound the obscure legal subtleties of the entire tractate in thirteen study-sessions. Torah study in the time of the latter Amoraim is therefore both more extensive and more complex than that of earlier times. This superiority in Torah, lamentably, does not bring tangible good: because earlier sages were more pious they were rewarded with miracles.

Admission of inferiority to earlier sages is a rabbinic commonplace generally expressed in the notion of the "decline of the generations."[62] The Amoraim claim, "If the ancients were sons of angels, then we are sons of men; if the ancients were sons of men, then we are like asses" (bShab 112b).[63] The same sensibility underpins the working assumption of the Talmud that an Amora cannot contradict a Tannaitic source, as Amoraim inherently have less authority than their forerunners. Given this historical perspective, the assertion of greater breadth of study is an unusually bold and self-confident gesture that shows full awareness of the extent to which Torah had proliferated in the Babylonian academies.

Note that the middle section of the tradition (B–C), which contains the claim of superiority, appears to be a later addition to a straightforward interchange between Rav Papa and his teacher Abaye (A–D). The dialogue reads smoothly without it, and the mention of Rav Yehuda is gratuitous. Moreover, the section is repeated verbatim in a similar tradition where Rabbah explains why, when he declared a fast, no rain came, although it did in earlier times. Rabbah's answer: the current generation is not worthy.[64] The Stammaim seem to have added the section to these Amoraic explanations, which imply a decrease in piety caused contemporary rabbis not to receive a reward where earlier sages did. The interpolation strengthens the question by insisting that, given the latter generations' superiority in knowledge of Torah, we should have expected them to receive even greater reward. Taken in and of itself, the section offers a concise statement of the breadth of study in later times as well as the consciousness of a vast increase from earlier generations. When it comes to study of Torah, the Stammaim do not see themselves as standing on the shoulders of their predecessors; they claim to be head and shoulders above them.

The Christian Academy at Nisibis

To date the rise of the Babylonian rabbinic academy to the fifth or sixth century coheres with the broader cultural climate. Hellenistic influence increased dramatically throughout Syria and northern Mesopotamia in the fifth and sixth centuries.[65] The Church Fathers Aphrahat (d. circa 350) and Ephrem (d. 373) wrote in Syriac and their writings exhibit a Semitic outlook; their works are largely free of the complex Christological formulations made possible by the philosophical terminology available in Greek and

Latin. In the succeeding centuries the Church Fathers within the Persian Empire expressed themselves in a thoroughly Hellenized idiom. More importantly, an influential Christian academy was founded at Nisibis in the late fifth century. Scholars have noted the value of the literature produced by this academy as a source of insights into the nature of Babylonian rabbinic institutions.

The "School of the Persians" had been located in Edessa in Eastern Syria from the late fourth century until 489 C.E. when it was forced out of the city (and the Roman Empire) as a result of a bitter Christological schism.[66] The school had been a champion of Nestorian (Dyophysite) Christianity. When the Council of Chalcedon (451 C.E.) failed to attain a satisfactory compromise, the Emperor Zeno ordered the closing of the school and all Nestorians to leave the empire. Under the leadership of Narsai the school moved within the borders of the Persian Empire and settled in Nisibis. Other Christian schools were also established in Persia at this time, in part due to the influx of Nestorians.[67]

In Nisibis the academy thrived and became an intellectual center of Christian learning within the Sasanian realm for several centuries.[68] The size varied over the years; various sources mention between 300 and 1,000 students.[69] Renowned for biblical exegesis, homiletics, and theology, the school produced a vast literature in Syriac, including hymns, liturgical texts, discourses, treatises, and commentaries. There is some evidence that philosophy was taught as well.[70]

Two sets of statutes or protocols (*kanona* = canons), the first drafted in 496 C.E., the second in 590 C.E., stand out among the literature preserved from the academy.[71] These set forth the structure and organization of the academy, the positions of leadership and their responsibilities, basic rules of conduct for students, and the everyday routine of study and prayer. Another important work is a document entitled "The Cause of the Foundation of the Schools," a speech delivered at the commencement of the academic year, written by a certain Barhadbeshabba in about 600 C.E.[72] The speech traces God's instruction from creation, through biblical, pagan, and Christian schools until the founding of the Nisibis academy, concluding with an exhortation to students and praise of Hinena, the leader of the school.

Gafni has noted several points of contact between this literature and Talmudic sources that suggest common academic structures and concerns. At Nisibis the school year was divided into two academic "sessions" (*motva*), a cognate to the term *metivta,* used for both "study-session" and "academy" in Talmudic sources.[73] The statutes mention that studies were interrupted during the summer months of Av and Tishrei (August–October), when students departed to earn a living, and "The Cause of the Foundation of the Schools" refers to the "summer semester" and "winter semester."[74] Similarly, a tradition ascribed to Rava instructs disciples, "I ask of you not to appear before me in the days of Nisan and the days of Tishrei in order that you not be burdened by your [need for] sustenance throughout the year" (bBer 35b).[75] The statutes mention a supervisor of students, a *resh qalita,* a term which Gafni conjectures may be related to the Talmudic title *resh kallah* given to various Amoraim, usually understood as the leader of a study-session.[76] The statutes provide that students who arrive early at the assembly should "leave one row (*sedra*) before the bench to be used for the brother-presbyters, and shall take places in the other rows."[77] The reference to set places, benches, and rows recalls the stories discussed above, such as Rav Kahana being seated in the first row, and the benches added to the academy of Rabban Gamaliel. Adam Becker observes that "The Cause of the Foundation of the Schools" mentions a "heavenly academy" and portrays the biblical patriarchs as scholarly predecessors.[78] Shaye Cohen has also noted that several references in these Syriac documents to "the established order" (*taksa*) seem to correspond to a Talmudic reference to the "Orders" or "Protocols (*sidrei*) of the [office of] Nasi" and the "Protocols of [the office of] Sage" in a late Bavli story about academic appointments.[79]

The School of Nisibis exemplifies what Becker calls the "scholastic culture" of late antique Syria and Mesopotamia, following José Cabézon's understanding of scholasticism as a cross-cultural category characterized by a focus on tradition and texts, an interest in language and interpretation, rationalism, and systematic analysis.[80] The type of Christian piety practiced at Nisibis did not emphasize solitary meditation, spiritual perfection, and contemplation, as did some monastic communities, but rather group study and biblical interpretation. Syriac sources in the sixth century also refer to the "scholastic" (*escholaya*), a type of educated Christian holy man distinct from a typical monk or bishop.[81] This kind of scholastic lifestyle and piety describes that of the rabbis in general and in particular the Stammaim, who dedicated themselves to the systematization, interpretation, and analysis of the earlier traditions.

The available evidence does not allow us to go beyond observing these general structural parallels to posit direct influence one way or the other. Rabbinic sources associate Nisibis with the (perhaps fictional) school of the early Tanna R. Yehuda b. Betera (mid second century C.E.).[82] While Nisibis is rarely mentioned in connection with later sages, it clearly included a Jewish community of some size. At all events, what we can say is that dating the rise of rabbinic academies to the fifth–sixth century C.E. fits well with developments within Persian Christianity and with the general cultural climate of Eastern Syria and Mesopotamia.

In sum, Bavli stories locate the sages in the study-house (*bet midrash*) to a far greater extent than do the Palestinian versions. The most plausible explanation for this tendency is that the Bavli storytellers revised Palestinian accounts in light of their situation. Since the Amoraim probably congregated in disciple circles, these storytellers were most likely the Stammaim. For them "study-house" refers to an academy; longer stories that bear signs of Stammaitic composition sometimes use the term "academy" (*yeshiva, metivta*) in addition to "study-house."[83] These sources picture a populous institution with numerous disciples seated in rows according to ability, a vision that correlates with that found in Geonic sources. Therefore, the rise of the Babylonian rabbinic academy should probably be dated to the Stammaitic period. Torah study in the Stammaitic academies attained greater esteem and greater complexity than that of previous eras. The next chapters examine some of the activities and characteristics of the Stammaitic academy.

Chapter 2

‿∶‿

Dialectics

Objections and Solutions

According to the story of R. Shimon bar Yohai, which we had occasion to mention in the previous chapter, the sage's weathered appearance after thirteen years of hiding in a cave so distressed his father-in-law, R. Pinhas b. Yair, that he lamented: "Alas that I see you so" (bShab 33b). R. Shimon, who had spent those long years studying Torah, responded, "Happy that you see me so. For if you did not see me so, you would not find me so [learned]." At this point a redactionial comment explains: "For originally when R. Shimon bar Yohai raised an objection, R. Pinhas b. Yair solved it with twelve solutions. Subsequently when R. Pinhas b. Yair objected, R. Shimon bar Yohai solved it with twenty-four solutions." The mark of R. Shimon's proficiency in Torah is not the breadth of his knowledge, nor the accuracy of his recall, nor his skill at determining the law, but rather his dialectical abilities. When engaging in the give-and-take of Talmudic discussion, he was now able to proliferate numerous solutions to every objection that R. Pinhas — no slouch in dialectic activity himself — advanced against his claims.

This assessment of dialectical ability as the highest dimension of Torah appears in several late Babylonian narratives which thematize "objections" (*qushiyot*), "solutions" (*paroqei*), "responses" (*teshuvot*), and "answers" (*teirutsei*). Another Bavli story relates how Rav Kahana's proficiency and apparent lack of proficiency in dialectics determined his status in the eyes of his colleagues (bBQ 117a). Upon arriving in the Land of Israel after fleeing Babylonia, Rav Kahana asked some students where he could find Resh Laqish. When they asked his business with the great sage, Rav Kahana "told them this objection and that objection, this solution and that solution." Not only did this display of dialectical acumen impress the students, who reported it to Resh Laqish, but Resh Laqish took pains to warn R. Yohanan, "A lion has come up from Babylonia. Let the Master look deeply into the lesson for tomorrow." Once again the storytellers have Rav Kahana prove his mettle as a scholar through his dialectical skill rather than another aspect of Torah knowledge.[1] His ability to propound objections and solutions earns the designation "lion," often used in the Bavli for a scholar of outstanding prowess.[2] The next day the sages appropriately seat Rav Kahana in the first row among the most learned students. But before he left Babylonia Rav Kahana had been warned by Rav not to raise difficulties against R. Yohanan's teaching for seven years, apparently out of the same concern expressed by Resh Laqish: that Rav Kahana might catch R. Yohanan off guard with his brilliant objections and cause the aged master to feel ashamed before his students.[3] The story continues:

> He [R. Yohanan] said a tradition and he [Rav Kahana] did not object. He said [another] tradition and he did not object. They seated him back through seven rows until he was in the last row. R. Yohanan said to Resh Laqish, "The lion you mentioned has become a fox."

> He [Rav Kahana] said, "May it be [God's] will that these seven rows take the place of the seven years that Rav told me [not to raise objections]." He stood up on his feet. He said, "Let the master go back to the beginning."

> He [R. Yohanan] said a tradition and he [Rav Kahana] objected [until] they placed him in the first row. He said a tradition and he objected. R. Yohanan was sitting on seven cushions. They removed a cushion from under him. He said a tradition and he objected to him, until they removed all the cushions from under him and he was sitting on the ground.

The position of both sages within the academic hierarchy depends on their capacity to object and respond. Rav Kahana is progressively relegated for failing to come up with objections and promoted when he objects, while R. Yohanan is demoted each time he cannot respond. Similarly, Rav Kahana's sobriquet switches from "lion" to "fox"—the weaker animal indicating inferior knowledge—when he fails to demonstrate dialectical prowess.

We find this link between academic rank and dialectical proficiency played out consistently. After Rabban Shimon b. Gamaliel ejects R. Natan and R. Meir from the academy because they plot to depose him from his position as Nasi, he finds himself in a difficult predicament: "They [R. Meir and R. Natan] would write objections on slips of paper and throw [them into the academy]. That which he [Rabban Shimon b. Gamaliel] solved, he solved. That which was not solved, they [R. Meir and R. Natan] wrote the solutions and threw them [in]. R. Yose said to them [the rabbis], 'Torah is outside and we are inside?' Rabban Shimon b. Gamaliel said to them, 'We will bring them in'" (bHor 13b). R. Yose protests the banishment because the other sages do not know as much Torah as R. Meir and R. Natan. He points out that the sages need these two scholars to contribute to their discussions, and the dissent compels Rabban Gamaliel to readmit them. Here too the story focuses on a specific type of expertise in Torah, the "objections" and "solutions" that characterize dialectical debate. R. Meir and R. Natan demonstrate their brilliance by submitting objections and solutions. And because Rabban Shimon b. Gamaliel's ability to solve objections is inferior to theirs, he must attenuate the punishment. Dialectical skill ultimately restores these rabbis to their positions within the academy. The story stops short of the idea that R. Natan and R. Meir should replace Rabban Shimon b. Gamaliel by virtue of their superior dialectical abilities. As we shall see in Chapter 5, the Bavli esteems lineage, and the storytellers' point, in part, is that those most proficient in Torah will not always occupy the top positions in the academic hierarchy. Knowledge of Torah and lineage stand in tension as competing bases for leadership of the academy. At all events, the type of Torah that counts is the capacity to respond and object, and on account of that capacity R. Meir and R. Natan reclaim their academic honors.

The description of Rabban Shimon b. Gamaliel's academy offered by yet another Bavli story expresses this link in a slightly different way: "When Rabban Shimon b. Gamaliel and R. Yehoshua b. Qorha were sitting on benches, R. Eleazar b. R. Shimon and Rabbi [Yehuda HaNasi] were sitting before them on the ground objecting and solving. They said: 'We drink their water yet they sit on the ground?!' They made benches for them and raised them up" (bBM 84b). Exactly who made the observation, whether the other students or Rabban Shimon b. Gamaliel and R. Yehoshua b. Qorha themselves, is unclear. But again the story equates objections and solutions with Torah — "drinking the water" of a sage is a common rabbinic metaphor for a disciple imbibing the Torah of his master.[4] The elevation from the ground to benches due to frequent objections and solutions perfectly inverts the reduction of R. Yohanan from his seat upon cushions to the ground due to the lack of cogent solutions to objections. We have then several variations of the topos: Rav Kahana moved backwards and forwards; R. Meir and R. Natan brought from the outside to the inside; and R. Yohanan, R. Eleazar b. R. Shimon, and Rabbi elevated and lowered. Dialectical ability bestows and removes academic status.

As the story continues, however, R. Eleazar b. R. Shimon expresses dissatisfaction with the new arrangement, for the parallel postures imply that he and Rabbi have equal ability.[5] To correct such an impression he turns to dialectics:

> He [R. Eleazar b. R. Shimon] thought: "Do they consider him equal to me?" Until that day, whenever Rabbi said something, R. Eleazar b. R. Shimon supported him. From that point onwards, whenever Rabbi said, "I have a response," R. Eleazar said to him, "Such-and-such is your response. This will be the response [to that]. You have surrounded us with bundles of responses that have no substance." Rabbi felt distressed. He went and told his father. He said to him, "My son, do not feel bad. For he is a lion, the son of a lion, while you are a lion, the son of a fox" (bBM 84b).

In these displays of intellectual virtuosity, R. Eleazar both anticipated Rabbi's response, predicting what his colleague would say, and immediately neutralized it with a response of his own. Rabbi's responses, though numerous ("bundles"), were evidently not of high quality. True dialectical skill involved not simply a proliferation of responses, but cogent arguments. The academic "lion" is again the master of debate.

These traditions suggest that dialectical argumentation was the type of Torah study most esteemed by the storytellers. Their passion for argumentation emerges in striking fashion in the account of the relationship between R. Yohanan and Resh Laqish. R. Yohanan brings Resh Laqish into the rabbinic fold, teaches him Torah and makes him "a great man," that is, a learned sage. After Resh Laqish's death, R. Yohanan becomes distraught at the loss of his study-partner. The rabbis of the academy try to "restore his mind" by providing him a replacement in R. Eleazar b. Pedat, "whose traditions are sharp." But their good intentions backfire, causing R. Yohanan to lament:

> Are you [R. Eleazar] like the Son of Laqish? When I made a statement, the Son of Laqish would object with twenty-four objections and I would solve them with twenty-four solutions, and thus our discussions expanded. But you say, "There is a teaching that supports you." Do I not know that my statements are accurate? He tore his clothes and went crying and saying, "Where are you Son of Laqish? Where are you Son of Laqish?" He could not be consoled. The sages prayed for mercy for him and he died. (bBM 84a)

For R. Yohanan, the lack of intense dialectical debate was essentially a fate worse than death. He craved heated intellectual combat, not a yes-man to confirm the veracity of his pronouncements. The description of his former discussions with Resh Laqish sheds some light on what was at stake. Through dialectical activity "discussions expanded"—new Torah was created as the relentless questioning opened up new avenues of analysis. Henceforth, when sages studied the issue, they could take up not only whatever traditions had existed previously, but the discussions of R. Yohanan and Resh Laqish as well. R. Eleazar's policy of supporting R. Yohanan, by contrast, entails stasis. Nothing is added to the corpus of rabbinic tradition, for R. Eleazar simply juxtaposes R. Yohanan's statements with supporting sources, presumably the sources upon which R. Yohanan based his claims in the first place. R. Yohanan knew that his statements are "accurate"; he did not know the dynamic possibilities that result from vigorous argumentation.

Note that the same antithesis of supporting as opposed to responding appears here as in the account of R. Eleazar b. R. Shimon and Rabbi. The difference is that R. Eleazar b. R. Shimon's responses were intended to stifle discussion. He preempted Rabbi's statements and cut off any interchange before it could develop, essentially terrorizing his less capable colleague into silence. For R. Yohanan and Resh Laqish the objections and responses function in the opposite way. They comprise the very stuff of analytical discussion, thereby creating an expansion, not limitation, of Torah. In both cases the capacity to propound objections and responses signals the brilliance of the sage.

Just as R. Yohanan thrived on a life of argumentation, so the rabbis looked forward to an eternity of debate in the next world. A late exegetical tradition relates that Judah, son of Jacob, caused himself to fall under a ban (*niddui*) which at first prevented him from entering the world to come. (This tradition is clearly late as it is an Aramaic addendum to a Hebrew midrash attributed to Palestinian sages, that is, a typical Stammaitic gloss.)[6] God relented when Moses prayed for mercy, but this did not rectify the situation completely:

(A) [Yet] they did not let him [Judah] enter the heavenly academy [because of the ban]. [Moses prayed,] *"[Hear, O Lord the voice of Judah] and restore him to his people" (Deut 33:7).*

(B) [Yet] he did not know how to engage in the give-and-take of debate with the sages. [Moses prayed], *"Let his hands strive for him" (ibid.)* (i.e. give him the strength to "fight" in academic debate).

(C) [Yet] he did not know how to solve an objection (*lefaroqei qushya*). [Moses prayed,] *"Help him against his foes" (ibid.).*[7]

We should expect that an afterlife without access to the heavenly academy would not satisfy the rabbis (A).[8] But the Bavli goes two steps further. A full reward in the world to come required not only participating in dialectical debate (B), but successful involvement, marked by the ability to respond to objections (C). Judah's otherworldly rehabilitation was therefore incomplete until God granted him such skill. Consistent with the narratives quoted above, the three stages of Judah's posthumous reward in this source (entry to the academy, participation in debate, successful argumentation) correspond to increasing status in the eyes of the Stammaim: the average rabbi had mastered tradition but lacked dialectical ability; those who engaged in debate held more prestige; while those who excelled in it were most esteemed. In the previous chapter we discussed the depiction of the heavenly academy as a projection of the situation of the Stammaim. Here we get a glimpse of the activity that dominates that academy: "the give-and-take of debate," objections, and solutions. And if they conceived of otherworldly bliss in such terms, then we can probably infer that lively, vigorous argumentation provided intellectual joy and exhilaration.

The hyperbole that characterizes some of these stories deserves comment. R. Yohanan and Resh Laqish routinely proffer twenty-four objections and solutions in their arguments, and similarly R. Shimon bar Yohai produces twenty-four solutions to each of Pinhas b. Yair's objections. Other Bavli sources also mention large numbers of arguments, although not in the context of dialectics per se. One tradition claims that "Doeg and Ahitofel asked four hundred problems concerning a tower that flies in the air, and not one was resolved."[9] In another story Dosa b. Harkinas warns the sages to be careful because his younger brother Yonatan has "three hundred responses to prove that the daughter's co-wife is permitted" (bYev 16a).[10] The story of the "Oven of Akhnai" relates that R. Eliezer "responded with all the responses in the world" in a futile effort to persuade the sages of his opinion (bBM 59b). Now at first one might think that the exaggerated number of "responses" functions as an indication of the cogency of that position: the sage propounded so many proofs that his claims should never be doubted. Yet R. Yohanan explicitly points out that his interchanges with Resh Laqish are unrelated to establishing the correct ruling. The four hundred problems about the flying tower are clearly hypothetical, and in any case no conclusions were reached. The story of Dosa and Yonatan b. Harkinas relates that Yonatan's position is wrong despite his hundreds of responses. For all of R. Eliezer's responses in the "Oven of Akhnai," the sages rule against him, although here the paradoxical story simultaneously indicates that God agreed with his opinion. The hyperbolic numbers rather point to the inherent worth of the most intricate and complex argumentation. To be able to trot out a prodigious number of arguments at will while immediately neutralizing challenges against one's points constituted the greatest proficiency in Torah.

Dialectical argumentation is among the clearest examples of a specifically Babylonian theme. The combination "objections and solutions" does not appear in the Yerushalmi or in other Palestinian sources. The story of Rav Kahana with its heavy emphasis on dialectical proficiency has no Yerushalmi parallel, nor does the story of R. Yohanan and Resh Laqish.[11] The Palestinian versions of the stories of R. Shimon bar Yohai and the cave, of R. Eleazar b. R. Shimon and Rabbi, and of Judah's posthumous predicament lack the scenes in which the sages demonstrate their dialectical skills,[12] as does the rather brief Yerushalmi version of R. Meir's demotion.[13] Because it was so important in their own culture, Bavli storytellers repeatedly added the theme to these Palestinian stories about sages. As for the disparity in proficiency between Rabbi and R. Eleazar b. R. Shimon, the Yerushalmi account presents it thus: "When R. Eleazar b. R. Shimon entered the house of assembly, Rabbi [Yehuda HaNasi's] face darkened. His father said to him, 'Truly, he is a lion the son of a lion, but you are a lion the son of a fox'" (yShab 10:5, 12c).[14] The "darkened face," a sign of consternation or distress, suggests that Rabbi feared that his colleague would outperform him or demonstrate superior knowledge. As in the Bavli, his father consoles him with the parable of the lion and the fox. But the type of expertise in Torah remains obscure; certainly there is no intimation that R. Eleazar b. R. Shimon possessed dialectical skill specifically. Here the Bavli storytellers have interpreted the indication that R. Eleazar b. R. Shimon was the greater sage in terms of their esteem for dialectical ability.

Further evidence of the difference between Palestine and Babylonia can be seen in the following tradition about King David:

Ruth Rabbah 4:3	bSanh 93b
I have observed a son of Jesse the Bethlehemite who is skilled in music (1 Sam 16:18) — in Bible	*I have observed a son of Jesse the Bethlehemite who is skilled in music (1 Sam 16:18)* — he knows how to question
he is mighty — in Mishna	*he is mighty* — he knows how to respond

a warrior — in Talmud	*a warrior* — he knows how to engage in give-and-take in the war of Torah
handsome in appearance — in good deeds. Another interpretation: he is able to infer one matter from another	*handsome in appearance* — he is able to infer one matter from another
sensible in speech — who proves his legal opinions	*sensible in speech* — who proves his legal opinions[15]
and the Lord is with him — the law follows his words.	*and the Lord is with him* — the law follows his words.

This tradition translates King David's talents and virtues into types of proficiency in Torah. But while *Ruth Rabbah,* a late Palestinian midrash, suffices with the general claims of his command of Bible, Mishna, and Talmud, the Bavli mentions dialectics specifically. Where the Palestinian source "rabbinizes" King David, the Bavli "Stammaizes" him as well.

Another clear example is provided by the different versions of the story of the deposition of Rabban Gamaliel.[16] In the Yerushalmi R. Eleazar b. Azariah is appointed to replace Rabban Gamaliel on the basis of his ancestry, that he is tenth generation in descent from Ezra. R. Akiba observes that R. Eleazar knows less Torah than he but is "more a descendant of great men." The Bavli attributes R. Eleazar's selection to a combination of wisdom, wealth, and ancestry.[17] Significantly, the type of wisdom required for a position of leadership is dialectical ability: "He is wise — so that if they object to him, he will solve it." Note again that academic status is contingent on skill in debate. The tradition implies that were R. Eleazar not able to solve objections directed toward him, his position atop the hierarchy would be in jeopardy.[18]

The closest Palestinian parallel to this theme is a tradition attributed to Rabbi, "R. Meir had a distinguished student who would [prove] that a [dead] reptile was pure and impure in one hundred ways." A variant in the name of R. Yohanan claims that, "[A judge] who does not know how to prove a [dead] reptile pure and impure in one hundred ways cannot begin the arguments for innocence [following a trial]" (ySanh 4:1, 22a).[19] While the talent described here bears some affinity to dialectical skill, it is not quite the same. These sources point rather to cleverness or intellectual adroitness, the ability to manufacture spurious arguments to prove the impossible (since the Torah explicitly states that a dead reptile is impure). Such theoretical exercises involve no dialogue or give-and-take or thinking quickly so as to parry objections. They more closely resemble the Bavli tradition of the four hundred problems about the flying tower. Interestingly, the Palestinian Amoraim appear ambivalent about such activity. After mentioning R. Meir's student the Yerushalmi continues: "They said: That student did not know how to teach [law]. R. Yaakov b. Disai said: That student was cut off from Mount Sinai." The problem seems to be that such skills draw attention away from authoritative law ("not know how to teach" correctly) and may even lead to erroneous rulings (hence "cut off from Mount Sinai"). For this reason the Yerushalmi disparages such endeavors. The Bavli, as we have seen, celebrates them. Here the parallel Bavli tradition (which claims that the student had 150 proofs) lacks the negative comments (bEruv 13b).[20] The only other tradition discussed above paralleled in Palestinian sources is that of Yonatan b. Harkinas's three hundred responses concerning the daughter's co-wife (yYev 1:6, 3a).[21]

The thematizing of dialectics is not only Babylonian, but late Babylonian, i.e., Stammaitic. Scholars have dated most of the sources adduced above to the Stammaitic stratum. Shamma Friedman devoted an influential article to the narrative complex that includes the accounts of R. Eleazar b. R. Shimon and Rabbi and of R. Yohanan and Resh Laqish, arguing that the Babylonian redactors substantially reworked two earlier Palestinian sources.[22] In the previous chapter we noted Daniel Sperber's contention that the story of Rav Kahana dates to the post-Amoraic period.[23] David Goodblatt has argued that the story of R. Meir's removal from the academy is replete with late Babylonian motifs.[24] The content, particularly the conception of the structure of the academy and the criteria for leadership, also suggests a post-Amoraic dating.[25] Elsewhere I have suggested that the Babylonian redactors revised the Yerushalmi's story of R. Shimon bar Yohai by transferring sources and adapting motifs from other passages in the Bavli.[26] The tradition of Judah's posthumous fate appears in an Aramaic addendum to a Hebrew midrash. The Aramaic is characteristic of the Stammaitic stratum, and, as noted above, the addendum does not appear in the Palestinian versions.[27] As we shall see in Chapter 8, references to "objections and responses" resemble dialectical practices mentioned in Geonic sources, a confluence similar to descriptions of the academy noted in Chapter 1.[28]

Why the Stammaim esteemed argumentation is not completely clear but may be related to their self-conception. They evidently saw themselves as living in a postclassical period after the conclusion of the era of their predecessors, the Amoraim. That they ceased attaching their names (or their teachers' names) to statements points to a substantive break with the past, a sense that prior modes of activity had come to an end. In the Introduction we mentioned the Talmudic traditions which claimed that the leading sages of the final generations of Amoraim, Rav Ashi and Ravina, were the last to possess the legislative authority to "instruct"—to formulate apodictic rulings and dicta (*meimrot*).[29] The Stammaim thus viewed the body of Amoraic legal rulings as a closed corpus. They accordingly dedicated themselves to the rigorous analysis and explanation of earlier sources.[30] They attempted to reconstruct the reasoning that justified Amoraic rulings, since the bulk of the reasoning had not been considered worthy of preservation or transmission during the Amoraic period. The Stammaim constructed hypothetical arguments to justify contradictory Amoraic opinions and formulated possible responses to those arguments. These types of activity involved dialectics, the formulation of "objections and responses," hence discursive argumentation became the dominant practice and most highly valued ability in Stammaitic times.[31]

The thematization of dialectics in these late Bavli stories correlates beautifully with the dialectical style of the Stammaitic layer. Likewise, the portrayal of dialectics as the true mark of academic ability supports Halivni's suggestion that a shift in values took place in the Stammaitic era.[32] Certainly other types of Torah study took place in the academy: determination of law, study and repetition of Tannaitic traditions, scriptural interpretation, even homiletical craft. While these enterprises were important—and no doubt proficiency in them all was expected—dialectics were the focus of Stammaitic life. In all probability, these stories point to the main type of Torah study practiced within the Stammaitic academy.

Pilpul

Related to the Bavli's celebration of dialectics is an emphasis on analytical skill. For example, we find high regard for *pilpul*. Although literally meaning "turn from side to side," hence "search, examine, investigate," *pilpul* was derived by the Bavli from "pepper" (*pilpel*) and refers to intellectual sharpness and acumen.[33] The term seems to be applied to a range of activity, including reasoning, interpretation and discussion, and need not always refer to sharpness in dialectics per se.[34] But in a general sense *pilpul* relates to the same concern for intellectual virtuosity that underlies dialectical ability. R. Hanina boasts, "Were the Torah, God forbid, to be forgotten in Israel, I would restore it by means of my dialectical arguments [*pilpuli*]."[35] He cannot mean that he would simply remember Torah, or he would say so explicitly. Rather, he seems to mean that from his knowledge of argumentation and his ability to reason he can reconstruct the original Torah. Similarly, a Bavli *baraita* relates that "[o]ne thousand seven hundred arguments *a minora ad maius,* scriptural analogies, and specifications of the Scribes were forgotten during the days of mourning for Moses." To which R. Abahu comments, "Nevertheless, Othniel b. Qenaz restored them as a result of his dialectics (*pilpulo*)."[36] Again the sense is that through adroit reasoning and dialectical skill Othniel recovered the hermeneutical traditions and detailed regulations that had been lost. He was able to work backward by means of analytical reasoning to arrive at the original traditions.

The Bavli's esteem for *pilpul* can be seen in an interesting tradition comparing the abilities of two rabbis: "When Rav Hisda and Rav Sheshet would meet, Rav Hisda's lips would tremble at Rav Sheshet's knowledge of Mishnaic traditions, while Rav Sheshet's whole body would tremble at Rav Hisda's dialectics (*pilpulei*)" (bEruv 67a). Rav Hisda feared lest Rav Sheshet should stump him with his superior skill at interpreting Tannaitic traditions or with his greater breadth of knowledge. Yet Rav Hisda's dialectical skills caused considerably more anxiety to Rav Sheshet, whose "whole body" trembled lest he fail to follow the complicated reasoning of his colleague. This tradition most likely is informing us not simply about the disparities between the relative talents of these particular sages but about academic ability in general. Those proficient in dialectical skill were held in the highest regard and engendered the most awe among their colleagues.

The situation in Palestine is difficult to determine, but there seems to be slightly less emphasis on *pilpul* there.[37] A Yerushalmi *baraita* states, "The collector of traditions (*sodran*) takes precedence over the dialectician (*pilpelan*)."[38] "Collecting" or "arranging" is usually associated with breadth of knowledge or precise recall of earlier traditions. Such knowledge, the *baraita* suggests, deserves more honor than does dialectical ability. However, the Amoraic discussion in the Yerushalmi continues: "Even one such as R. Imi? He said to him, 'Leave aside the case of R. Imi. He is a superb dialectician.'"[39] So a master of dialectics still garners respect. Yet the general Palestinian hierarchy finds some support in a tradition reporting that an enquiry was sent to Palestine whether a "Sinai" or an "Uprooter of Mountains" takes precedence (bHor 14a; bBer 64a).[40] A "Sinai" is a scholar with a comprehensive and exact knowledge of Mishnaic traditions, a recall as precise as when "they were given on Mt Sinai."[41] An "Uprooter of Mountains" is a master of dialectics.[42] The Palestinians sent back to Babylonia: "A Sinai takes precedence, as we have a tradition: All depend on the owner of wheat." An "owner of wheat" appears to be synonymous with "Sinai," a sage with solid knowledge of traditions. Hence the Palestinians reportedly instructed their Babylonian investigators to give precedence to comprehensive knowledge over dialectical skill. A similar ranking appears in a *baraita* found elsewhere in the Bavli.[43] This point should not be pressed to an extreme, since Palestinian sages, like any elite intellectual class, obviously valued sharpness and reasoning ability as well. The issue is one of emphasis, and there seems to be a subtle but discernible preference for *pilpul* /dialectics in the Bavli.[44]

Several other Bavli traditions suggest that different types of study characterized the two centers. A brief anecdote reports, "When R. Zeira went up to the Land of Israel, he observed one hundred fasts to forget the Babylonian learning (*gemara*) in order that it not trouble him (bBM 85a)." Rashi explains: "The Amoraim in the Land of Israel were not disputatious . . . and they reconciled [contradictory] reasons without objections and solutions."[45] In Palestine the sages resolved their legal difficulties without engaging in the argumentative process of "objections and solutions" to examine all sides of the question. R. Zeira apparently did not wish to be encumbered by the proliferation of arguments typical of the Babylonian method but rather to focus on neat and tidy explanations to clarify matters. That the complex argumentation glorified in the Bavli could simultaneously be "troubling" is seconded by a surprisingly self-reflective midrash to Lam 3:6: "*He has made me dwell in darkness like those long dead*. R. Yirmiah said: This is the Talmud (or "learning") of Babylonia" (bSanh 24a). Extended and artificial debate, for all its intellectual appeal, can also obfuscate an issue. This contrast in styles also appears in a report of eulogies for deceased scholars:

> Resh Laqish eulogized a certain disciple of the rabbis who often spent time in the Land of Israel and who used to repeat laws before twenty-four rows of students, "Alas! The Land of Israel has lost a great man."

> A certain man who repeated halakhot, Sifra, Sifre, and Tosefta died. They came before Rav Nahman and said, "Let the master eulogize him." He said, "How can we eulogize him? Behold this bag of books who has been lost!" (bMeg 28b)

Resh Laqish, the Palestinian, praised a sage who taught fixed laws — possibly referring to Mishnaic traditions — to others. By contrast the Babylonian Rav Nahman disparaged a sage of considerably more prowess who had mastered not only halakhot but other traditions as well. Such a sage was still simply a "bag of books," a repository of information, but lacked the analytical ability acclaimed in Babylonia. Here we have another internal tradition that recognizes the difference between the type of study practiced in the two rabbinic centers. Even more telling, the fourth generation Babylonian sage Rami bar Hama reportedly would not count a certain R. Menashiah b.

Tahalifa among the quorum of three necessary for the grace after meals, even though his colleague "had learned Sifra, Sifre, and halakhah" (bBer 47b). Rami trivialized memorization of traditions to such an extent that he equated R. Menashiah with an *am ha'arets* (ignoramus), whom the sages also excluded from participating in the grace.[46]

Babylonian nicknames for scholars and the metaphors for their talents likewise recognize sharpness.[47] Upon hearing Abaye explain the midrashic derivation of a point of inheritance law, Rava remarked, "A sharp knife severs the verse" (bBB 111b).[48] Elsewhere Abaye applies the same description to his teacher Rabbah's biblical exegesis (bArakh 26a). When Abaye could not resolve a complicated legal question, R. Adda b. Mattena referred the case to Rava, "whose knife is sharp" (bHul 77a).[49] Rava observed that sages from Mahoza are sharp because they drink the waters of the Hideqel (= Tigris; the Hebrew word *had* means "sharp").[50] Shmuel regularly calls Rav Yehudah *Shinena*, "sharp one," that is, "keen scholar," probably from the root *sh-n-n*, to be pointed or sharp.[51] These phrases seem to be Amoraic, which suggests that acute reasoning, if not dialectics per se, was highly valued among later Babylonian Amoraim.[52] Esteem for sharpness is rare in Palestinian sources.[53]

Study–Partners

The Bavli's emphasis on the importance of a study-partner with whom a sage learns Torah may also be related to its high regard for dialectics. This nexus is apparent in the story of R. Yohanan and Resh Laqish discussed above (bBM 84a). When R. Yohanan despairs at the death of Resh Laqish, the sages try to comfort him by providing a replacement study-partner. Their attempt fails, however, because R. Eleazar b. Pedat does not engage R. Yohanan in dialectical argumentation. R. Yohanan suffers not from the loss of a friend or student but the absence of an equal study-partner with whom to debate. That death would be preferable to such solitude is implied in another Bavli story too. Honi the Circle-Drawer returns to the study-house after a seventy-year nap (bTa 23a). The sages, however, cannot believe he is who he claims to be and do not respect him sufficiently. Honi thereupon prays for death and dies, at which point Rava comments: "Hence the saying, 'Either companionship or death.'" Honi's misery partially results from the shame he feels at not being honored, which will be discussed in Chapter 4. But the concluding proverb emphasizes the absence of a "companion," in this context referring to a study-partner in the academy. Another Bavli story relates that Levi used to "sit with" (= study together with) R. Efes. When the latter died, Levi "had no one to sit with" and therefore left Palestine and came to Babylonia, where he presumably found scholarly company and avoided the bleak fate suffered by R. Yohanan and Honi (bKet 103b).

Several exegetical traditions found in the Bavli laud study with a partner and condemn solitary study:

> R. Hama b. Hanina said: What is the meaning of the verse, *As iron sharpens iron, so a man sharpens the wit of his friend (Prov 27:17)*? Just as in the case of iron, one [piece] of iron sharpens another, so scholars sharpen each other in legal [debate].

> Rabba bar bar Hama said: Why are words of Torah compared to fire . . . ? To teach you: Just as fire does not ignite by itself, so words of Torah do not endure for [one who studies] by himself.

> This coheres with what R. Yose bar Hanina said: *A sword against the diviners* (badim) *(Jer 50:36)*. Let a sword be against the enemies of scholars[54] who busy themselves in Torah by themselves [*bad bevad*]. Not only that, but they become foolish. . . . Not only that, but they sin.[55]

The first two traditions highlight the mutual advantage of study in partnership. R. Aha bar Hanina's midrash again alludes to dialectical proficiency. The problem is not simply that a student is more prone to forget or tends to be lazier when studying alone — as Rabba bar bar Hama seems to suggest — but that study with a partner increases intellectual ability. By debating back and forth two scholars "sharpen" (*mehadedin*) each others' minds. The conception of learning depicted here is that of sages arguing with one another so as to improve their analytical skill, not that of a master repeating traditions before his students who commit them to memory. Consistent with these traditions, R. Tanhum b. R. Hiyya advises: "Form yourselves into groups when you study Torah, since Torah can only be acquired in fellowship (*bahavura*) (bBer 63b)." Yet another Bavli tradition promises great reward for those "who love to study among a multitude" (bMak 10a).

In this case it is difficult to determine whether we are dealing with a specifically Babylonian concern or a value shared with Palestinians.[56] The story of R. Yohanan, as noted above, is of late Babylonian provenance. The Yerushalmi version of the story of Honi lacks this scene, and the story of Levi and R. Efes has no Palestinian parallel.[57] While most of the exegetical traditions cited above are attributed to Palestinian sages, the only parallel found in Palestinian sources themselves is that of R. Hama bar Hanina. Here too there may be a subtle difference. The version in *Genesis Rabbah* concludes,

"Just as in the case of iron, one [piece] of iron sharpens another, so scholars improve each other."[58] While the analogy implies that the improvement relates to "sharpening," there is no mention of debate, as there is in the Bavli. Two scholars may improve one another by inspiring greater discipline or helping each other memorize traditions. We also find a tradition attributed to R. Yohanan of Anatot in the Yerushalmi: "It is as certain as the covenant that one who labors at his learning in private will not quickly forget" (yBer 9a, 5:1). This praise of private study seems at odds with the denunciations in the Bavli. While Yerushalmi stories often involve two sages studying together, they rarely insist that this is a superior arrangement.[59] At all events, traditions that place a positive value on studying with a partner appear almost exclusively in the Bavli.

Chapter 3

◌⸱◌

Violence

Readers of Bavli stories are often struck by the hostile and threatening manner with which the sages address one another: "Three hate each other, and these are they: dogs, fowl, and [Zoroastrian] priests. And some say: prostitutes. And some say, the scholars of Babylonia" (bPes 113b). Some rabbinic exchanges seem more suited to spiteful enemies than colleagues dedicated to a common religion and worldview; the citation suggests that this impression was not lost on the sages themselves.[1] When R. Hiyya becomes annoyed upon seeing a sage observe a legal stringency, potentially a display of ostentatious piety, Rabbi tells him that the sage may be a certain Yehuda b. Qenosa "whose deeds are all for the sake of heaven." To this R. Hiyya remarks, "Were you not Yehuda b. Qenosa I would have cut off your legs with an iron saw" (bBQ 81b). Yehuda's motives were beyond reproach, but anyone else would have been showing off and deserving of a very severe punishment. The Yerushalmi contains a story with a similar plot but involving different characters. In this version when R. Yehoshua tells Rabban Gamaliel that Yehuda b. Pappos's deeds are all for the sake of heaven, Rabban Gamaliel simply responds by questioning whether Yehuda nonetheless violates rabbinic mores by abiding by the stringency. A legal discussion ensues; there is no threat of dismemberment.[2] Even if we take R. Hiyya's outburst in a metaphoric sense, it seems exceedingly fierce.

Such assertions of physical violence are not infrequent. In bHag 3b R. Eliezer commands R. Yose b. Durmaskit, "Extend your hand and take out your eye"—and R. Yose complies! The reason for his wrath is that R. Yose failed to honor R. Eliezer with the deferential praise, "We are your disciples and we drink your waters," when R. Eliezer asked what had transpired in the study-house. A slight insult to R. Eliezer's honor, probably a mere oversight, is punished by mutilation (although the redactors inform us that R. Eliezer's prayers subsequently restored R. Yose's sight.) A parallel to this story appears in tYad 2:16, but there R. Yose makes the deferential response and R. Eliezer makes no rebuke, much less an order to self-mutilate. There are also other prominant signs of Stammaitic intervention that suggest that the violent motif was added to the Tannaitic source when the redactors composed the *sugya*.[3]

Yet another story involving physical deformity appears in bBB 89a. When "those of the Exilarch's house" taught that market overseers may regulate both measures and prices, Shmuel told Qarna to instruct them that overseers may regulate only measures. Qarna, however, apparently afraid of the Exilarch's power, taught that overseers may indeed regulate both. The story continues: "He [Shmuel] said to him, 'Is your name Qarna? Let a horn (*qarna*) come forth from your eye.' A horn came forth from his eye." Now *qarna* means horn, so there is an onomastic pun at work.[4] But again we see the speed with which the Bavli's sages imprecate one another. The Yerushalmi contains a similar story involving Rav and Qarna, but Rav makes no hurtful comment despite the fact that Qarna does not carry out his instructions.[5] Given such malicious sentiments, it is not surprising to find a menacing midrash to Deut 20:19, "You may eat of them (trees) but do not cut them down": "If a scholar is worthy, eat (learn) from him and do not cut him down; but if he is not worthy then cut him down and destroy him" (bTa 7a).[6] An exemplification of this attitude appears in another midrashic tradition, which relates that when Joshua forgot 300 laws and had doubts about 700 others, "all of Israel rose up to kill him" (bTem 16a). While it is hard to know how far to press this midrash as a reflection of the relations among sages, it may imply that poor performance was punished severely. In other cases, unfriendly behavior seems simply to have been the norm: Rabbi recounts that, "When I went to learn Torah with R. Eleazar b. Shamoa, his disciples ganged up on me like the cocks of Bet Buqia" (bYev 84a).[7]

The Violence of Debate

The brief comparisons with the Palestinian versions of many of these sources suggest that hostility among sages was predominantly a Babylonian issue. Indeed, the difference between the two rabbinic centers was acknowledged by the sages themselves:

> R. Oshayya said: What is [the meaning] of the verse, *I got two staffs, one of which I named* Noam *(Grace) and the other I named* Hovlim *(Damages) (Zech 11:7)?*
> *Grace* — these are the scholars in the Land of Israel who are gracious (*manimin*) to each other in halakhic [debate].

Damages—these are the scholars in Babylonia who damage (*mehablin*) each other in halakhic [debate].

It is written, *They are the two sons of oil (Zech 4:14)*, and *By it are two olive trees (Zech 4:3):*
R. Yizhaq said: *Oil*—this refers to the sages of the Land of Israel who are as pleasant (*nohin*) toward each other in halakhic [debate] as olive oil. *Olive trees*—this refers to the sages of Babylonia who are bitter toward each other in halakhic [debate] as olive trees. (bSanh 24a)[8]

R. Oshayya and R. Yizhaq contrast the polite interactions of Palestinian sages with the violent interchanges and bitter sentiments of their Babylonian colleagues.[9] The animosity apparently derives from the intensity with which the rabbis debated points of law, each arguing passionately for his opinion. Despite the representations of actual physical violence in the stories discussed above, the damage is verbal: the Babylonians insult, embarrass, or disparage their fellow sages while contesting points of law.

Because R. Oshayya and R. Yizhaq specifically mention legal debate, it is there that we might probe for the source of the violence. Many Bavli stories in fact use violent imagery in the context of argumentation. Dosa b. Harkinas warns the sages of his brother Yonatan: "Be careful lest he overwhelm (*yeqapeah;* literally, "strike") you with laws, for he has three hundred responses concerning the daughter's co-wife that she is permitted" (bYev 16a). Dosa and the sages believe that a daughter's co-wife is forbidden, so the three hundred arguments are spurious. To be bombarded by numerous responses, perhaps voiced in an antagonistic or assertive manner, apparently felt like a physical attack. The Palestinian version lacks the imagery: Dosa simply says,"Be careful of him for he has three hundred responses concerning the daughter's co-wife" (yYev 1:6, 3a). Similarly, after R. Meir dies, R. Yehuda instructs his own students, "Do not let the students of R. Meir enter here because they are disputatious; they do not come to learn Torah but to overwhelm me (literally, "strike me") with laws."[10] In the continuation of the story, a student of Meir enters and states a puzzling ruling in his master's name. R. Yehuda becomes angry, remarking that this was precisely the type of incident he wished to avoid. Thus legal challenges and complex questions advanced by pugnacious sages felt like personal assaults. The Palestinian version again omits the violent figure and gives no reason for the exclusion: "R. Yehuda ordered and said, 'Do not let the students of Meir enter here'" (yQid 2:8, 63a). The Bavli storytellers may have sought an explanation for the unusual ban on entry and found it in a common problem of their culture. Likewise, when Rav Safra pointed out a flaw in the decision of three colleagues who had formed a court, Rava remarked, "R. Safra struck down (*qaphinhu*) three ordained masters" (bGit 29b). Rashi comments, "He cut off their legs, for they could no longer find a basis for their decision."[11] The Bavli version (though not the Yerushalmi's) of the "Oven of Akhnai" relates that although R. Eliezer propounded "all the arguments in the world" proving that the oven was pure, the sages "surrounded him [R. Eliezer] with words like this snake and ruled it impure" (bBM 59a–b).[12] A snake surrounds its victim, suffocating it to death. In the perception of the Bavli storytellers, the sages' rejections of R. Eliezer's arguments were as treacherous as a dangerous snake.

In the course of argumentation, unanswerable objections seem to have been experienced as sharp blows. A sage's position was cut down, and with it his ego. In bMe 7b, for example, R. Yohanan rejects Resh Laqish's suggestion with such decisiveness that Resh Laqish "was silent," that is, he had no response. Whereupon R. Yohanan exclaimed, "I have cut off the legs of that child" (Resh Laqish was younger, hence a "child" in R. Yohanan's eyes). Thus the victor of an argument feels that he has brutalized his opponent. A sage who raises an unanswerable difficulty is said to have "thrown an axe at it."[13] A particularly chilling expression of rabbinic hostility can be found in a Bavli *baraita* at bPes 69a. R. Eliezer tells R. Akiba, "You responded to me with [the law of] slaughtering; by slaughtering you will die," an allusion to Akiba's martyrdom at the hands of the Romans.[14] The *baraita* is based on mPes 6:2, in which R. Akiba and R. Yehoshua dispute R. Eliezer's ruling concerning the slaughter of the Passover sacrifice on the Sabbath. This Mishna contains one of the most extended and complex dialectical interchanges in Tannaitic sources. R. Akiba even advances a spurious argument to illustrate the weakness of R. Eliezer's ruling, prompting R. Eliezer to protest, "Akiba, you have uprooted that which is written in the Torah!" It is not accidental that the Bavli links R. Eliezer's tragic prophecy — assuming that his statement is not meant as a horrifically mean-spirited prayer or hope — to this Mishna. R. Akiba's ingenious "response," which concludes the argument, so distresses R. Eliezer that he responds in kind. The "measure-for-measure" theme, I am suggesting, operates on two levels: slaughter is both the topic of the debate and R. Eliezer's experience in the eyes of the Bavli storytellers. At all events, to prognosticate the awful death of a colleague because he bests one in debate illustrates the viciousness of the Bavli's intellectual climate. And we find even more shocking accounts. When Rav Papa made a brilliant point in Abaye's presence, Abaye inquired as to the where-abouts of Rav Papa's parents, and upon learning that they lived in town, "set his eyes upon them and they died" (bYev 106a).

Another story of Resh Laqish and R. Yohanan may help us understand how halakhic debate degenerates into verbal "damage." A late Bavli narrative relates that R. Yohanan encountered a brigand named Resh Laqish, recruited him, taught him Torah, made him a sage and married him to his own sister (bBM 84a).[15] The story continues:

> One day they disagreed in the academy:
>> *The sword and the knife and the dagger and the saw and the spear — when are they subject to impurity? When their manufacture is complete.*
>
> And when is their manufacture complete? R. Yohanan said, "When they temper them in an oven." Resh Laqish said, "When they furbish them in water." He [R. Yohanan] said to him, "A brigand knows brigandage." He [Resh Laqish] said to him, "So how did you benefit me? There [when I was a brigand leader] they called me 'Master.' Here they call me 'Master.'" He said to him, "I benefited you in bringing you under the wings of the Divine Presence." R. Yohanan felt insulted (*halish daatei*). Resh Laqish became ill (*halish*) (as punishment for causing R. Yohanan to feel hurt).

Two brothers-in-law, also friends and colleagues, disagree over a point of law: at what stage is the process of manufacturing a sword complete such that it becomes susceptible to impurity. Their dispute quickly turns to insults: annoyed that his study-partner rejects his opinion, R. Yohanan calls Resh Laqish a brigand, snidely reminding him of his sordid past. Resh Laqish in turn rejects everything that R. Yohanan did to make him a sage, causing his former teacher to feel great anguish. Tragedy ensues; the story relates that despite R. Yohanan's sister's entreaties on behalf of her husband, he shows no mercy and Resh Laqish dies. We sense how rejection of one's opinion easily can be interpreted as personal rejection, how an attack on one's position can be confused with an attack on one's person. As a result, a sage lashes out against his opponent rather than against his opponent's claims. The more intense the debate, the greater the potential that it will break down into insults.

Here the topic of the debate, the manufacture of a weapon, and the allusions to brigandage contribute to the bellicose climate.[16] That Resh Laqish equates a "master," literally, a "rabbi" (*rabbi*), of brigandage and a rabbinic master suggests that the two enterprises have much in common. At the outset of the story R. Yohanan in fact recruits Resh Laqish with the exhortation, "Your strength for Torah," after seeing him display great physical prowess by vaulting over the Jordan River. Resh Laqish thus exchanges physical ability for mental aptitude and mastery over brigands for rabbinic mastery. He also exchanges an environment of physical violence (swords and brigandage) for verbal violence, namely disputes that breed insults and *ad hominem* attacks. Ironically, as we discussed in the previous chapter, the story proceeds with R. Yohanan longing for Resh Laqish and their intricate debates to such an extent that he goes out of his mind and dies. Relationships among Babylonian sages were evidently a very tricky business.[17] They depended on study-partners for rigorous argumentation but simultaneously risked insulting their partners in the heat of the debate. A razor's edge seems to have separated intense argumentation — the prerequisite for rabbinic life — from verbal insults that could cause embarrassment and (social and metaphoric) death.[18]

Descriptions of rabbinic debates in the Bavli routinely employ words connoting antagonism and physical struggle. A story in bKet 103b begins, "When R. Hanina and R. Hiyya were striving (*mintsu*), R. Hanina said to R. Hiyya, 'Do you strive with me? Were the Torah, God forbid, to be forgotten in Israel, I would restore it by means of my dialectical arguments.'" The sages were simply disputing, that is, "striving," over a point of law, and R. Hanina warned that because of his skill, R. Hiyya was sure to lose. But the storyteller uses a verb that means to quarrel and fight.[19] In the story of the Oven of Akhnai, R. Yirmiah exclaims, "When sages defeat (*menatshim*) each other in law, what is it for you?" and God subsequently concedes, "My sons have defeated me!" (bBM 59a–b). The verb "defeat" (*n-ts-ḥ*) primarily refers to conquest in physical confrontations and battle, and is applied in a secondary sense to victory in argumentation. A midrash found in bSanh 105a calls the answer of the "community of Israel" to the prophet Jeremiah a "conquering response" (*teshuva nitsehet*).[20] The technical terminology of the Bavli even takes on this bellicose character. The term *matqif leih,* literally "he attacked him," that is, "he objected to his opinion," often introduces a challenge to a sage's pronouncements. Interestingly, this expression is used first by third generation Amoraim, and regularly in subsequent generations.[21] There is a parallel increase in the amount of dialectical argumentation attributed to sages of the latter Amoraic generations.[22] Thus the preference for dialectical debate constituted by "objections and solutions," as described in the previous chapter, goes hand in hand with combative terminology.

The Wars of Torah

A common metaphor for the rabbinic vocation is the "wars of Torah" — this we find in both Babylonian and Palestinian sources.[23] The sages conceived of their struggles to learn Torah, perform the commandments, and help their fellow Jews lead pious lives as a holy war. Where their biblical ancestors fought battles against the inhabitants of Canaan to carry out God's plan, so they struggled against Roman and Persian oppressors, heretics, nonrabbinic Jews, the evil impulse, sin, laziness, and suchlike. However much the sages perceived themselves as a scholastic class of philosophers, they simultaneously saw themselves as soldiers waging war. This self-conception helps explain the violent tenor of rabbinic interactions.

Bavli interpretations of biblical passages frequently render warlike imagery in terms of the "war of Torah." A midrash attributed to R. Yohanan on Prov 24:6, "For by stratagems (*tahbulot*) you wage war," comments, "In whom do you find the war of Torah? In one who possesses bundles (*havilot*) of Mishna" (bSanh 42a). The "stratagem" that serves the sages is not expertise in military tactics but knowledge of legal sources. In bMeg 15b R. Eleazar interprets Isa 28:6, "Those who repel attacks at the gate," as "those who give-and-take in the war of Torah."[24] He analogizes the thrusts and parries of the defenders of a city to the verbal "give-and-take" involved in debate. We saw two similar examples of this conception of academic debate in the discussion of dialectics (Chap. 2). The midrash concerning Moses's petitions that Judah be allowed to enter the heavenly academy interprets the phrase from Deut 33:7, "let his hands strive for him," as the ability "to engage in the give-and-take of debate" and the phrase, "help him against his foes," as "solving an objection."[25] Similarly, the midrash rabbinizing the description of King David, "he is mighty, a warrior" (1 Sam 16:18), explains, "he knows how to respond" and "he knows how to give-and-take in the wars of Torah."[26] Rav Kahana interprets Ps 45:4, "Gird your sword upon your thigh, O hero," in terms of "words of Torah." As Rashi explains, "Be careful to review your studies such that they will be ready for you to bring proof in the course of debate, just as the sword on the thigh of the hero [is ready] to triumph in battle."[27]

If biblical imagery of battle translates into discussions of Torah, then biblical foes turn into opponents:

> [*Happy is the man who fills his quiver with them; they shall not be put to shame*] *When they contend with the enemy in the gate (Ps 127:5)*. R. Hiyya bar Abba said: "What is *the enemy in the gate*? Even a father and son or a teacher and disciple who busy themselves with Torah in one gate become enemies toward each other, but they do not move from there until they become friends with one another." (bQid 30b)

There is a nice play here on the rabbinic use of "gate" (Hebrew: *shaar* = Aramaic: *bava*), which refers to the divisions of lengthy tractates; the first three divisions of the tractate of damages are called *Bava Qama* (first gate), *Bava Metsia* (middle gate), and *Bava Batra* (last gate). A soldier contending with "an enemy in the gate" becomes a sage disputing with his colleague over a point of rabbinic law. Consistent with the traditions we have seen, Rashi comments that they become enemies "because they object against each other and neither accepts the other's opinion."[28] While R. Hiyya bar Abba optimistically claims that fathers and sons and teachers and their students resume amiable relations once they cease their debate, we can well imagine that unrelated sages, especially those with personality conflicts or prior histories of bad feelings, might not be so quick to cool off. The result: scholars of Babylonia hate one another, as the tradition quoted at the outset of this chapter relates.[29]

Several sources apply military imagery to the rabbinic academy even independent of the exegesis of biblical verses. In the story of the deposition of Rabban Gamaliel, the Nasi tells a student: "Wait until the shield-bearers enter the study-house" (bBer 27b). Rashi explains this reference, which the Yerushalmi's version omits: "the sages, who combat each other in halakhic debate."[30] A metaphoric shield evidently helps defend against verbal attacks. We have had occasion to mention the story of the Shammaites' outnumbering the Hillelites and decreeing eighteen edicts.[31] In the Bavli's retelling, "[t]hey stuck a sword in the study-house. They said: Let he who would enter, enter. But let he who would depart, not depart" (bShab 17a).[32] Such disturbing memories perhaps explain the proviso, "One may not enter the study house with weapons" (bSanh 82a). While metaphoric shields protect against metaphoric warfare, they might not help against real weapons and actual bloodshed.

Orality and Violence

How are we to explain this prominent thematization of violence? Several factors should be taken into account. First, the discipline of law — study, practice, judicial activity, and enforcement — generally involves conflict and the exertion of force. Many cultures accordingly portray legal interactions with metaphors of war and combat. Greco-Roman sources, for example, frequently analogize speaking in court and debating in public to battle.[33] While rabbinic law clearly has some idiosyncrasies such as the hefty component of biblical exegesis, it shares the oppositional structure with other societies.

Second, although the sages were highly literate, they functioned in a predominantly oral cultural milieu.[34] The rabbis distinguished the Bible, "the Written Torah," from rabbinic tradition, "the Oral Torah," and insisted that the two types of revelation retain their distinct characters. All sages committed to memory the traditions they received from the mouths of their masters. In addition, a professional class of memorizers known as *tannaim*, literally "repeaters," served as repositories for oral texts. These "living books" possessed excellent memories (though not necessarily excellent intellects) and were called upon to repeat traditions before a master and his disciples.[35] Individual sages may have taken notes or jotted down rabbinic traditions for private study, but these unofficial texts had no authority and were not adduced during official study-sessions.[36] As Martin Jaffee has argued, performance must be distinguished from composition, and public from private use.[37] When the sages performed by reciting, interpreting, and debating in formal sessions, they worked from memory. Furthermore, texts in antiquity were expensive and difficult to procure, so that memory played a much greater role than it did after the printing press facilitated the mass production of books. Even cultures with long traditions of literacy functioned as "residually oral cultures" in which significant amounts of information were committed to memory. Both technical and ideological reasons thus contributed to the rabbis functioning in an oral matrix. Yaakov Elman accordingly uses the expression "pervasive orality" to describe Babylonian rabbinic culture, a situation that prevailed well into the Geonic period, as we know explicitly from later sources.[38]

Oral and predominantly oral cultures typically evince a more violent tenor than cultures in which writing is the dominant mode of expression. Literate cultures often conduct social and interpersonal dealings through exchanges of texts. Writing mediates the interaction and attenuates the immediacy of the experience. In oral cultures, however, social intercourse is always face-to-face. Combative and hostile interactions will therefore be experienced more acutely in oral than literate cultures. For this reason Walter Ong describes oral cultures as "agonist":

> Many, if not all, oral or residually oral cultures strike literates as extraordinarily agonist in their verbal performance and indeed in their lifestyle. Writing fosters abstractions that disengage knowledge from the arena where human beings struggle with one another. It separates the knower from the known. By keeping knowledge embedded in the human life world, orality situates knowledge within a context of struggle.
>
> . . . [V]iolence in oral art forms is also connected with the structure of orality itself. When all verbal communication must be by direct word of mouth, involved in the give-and-take dynamics of sound, interpersonal relations are kept high — both attractions and, even more, antagonisms.[39]

Discussions and disputes conducted through letters or publications are more easily limited to the topic at issue, as the parties tend to recede to the background. The text is present, not the opponent, so the debate focuses on the issue rather than the individual. Time passes between the exchanges, which allows both sides to calm down, rethink the matter and measure their response before the next reply. Debates in oral milieus involve opponents speaking directly to one another. Topics are inevitably identified with their proponents, not apprehended as abstract issues. Conversation is direct, unmediated, and often fast-paced, which can prompt tempers to flare and insults or fists to be hurled. Of course written exchanges can include insults, nastiness, and the most vicious polemics.[40] But no matter how incensed one becomes, one cannot lash out and physically attack an opponent who is not present.

Violent and military imagery found in Babylonian rabbinic sources should be attributed in part to the oral cultural milieu. This is not to say that the sages actually fought or behaved violently. The point is that the sages experienced the study-house and academy as a hostile, combative environment, and that experience colored numerous sources and especially narrative traditions.

Palestinian sages, to a certain extent, shared the oral matrix and legal discipline with the Babylonians, and consequently we find some military metaphors and violent imagery in Palestinian documents and attributed to Palestinian sages in the Bavli. For example, in tYev 1:10 R. Yehoshua declines to answer a legal query directly, protesting: "Why do you interpose my head between two great mountains, the House of Hillel and the House of Shammai, lest they crush my skull."[41] Similarly, R. Zeira expresses reluctance to venture into a dispute between the Houses: "If I did not wish to raise my head among lions, I would say . . ." (yShab 1:5, 4a).[42] Yet the violent character is much more pronounced in the Bavli, as evidenced both by comparisons of parallel traditions and the explicit testimony of rabbinic sources.[43] The accentuated Babylonian level resulted in part from the fact that writing was much more common among Palestinian rabbis and throughout Greco-Roman culture in general.[44] Zoroastrian texts, for example, were passed down orally for well over a millennium, and were not preserved in writing until the sixth century C.E. Even then the written copies had impact on the actual practice of the religion only in a handful of central temples.[45]

The main reason, however, for the thematization of violence in the Bavli relates to the topics discussed in the previous two chapters, the highly structured Stammaitic academy and the emphasis placed on dialectical debate. Argumentation embodied verbal struggle. Through objections, solutions, answers, and responses a sage attempted to prove his opinion correct and his opponent's wrong, to win the debate and defeat the other side. Since status and, to a certain extent, rank within the academy depended on dialectical ability, the Stammaim devoted their energy to prevailing in academic debates. We can imagine that they seized available opportunities to show off their skill by directing vicious objections against others. A sage who stuck his neck out, so to speak, to voice his opinion risked being bombarded with objections. To participate in the soul of academic life therefore entailed entering into verbal battles on a daily basis. For the Stammaim, in other words, the academy was a competitive environment characterized more by struggle than by mutual collaboration. Combine the valorization of argumentation and competitive spirit with the "agonist" ethos of the oral milieu and you have a hostile climate, even if the sages were on their best behavior. Given the egos involved, high stakes, and an irritating (or "disputatious") personality or two, arguments sometimes turned to insults and *ad hominem* assaults, raising the level of contentiousness to an even higher pitch.

In Palestine argumentation played a role in rabbinic life but was neither the focus of activity nor the touchstone that determined status. Sages with weak dialectical skills could gain respect by mastering traditions and recalling them accurately—perhaps even more respect than the dialectician.[46] Less jockeying for ranks took place in the smaller Palestinian disciple circles and schools than in the larger Babylonian academies. Palestinian sages certainly considered themselves to be engaged in the general "war of Torah" as a personal spiritual discipline and religious struggle within the wider Jewish community.[47] They sometimes functioned as judges, litigants, and witnesses in judicial settings. But they apparently did not experience the same intensity of dialectical argumentation that prevailed in the Stammaitic academies in Babylonia.[48] Note that most of the traditions containing violent imagery which are surveyed above are set in the context of halakhic debate.

A final factor that contributes to the Bavli's thematization of violence is the significance of shame in Babylonian rabbinic culture, which will be discussed in the next chapter. To suffer public humiliation was among the most terrible experiences; to humiliate someone else among the greatest sins. Insults and verbal attacks intended to embarrass another person were experienced in a very real way, almost tantamount to physical violence. So while verbal violence is attested in both Palestinian and Babylonian Amoraic traditions, it is most pronounced in the Bavli, on account of the combative ethos of Stammaitic times.

Graciousness

According to a rabbinic legend preserved in both Talmuds, the primacy of the House of Hillel over the House of Shammai was decided by a heavenly voice that stated, "Both these and those are the words of the living God. But the Law follows the House of Hillel" (bEruv 13b; yBer 1:6, 3b).[49] While the Yerushalmi suffices with this tradition, in quintessential Talmudic style, the Bavli seeks to know more:

> And since "both these and those are the words of the living God," why did the House of Hillel merit that the law be established according to their [words]?

> Because they were gracious (*nohim*) and modest (*aluvin*), and they would teach their words and the words of the House of Shammai. Not only that, but they [were so modest that they] would mention the words of the House of Shammai before their own words. (bEruv 13b)[50]

This rationale is surprising in light of both the Bavli's privileging of dialectics and its violent academic climate. We might have expected the Bavli to have attributed the divine preference for the House of Hillel to their superior dialectical skill or "sharpness." Instead the Bavli claims that God sided with Hillelite legal opinions on account of their benevolent disposition and humility.

This tradition should probably be understood as an attempt to ameliorate the hostile environment that prevailed within the Babylonian academies. By portraying the character of the early sages as gracious and claiming that God rewarded them on that account, the storytellers construct an exemplary model for the contentious students of their times.[51] Recall that the tradition cited above contrasting the sages of the two rabbinic centers describes the Palestinians as gracious (*manimin*) and pleasant (*nohin*). Here too the purpose, in part, was to present a more salutary model for Babylonian sages to emulate. In fact, we find a considerable number of prescriptive traditions in the Bavli urging sages to be modest and cordial. Two sayings attributed to Resh Laqish assert that God pays attention to two scholars "who are gracious to each other in legal debate" and who "listen to each other in legal debate" (bShab 63a). According to R. Hanina b. Idi, "Words of Torah endure only for one who has a humble disposition" (bTa 7a). R. Yohanan relates, "Words of Torah endure only for one who behaves as if he is nothing" (bSot 21b). Similarly, R. Eleazar interpreted "bed of spices" (Song 5:13) to teach that "if a man acts as a bed upon which all tread, and as spices with which all perfume themselves, then his learning will be preserved" (bEruv 54a). The sense of the analogy to spices is that a sage should behave pleasantly, just as the spices give off a pleasant aroma.[52] Of course modesty and humility are standard rabbinic virtues emphasized in dozens of sources.[53] The aforecited traditions, however, are set in a context of rabbinic study in that they mention either relations between students or reward of superior knowledge. While these traditions are attributed to Palestinians, I am aware of neither parallels nor similar traditions in the Yerushalmi.

The Stammaim provide numerous accounts reflecting the verbal violence and hostility that prevailed within the late Babylonian academies. They were well aware of the detrimental effects of this climate and the wounds suffered by offended parties. They tried to improve the academic ethos by stressing the importance of cordial relations, creating exemplary models of earlier sages who behaved modestly, and promising reward to scholars who maintained a humble attitude while engaging in debate. They also repeatedly cautioned students of the severe consequences that would result from shaming their colleagues — to this topic we now turn.

Chapter 4

⌣∴⌣

Shame

Once Rabban Gamaliel said, "Summon seven [sages] to my upper-story tomorrow morning [in order to intercalate the year]."[1]

When he arrived there he found eight. He said, "He who came up here without permission — let him descend." Samuel the Little stood up and said, "It was I who came up here without permission. I did not come here to intercalate the year, but I needed to learn the practical law [of how intercalation is done]." He [Gamaliel] said to him, "Sit down, my son, sit down. It is fitting that all years be intercalated with your [participation]. However, the sages have said, 'The intercalation of the year may be done only by those who were invited.'"

And it was not Samuel the Little [who had not been invited] but another man. But he [Samuel] acted this way to avoid shaming [his colleague]. (bSanh 11a)

T he first two sections of this story illustrate the zeal necessary to become a master of Torah. So dedicated was Samuel the Little to learn the details of a rare point of law, the procedure for intercalating the year, that he appeared uninvited at an elite gathering of sages. Torah must be actively pursued, not passively absorbed.[2] The last section, however, changes the slant of the story and teaches a completely different lesson: that one must do everything possible to spare another person from experiencing shame. Samuel the Little told a white lie and risked being reprimanded to protect the feelings of his colleague, whose motives for intruding upon the assembly are unknown.

This final addendum is clearly the work of the Stammaim. It is in Aramaic, while the first two sections are in Hebrew (the italics illustrate the linguistic shift). The Stammaitic stratum of the Bavli is mostly Aramaic, and such Aramaic addenda to Hebrew statements of the Amoraim are among the clearest signposts of Stammaitic activity.[3] Furthermore, the version of the story that appears in the Yerushalmi, although not identical to the Bavli's, lacks the final section (ySanh 1:2, 18c). Rabban Gamaliel offers a similar comforting comment to Samuel the Little, that he considers Samuel worthy in principle to intercalate the year, and the story concludes with the narrator informing us that they did not perform the intercalation on that day but upon the next. Samuel himself, not another sage, intruded on the gathering. Shame is never mentioned. Thus both form-criticism (the Aramaic vs. Hebrew) and source-criticism (comparing the Yerushalmi's version) suggest that the Stammaim reworked a Palestinian source.[4]

When we compare Talmudic stories we often find that the Bavli version stresses the theme of shame where the Yerushalmi does not mention it. Let us look at another example.

yShab 6:9, 8d	*bShab 156b*
Two students of R. Hanina went out to cut wood. A certain astrologer saw them. He said, "These two will go out but not return."	From the case of Shmuel too [we learn that] 'Israel has no constellation.'[5] Shmuel and Ablet [a Persian sage] were sitting, and certain men passed by [on the way to] the fields. Ablet said to Shmuel, "That man is going but will not return, for a snake will bite him and he will die." Shmuel said to him, "He will go and return."
When they went out they came upon a certain old man. He said to them, "Give me alms, for it has been three days since I have tasted anything." They had a loaf of bread. They cut it in half and gave it to him." He ate and prayed for them. He said to them, "May your souls be preserved this day just as you have preserved my soul for me this day." They went out safely and came back safely.	They were still sitting while he went and returned.

There were some men there who had heard his [the astrologer's] words. They said to him, "Did you not say, 'These two will go out but not return'"? He said, "There is here a man of lies [=me] whose astrology is lies." Even so they went and searched and found a snake, half in this one's load and half in the other's.

Ablet stood up and cast off his [the man's] bag. He found there a snake sliced apart and cut into two pieces.

They said, "What good deed did you do today?" They told him the deed.

Shmuel said to him [the man], "What have you done?" He said to him, "Every day we toss all our bread together (into a basket) and we eat. Today there was one among us who had no bread, and he felt ashamed. I said to them, 'I will get up and toss (the bread in the basket).' When I got to him I pretended as if I took from him in order that he not be ashamed." He [Shmuel] said to him, "You did a righteous deed (*tsedaqa*)!"

He [the astrologer] said, "What can I do? For the God of the Jews is appeased by half a loaf."

Shmuel went forth and expounded, "Righteousness (*tsedaqa*) saves from death, not only from an unusual death, but from death itself."[6]

The two stories share the same basic plot: a gentile astrologer predicts that a Jew (or two Jews) will die. The Jew performs a righteous deed and is rewarded with a type of miracle, the inadvertent killing of the snake that had entered his pack and was "destined" to kill him. The stars therefore do not determine the fate of Jews, at least not conclusively. Rather, the performance of righteous deeds (*mitsvot*) and presumably sins, which respectively earn rewards and trigger punishment, is the decisive influence on a Jew's life. There are a number of differences. To list but a few: the Bavli introduces the story as a conflict in predictive power between a rabbi and a gentile sage and concludes with the rabbi expounding the moral. In the Yerushalmi the opposition is implicit; no sage rejects the astrologer's assertion. Ablet predicts that the man will be killed by a snake; the astrologer in the Yerushalmi simply foretells that the men will not return.

Of interest to us is the nature of the meritorious deed that bestows life. In the Yerushalmi the two sages give charity, feeding a hungry man. In the Bavli, the hero prevents a co-worker from being shamed. He does not feed the poor man or even give him alms; apparently all the workers will share the potluck meal even if they do not contribute. By pretending that the man had proffered food the hero enables him to eat without embarrassment. Again it seems that the Bavli storytellers have reworked a story similar to the version preserved in the Yerushalmi. For in the Yerushalmi the cutting of the snake fits neatly: when the sages replaced the knife after slicing their loaf they happened to kill the snake. And they went out to cut wood, so we know that they carry a knife or axe. A measure-for-measure theme is generated: they cut their bread in half, God or providence cuts the snake in half. As the old man explicitly prays: they sustained a life, so God sustained their lives. The Bavli version lacks a connection between the hero's deed and the severed snake. Nor is it clear exactly how or when the snake was cut. Rashi fills in the narrative gap: "he had cut it (the snake) with the reeds without knowing it."[7] Yet the story does not mention reeds either. Moreover, the scenario of workers combining their food seems contrived. The storytellers probably devised this strange supping method in order to incorporate the theme of shame. In any event, whatever the precise history of the tradition, shame, absent from a Palestinian story, becomes the focus of the Babylonian version.

In this thematization of shame there is more at stake than an interesting variation in the ethical interests of the two Talmuds. The Bavli's emphasis on shame ultimately relates to important aspects of Babylonian academic life: *Many of the sources that deal with shame pertain directly to the academy or to relations between sages.* In other words, we are dealing with a specific academic concern, not merely an ethic that the Bavli deems essential to general Jewish social relations. A fine example of this phenomenon is the well-known story of the Oven of Akhnai, which I wish to consider at some length due to its centrality to this topic (bBM 59a–b).[8] The first half of the story centers on the nature of the legal process and the interpretive authority of the sages.[9] R. Eliezer and the sages disagree about the purity of an oven constructed in an unusual way.[10] The sages reject R. Eliezer's arguments, the miracles he performs, and even a heavenly voice pronouncing him correct. This conflict illustrates both the potential gap between the original, divine intent of the Torah and rabbinic interpretation and also the paradox that the sages are simultaneously aware of, and partially responsible for that gap. The second half of the story takes a different tack. The sages ban R. Eliezer and burn his purities. When R. Akiba informs R. Eliezer of the ban, R. Eliezer weeps at the degradation and humiliation. God punishes the sages for retaliating against R. Eliezer by devastating the crops and by almost drowning Rabban Gamaliel, the Nasi, who apparently bears primary responsibility for the ban. The story concludes:

> Imma Shalom, the wife of R. Eliezer, was the sister of Rabban Gamaliel. After that event she never allowed him [Eliezer] to fall on his face [and pray]. That day was the new month and a poor man came and stood at the door. While she was giving him bread she found that he [Eliezer] had fallen on his face. She said, "Stand up. You have killed my brother." Meanwhile the shofar [blast] went out from the House of Rabban Gamaliel [signalling that he had died]. He said to her, "How did you know?" She said to him, "Thus I have received a tradition from my father's house: 'All the gates are locked except for the gates of verbal wronging.'"

Imma Shalom futilely attempts to prevent R. Eliezer from pouring out his heart in prayer, for she knows from the near drowning that her brother is in grave danger. A distraction gives R. Eliezer the opportunity, he expresses his pain at the humiliating treatment, and Rabban Gamaliel immediately dies. The final line of the story points explicitly to Rabban Gamaliel's sin: verbal wronging (*onaat devarim*).

"Verbal wronging," a rabbinic term lacking a precise English equivalent, comprises a broad prohibition against all types of harmful speech, including humiliation, shame, and insults. Imma Shalom's final comment explains the magnitude of this sin. While God may have locked the "gates of prayer" or even the "gates of tears," meaning that he may ignore prayers and weeping due to the rupture caused by the destruction of the temple, he always responds to the pain of the victim of verbal wronging. An explicit interpretive key to the story blames the sages for having verbally wronged R. Eliezer through their retributive ban and the pernicious impact of that news.

Not only does the conclusion of the story point to verbal wronging, the redactional context focuses attention on this theme. The story appears in the section of Talmud that comments on mBM 4:10, which articulates the prohibition and provides several examples.[11] Preceding the story is an aggadic *sugya* comprised of additional traditions about the nature and severity of this sin. A few excerpts are worth citing, as they provide further illustration of the Bavli's sentiments:

(A) A Tanna taught before Rav Nahman bar Yizhaq, "Whoever whitens the face (= embarrasses) of another in public, it is as if he sheds his blood." He said to him, "You have spoken well. For the red [color] leaves and white comes."

(B) Abaye said to Rav Dimi, "What are they careful about in the West (= Israel)?" He said to him, "About whitening the face, as R. Hanina said, 'All who descend to Gehennom rise except for three who descend and do not rise. And these are they: He who calls his fellow by a nickname, and he who whitens the face of his fellow in public, and he who has intercourse with a married woman.'"

(C) Rabbi bar bar Hanna said in the name of R. Yohanan, "It is better for a man to have intercourse with a married woman, but let him not whiten the face of his fellow in public."

(D) "It is better for a man to throw himself into a fiery furnace, and let him not whiten the face of his fellow in public."

(E) Rav Hisda said, "All the gates have been locked except for the gates of wronging." R. Eleazar said, "[Punishment] for all [sins] is by a messenger except for wronging."

We have an impressive collection of denunciations of shame and verbal wronging. The sin is worse than adultery (C), equated with bloodshed (A), punished directly by God (E) with eternal perdition (B), and should be avoided even at the cost of death (D). Rav Hisda's saying about the locked gates (E) is the very tradition that Imma Shalom ascribes to "her father's house" and which provides the explicit redactional link to the story. In this context, the story functions primarily to illustrate how the sin of verbal wronging bears extremely severe consequences. The first half of the story, which focuses on the paradoxes about interpretive authority and rabbinic legislative autonomy, fades into the background. It serves as an introduction, a lengthy exposition, to the real concern of the story.

Support for this interpretation can be found once again by comparing the Yerushalmi's version, which closely parallels the first half of the story.[12] In this account, however, R. Eliezer reacts with anger, not tears, when informed of the ban. The destruction of crops results not from divine punishment for the sages' treatment of R. Eliezer but from the wrathful unleashing of his supernatural powers. More important, the second half of the Yerushalmi's story diverges completely. Neither Rabban Gamaliel nor Imma Shalom nor verbal wronging are mentioned, and there is neither potential drowning nor threat to the life of any sage, much less a death. Instead the story concludes with additional debasement of R. Eliezer. Whereas the Bavli story construes R. Eliezer as the victim and punishes the sages for wronging him, the Yerushalmi presents him as the culprit and punishes him for opposing the sages. We have another example to add to the two stories discussed above where the Bavli thematizes shame / verbal wronging while the Yerushalmi lacks it completely.

The Yerushalmi story appears in Tractate Moed Qatan juxtaposed with a Mishna that mentions the ban and following a series of stories about individuals who were banned.[13] I have argued elsewhere that the Bavli version shows clear signs of reworking by the Stammaim.[14] It seems that they revised a version similar to that of the Yerushalmi and recontextualized it in Tractate Bava Metsia in relation to a Mishna that mentions verbal wronging. While the Yerushalmi focuses on the ban and the consequences of opposing the sages, the Stammaim changed the story and its context to emphasize the verbal wronging and shaming of R. Eliezer.[15] And by integrating the theme of shame into that story, they made an extremely bold statement: *despite* the importance of rabbinic authority and the integrity of the legal process, the sin of verbal wronging outweighs them both.

Shame and the Late Babylonian Academy

The key question is, What explains the Bavli's heightened focus on shame? The answer relates to the complex of factors discussed in the previous chapters: the highly structured academy, dialectical argumentation, and verbal violence. To begin to see these interrelations, let us take note again of the differences in the versions of a brief tradition discussed in the Introduction. When asked a question concerning a Mishna in Tractate Bikkurim, R. Eleazar responds as follows:

yBik 1:8, 64d
R. Eleazar said to him: "You ask about a matter which the sages of the assembly-house still need [to explain]."

bBB 81a–b
He [R. Eleazar] said to him, "Do you ask me in the study-house about a matter which former scholars did not explain in order to shame me?"

In the Yerushalmi R. Eleazar simply points out that the question pertains to an exceedingly difficult issue, a matter that the sages have yet to resolve. That is why he has no answer for his colleague. In the Bavli, R. Eleazar reproaches the interlocutor with a rhetorical question implying that the initial query was inappropriate. Difficult issues should not be asked *in the study-house* because failure to answer results in *shame*. A rabbi who cannot answer a question directed at him will lose face before the sages and students who witness the incident in the study-house. Note that in the Yerushalmi the "assembly-house" functions simply as a modifier for "the sages"; we do not know where the encounter took place. But in the Bavli the "study-house" is the locus of the event and, more importantly, the cause of the problem. This variation tallies well with the shift described in Chapter 1, that the Bavli tends to locate events in the study-house, which often signifies the Babylonian academy.[16] In the heavily populated academy, a sage's inability to answer is manifest to all.

R. Eliezer's aversion to queries may seem surprising in light of the Bavli's evaluation of the questions, objections, and responses of dialectical argumentation as the highest form of academic ability (as discussed in Chap. 2). Yet because of the potential for queries to cause shame, that is precisely the stance taken by several sources. R. Hiyya rebuked Rav when he once asked an unanticipated question of Rabbi Yehuda HaNasi: "Did I not say to you that when Rabbi [Yehuda HaNasi] is occupied with one tractate you should not ask him about another tractate. Perhaps he will not be acquainted with it. Were Rabbi [Yehuda HaNasi] not a great man, you would have shamed him, for he would have taught an incorrect teaching. In this case, however, he taught you correctly (bShab 3a–b)." Fortunately Rabbi Yehuda HaNasi happened to know the answer to Rav's question. Had he not known, or had he answered incorrectly, he would have been shamed. Off-topic questions, likely to catch even the most erudite masters unprepared, simply should not be asked. Surprisingly, even questions related to the topic at hand perhaps should be avoided. An anecdote relates that Rav Shimi bar Ashi would regularly attend the lectures of Rav Papa and "would make many objections." Once he came upon his master praying, "May the Merciful One save me from the shame of Shimi." Shimi therefore "resolved to be silent and not to make objections again" (bTa 9b).[17] In this case Shimi did not intend to embarrass his teacher, but his objections were too good. When he found out how much distress he caused Rav Papa, he stopped objecting. Elsewhere the Bavli explicitly warns students against asking questions that their teachers cannot answer. R. Hiyya interpreted Prov 23:1–2, which begins, *When you sit down to dine with a ruler,* in terms of "a student sitting before his master," as follows: "If a student knows that his master can respond with the answer, let him ask. If not, *Consider who is before you. Thrust a knife into your gullet if you have a large appetite (Prov 23:1–2),* and leave him be" (bHul 6a). Rashi explains that the student should restrain his mouth (as if a knife were against his throat) and not embarrass his teacher. He should "kill" his appetite for knowledge and leave his teacher alone.[18]

We thus find an interesting paradox in the Bavli's attitude toward dialectics. On the one hand, to propound questions and objections is the goal of academic life and an important measure of status. On the other, questions and objections should be propounded with great caution, even avoided in certain circumstances, because they may embarrass a scholar who cannot provide the requisite answer. This tension is particularly evident in an account of a conflict between Rav Amram and Rabbah (bBM 20b). When Rav Amram advanced a solid objection to Rabbah's argument, Rabbah insulted Rav Amram before responding. Thereupon, the column supporting the study-house split in two. Each sage claimed the column ruptured in protest for the way he was treated.[19] Rav Amram believed Rabbah's insult provoked the supernatural portent. Rabbah believed that Rav Amram ought not to have asked him a difficult question that might have shamed him. That the storyteller leaves this question open suggests that both perspectives are plausible.

In these sources the questioners harbored no ill will towards their colleagues, and yet the possibility of accidentally shaming them mandated caution. How much the more so did sages constitute acute sources of danger when motivated by base intentions! When Rav Avia once angered Rava by sitting with muddy shoes upon his couch, Rava "wished to distress him," so he posed a formidable question. Rav Avia knew the answer, prompting Rav Nahman b. Yizhaq to observe, "Blessed be the Merciful One that Rava did not shame Rav Avia" (bShab 46a–b). In this case Rava's attack failed; presently we shall see why Rav Nahman was so relieved that no shame resulted. A more malicious example appears in the story of the attempted deposition of Rabban Shimon b. Gamaliel (bHor 13b–14a).[20] At the outset of the story Rabban Shimon b. Gamaliel, the Nasi, wishes to create a distinction between the honor shown to him and the honor shown to R. Meir and R. Natan, who hold the second and third positions in the academic hierarchy.[21] He therefore changes the way the students rise in honor when his colleagues enter the academy. In return R. Meir and R. Natan plot to challenge Rabban Gamaliel to teach Uqtsin, an obscure tractate which he does not know, when he enters the academy on the morrow. In this way they hope to depose him and to each move up one rank. When Rabbi Yaakov b. Qudshai hears of the plot he remarks, "Perhaps, God forbid, it will result in shame?" and tips off Rabban Gamaliel, who proceeds to study the tractate. The two scholars challenge the Nasi as planned, but he has boned up on the material and even stymies his rivals. Rabban Gamaliel acknowledges, "Had I not learned it, you would have shamed me," and immediately he banishes his opponents from the academy. Again the failure to answer a question, in this case the call to expound a particular subject, would have humiliated a sage. Only the lucky intervention of a colleague, horrified at the prospect of shame, obviates the situation.

The plot of this story turns almost entirely on shame and its interrelated component, honor, so we should pay close attention to the confluence of the factors we have been tracing. When Rabban Gamaliel reduces the two sages' honor, they feel ashamed and respond in kind, by attempting to shame him. Consider the impact of shame upon academic rank. R. Meir and R. Natan assume that they can depose the Nasi by exposing his lack of knowledge and thus shaming him. This helps explain why avoiding shame is so important. Maintaining one's position in the academic hierarchy depended, to some extent, on not being shamed. It was not simply that a sage would feel like a fool or lose self-esteem for not knowing the answer, but that he might either officially be demoted or lose his unofficial rank in the eyes of his colleagues. The Bavli's version of the story of Honi the Circle Drawer reveals the catastrophic results of loss of status. After a seventy-year nap Honi returns to the study-house. The sages, however, cannot believe he is really Honi: "They did not believe him, and they did not treat him with the honor that he deserved. He prayed for mercy and his soul departed" (bTa 23a).[22] Here again the lack of honor is equivalent to the experience of shame. For the Bavli storytellers, death is preferable to such a state.

The story of Rabban Shimon b. Gamaliel also illuminates the public dimension of shame. Almost by definition shame presupposes an audience. One feels humiliated at the loss of face before others.[23] R. Meir and R. Natan accordingly wait until the next day, when Rabban Shimon Gamaliel enters the academy, presumably in the presence of the students mentioned at the outset of the story, in order to challenge him. Everyone seems to know that there are gaps in Rabban Shimon b. Gamaliel's knowledge, that Rabbis Meir and Natan are the superior scholars. The danger is that his lack of knowledge will be publicly exposed. Thus the Bavli's concern with shame is partially a product of the populated academic institution we discussed in Chapter 1. That issues were debated in the presence of numerous students made academic interactions "public." Recall that the traditions introducing the "Oven of Akhnai" cited above repeatedly denounce one who "whitens the face of his fellow *in public*" (A, B, C, D). Fittingly, the Bavli's story of Avdan, which provides one of the most vivid descriptions of a study-house packed with students, also provides one of the most vivid descriptions of the effects of shame.[24] After Avdan exchanges insults with R. Ishmael b. Yose, Rabbi embarrasses him before the assembled students. The consequences are ugly: "Avdan became leprous, his sons drowned, and his daughters-in-law annulled [their levirate marriages]" (bYev 105b). Nevertheless, Rav Nahman bar Yizhaq later reflected, "Blessed be the Merciful One who shamed Avdan in this world." Avdan received appropriate punishment for insulting R. Ishmael b. R. Yose and thus avoided punishment in the world to come. Here too we sense the horrors of shame in the eyes of the storytellers.[25]

Study within the academy, for the Stammaim, was a risky endeavor in which dangers constantly lurked. A midrashic tradition of King David's academy reflects the vulnerability to humiliation that the sages constantly experienced.

> David said before the Holy One, Blessed be He: "Master of the Universe. It is revealed and known before you that were they to tear my flesh, my blood would not flow out. But even when we are studying the [laws of] leprosy and tent-impurity, they interrupt their studies and say to me, 'David: He who has intercourse with a married woman — how is he put to death?' And I say to them, 'He who has intercourse with a married woman is put to death by strangulation, but he retains his share in the world to come. Yet the one who whitens the face of his fellow in public — he has no share in the world to come.'" (bSanh 107a)[26]

King David's nasty colleagues enjoy shaming him by alluding to his adulterous relationship with Batsheva. Even when they are studying the most obscure and unrelated topics, complicated laws of purity, they raise the question of the punishment for adultery, obviously intending to remind him of his sin. For David, this humiliation is worse than corporeal violence. He claims that while he would not bleed even if physically attacked, the verbal assault "whitens his face" as if the blood flowed out. Not only did a sage risk humiliation by not being able to respond to an objection, he could be humiliated by questions with covert references to the embarrassing events of his past.[27]

Honi's death, Avdan's massive reaction, and King David's suffering take us back to the theme of verbal violence discussed in the previous chapter. If the sages could cause such injuries to one another, we can well understand why R. Oshayya should have claimed that the Babylonians "damage each other in legal [debate]."[28] Another midrashic tradition explains the name of Saul's son Mephiboshet — "for he used to shame David's face in legal [debate]," — making a play on *mipeh*, "from the mouth," and *boshet*, "shame" (bBer 4a). The correspondence between this midrashic etymology and R. Oshayya's description confirms that verbal violence and shame are linked.

But as we have seen, there was danger on both sides, for both the offender and offended. Rabban Gamaliel died for perpetrating the verbal wronging of R. Eliezer; David admonishes his colleagues that they will have no share in the world to come. Recall that in the story of Rav Kahana discussed in Chapter 2, Rav warned Rav Kahana not to ask questions of R. Yohanan for seven years, lest he shame him.[29] Eventually Rav Kahana does offer objections that R. Yohanan cannot answer. When R. Yohanan sees Rav Kahana's split lip, he mistakenly thinks that Rav Kahana is laughing at him, feels embarrassed, and Rav Kahana dies as punishment (although R. Yohanan succeeds at resurrecting him when apprised of the error.) Finally, a strange tradition relates that once Rav Ahilai came to harm in a case when Rava believed no harm should result. Rava, however, did not consider this affliction to contradict his view because, "Rav Ahilai objected to him during his study-session" (bPes 110a). The true cause of Rav Ahilai's suffering was divine punishment for raising difficulties when Rava lectured before the assembly, potentially shaming him. Both to cause shame and to experience shame had violent consequences. Thus R. Shimon reportedly offered the departing blessing: "May it be God's will that you neither be shamed nor shame others (bMQ 9b)."[30]

Palestinian Sources on Shame

We can now understand why the Bavli emphasizes shame to a much greater extent than the Yerushalmi and other Palestinian compilations. The conditions that rendered the potential for shame so acute were primarily found in Babylonia during Stammaitic times: the assessment of dialectical argumentation as the acme of academic ability and the institutionalized academy where numerous sages were present. Study of Torah in the Stammaitic academies was probably conducted in a dialectical fashion in which sages endeavored to display their talents through propounding objections and quickly responding to challenges. A sage who could not answer an objection lost status and perhaps rank in the eyes of his colleagues, that is, he felt ashamed. In Palestine, where other types of knowledge were valued more than argumentation, the failure to respond did not entail such consequences. Moreover, the oral milieu rendered questions and objections *ad hominem*.[31] The directness contributed to a sense of personal assault, hence the experience of the academy as a place of verbal violence and danger. The injuries suffered were not physical, but emotional: shame and humiliation. True, Palestinian sages could have experienced shame in other ways, perhaps by making a mistake in the formulation of a Mishna due to faulty memory.

But such setbacks are much more in the control of the sage himself. It is unlike the Babylonian predicament of being vulnerable to brilliant objections unleashed by numerous scholars and demanding immediate response. Second, the presence of numerous students in the Stammaitic academy meant that interactions were public. In disciple circles or small schools, such as those of Palestine and Amoraic Babylonia, where a few students studied with one master, there was less of an audience, hence less potential to feel ashamed. Furthermore, if academic position depended on performance, as several of the sources suggest, then a great deal was at stake in Babylonia. A sage who failed to perform risked being demoted. Loss of position inevitably involves loss of face, that is, shame.

None of this denies that Palestinian compilations take a strong stand against shaming others. The importance of honor and shame in Mediterranean societies is well known.[32] Palestinian sources warn against shaming others in the context of typical social relations.[33] Several Yerushalmi stories teach that parents should be honored and not shamed no matter how demeaning their behavior.[34] The ethic of not shaming the poor by exposing their needs is particularly common.[35] A Palestinian midrashic tradition even traces the destruction of the temple to the public shaming of a certain Bar Qamtza who had been invited to his enemy's dinner party by mistake.[36] However, what we do not find in the Yerushalmi is the theme of shame *in an academic setting.*[37] All the sources discussed above either lack parallels in the Yerushalmi or have parallels that lack mention of shame. For the Bavli, as opposed to the Yerushalmi, shame was an academic problem that attracted significant attention.

The degree to which shame plays a role in the lengthy, highly developed Bavli narratives bearing signs of Stammaitic composition or reworking is remarkable. Readers have undoubtedly observed how the same stories are repeatedly adduced. The very sources that thematize objections and solutions, violence, and the populated academy also thematize shame. These include the story of Rav Kahana's visit to R. Yohanan's academy, the "Oven of Akhnai," the attempted deposition of Rabban Shimon b. Gamaliel, the shaming of Avdan, and Honi's return to the study-house.[38] In the stories of the tragic deaths of R. Yohanan and Resh Laqish and of the tensions between R. Eleazar and R. Yehuda HaNasi the characters feel insulted, although "shame" per se is not mentioned.[39] This coherence of themes in late narratives points again to the Stammaitic setting.

Chapter 5

⌣∶⌣

Lineage and Rabbinic Leadership

Rabbi [Yehuda HaNasi] was planning for his son's [marriage] into the family of
R. Hiyya. When he was about to write the marriage contract, the girl died. Rabbi
said, "Is there, God forbid, a taint [in her lineage]?" They sat down and investi-
gated the families. [They found that] Rabbi descended from Shefatiah, the son of
Avital [wife of King David]. Rabbi Hiyya descended from Shimi, the brother of
[King] David. He [Rabbi] said, "Were there not a problem, she would not have
died." (bKet 62b)[1]

To the modern reader, Rabbi's reaction is bizarre. The sage feels distress when his daughter-in-law dies not because of the tragedy itself,
nor because his son might be disappointed, but because he came close
to arranging a "poor" union. The premature death he attributes to a provi-
dential intervention that obviated the marriage, as if a fundamental law of
the universe had been jeopardized. And the flaw in the match is what seems
to be a very minor inequity in the genealogy of the two families: direct descent from King David versus descent from King David's brother. We might
have expected the story to tell that the prospective family was disqualified on
account of tainted lineage (*mamzerut*), in which case the union would violate a real legal prohibition, or perhaps because of lower-class origins. Not
so; R. Hiyya is a leading scholar who boasts high lineage—but not high
enough. That he descends from King David's brother, not directly from
King David's wife, is considered a "taint" (*pesula*), the language normally
reserved for offspring of forbidden sexual relations. One is reminded of
eighteenth-century European nobility who would not consider marrying
into families that traced their titles to the fourteenth century if their own

dated to the thirteenth. Yet, for the storyteller, the seriousness of this issue explains the death of an innocent girl.

This story is a Babylonian fiction. There is not one hint of this event in Palestinian sources, and the putative genealogies contradict those given in the Yerushalmi.[2] The story's focus is a quintessential concern of Babylonian sages: lineage (*yihus*). This chapter begins by discussing the esteem for lineage in Babylonia and the factors that contributed to its high valuation.[3] The second half of the chapter considers the ways in which lineage impacted academic rank and how exalted lineage may have been a prerequisite to the leading positions in the academic hierarchy. In this respect the chapter continues the exploration of the organization and dynamics of the Stammaitic academies of the previous chapters.

Far more than their Palestinian brethren, Babylonian Jews valued noble pedigree. Consider the following versions of a story found in both Talmuds:

yKet 2:5, 26c	*bKet 22a*
A woman in a certain place. . . . said, "I am a married woman," and the next day she said, "I am divorced." They said to her, "Yesterday you said one thing and today you say something different?"	Once there was a noble (*gedola*) woman, who was great in beauty, and men were eager to betroth her. She told them, "I am already betrothed." Later on she betrothed herself. The sages said to her, "What explains why you acted this way?"
She said to them, "On account of a group of immoral men who approached me to have sex."	She said to them, "At first, when men *who were not fit (meḥuganim)* approached me, I said that I was betrothed. But subsequently, when men *who were fit* approached me, I arose and betrothed myself."
R. Avin said in the name of R. Ila: "Because she gave a solid reason for her [change] in claim, she is believed."	This is the law that R. Aha, Overseer of the Tower, brought to the sages in Usha: If she gave a solid reason for her [change of] claim, she is believed.

At first sight the two stories, which occur in identical contexts in the two Talmuds, are similar in substance. Yet the woman's predicament is in fact very different. In the Yerushalmi, immoral men want to have sex with her, apparently concluding from her status as a divorcee that she is available or of loose morals.[4] She lies to avoid this outright sin and is believed because she provides a cogent reason for the false claim. In the Bavli, by contrast, the men are interested in betrothing her, not in committing a sin, and she lies to avoid a poor match. The term *hogen / mehugan* derives from a Semitic root whose base meaning is "noble," "fine," "of good birth."[5] It also may have assimilated the meaning of the term *hugnos,* the Hebrew cognate of the Greek *eu genes,* "of good birth," the source of the English "eugenic."[6] In a secondary sense *mehugan* came to mean "fitting" or "worthy," and is used in a variety of contexts: "worthy (talented) student" (bTa 7a), men who are "not worthy" (immoral) and pretend to be poor so as to receive charity (bBQ 16b), and so forth. Here the fact that she is a "noble woman" suggests that the base meaning is intended, or at least the typical equation of lineage and character assumed in class-oriented societies: the men possessed poor lineage *and therefore* poor (unfit) character.[7] In principle the Bavli would probably agree with the case presented in the Yerushalmi. Nevertheless, the change in scenario points to different moral concerns in the two rabbinic centers. Where the Yerushalmi targets promiscuity, a violation of sexual morality, the Bavli focuses on an unfit marriage, a transgression of social status.

The Bavli's interest in lineage extends beyond a concern for appropriate marriages. Let us look at another contrast between versions of a story that appears in both Talmuds. Earlier we discussed the story of a failed Babylonian attempt to arrogate the right to intercalate the calendar, a traditional prerogative of the sages of the Land of Israel.[8] In both accounts Palestinian sages send two scholars to Hananiah, the nephew of R. Yehoshua, warning him to desist from such activity:

ySanh 1:2, 19a	bBer 63a
Rabbi [Yehuda HaNasi] sent three letters to him [Hananiah] with R. Yizhaq and R. Natan.	They sent to him [Hananiah] two scholars, R. Yose b. Kefar and the grandson of Zecharia b. Qevutal.
(1) In one he wrote, "To his holiness Hananiah."	When he [Hananiah] saw them he said to them, "Why have you come?" They said to him, "We have come to study Torah."
(2) And in one he wrote, "The kids you left behind have become goats."	
(3) And in one he wrote, "If you do not accept [that the intercalation must be done in the Land of Israel] . . ."	

(1) He [Hananiah] read the first and honored them [R. Yizhaq and R. Natan.]	He announced concerning them, "These men are the luminaries of the generation, and their ancestors
(2) He read the second and honored them.	served in the Temple, as we learned, *Zecharia b. Qevutal said, 'Many*
(3) He read the third and wanted to dishonor them . . .	*times I read to him [the High Priest] from the Book of Daniel' (Mishna Yoma 1:6)."*[9]

In the Yerushalmi, Hananiah honors the two sages, R. Yizhaq and R. Natan, on account of the content of their first two letters, a salutatory greeting and an assertion that the Palestinian sages have matured. In the Bavli he honors the emissaries because of their knowledge of Torah ("luminaries of the generation") and their lineage: he announces that they descended from leading priests.[10] The high regard for lineage is probably responsible for the change of the identity of the emissaries to R. Yose b. Kefar and an unnamed grandson of Zecharia b. Qevutal. This grandson is never mentioned elsewhere; the storyteller fictionalized such a character to create a sage whose lineage descended from a leading priest. (The other sages, R. Yizhaq, R. Natan, and R. Yose b. Kefar, are all late Tannaim, mentioned infrequently in the Tosefta and halakhic midrashim.[11] R. Yose b. Kefar was apparently selected because the storyteller believed that his ancestors also served in the temple, although there is no source to that effect.[12]) The Babylonian storyteller was probably troubled that Hananiah honored the emissaries for trivial reasons. He reworked the story such that his Babylonian audience could understand why visitors immediately would be shown respect: they were sages of exalted lineage.

This surprisingly deep current within Babylonian rabbinic culture probably has its roots in the early Second Temple Period. From its inception the Babylonian Jewish community seems to have zealously guarded its pedigrees as a necessary strategy to prevent assimilation within the larger society.[13] Whatever its historical basis, by the Talmudic period Babylonian sages asserted that Babylonian lineage was the purest among all Jewish communities. Evidence for this claim they mustered from a pseudohistorical Mishnaic tradition that the Jews who returned to Judea with Ezra were divided into ten genealogical classifications: priests, Levites, Israelites, converts, *mamzerim,*[14] and other categories of Jews of tainted descent. Babylonian Amoraim interpreted this to mean that Ezra *removed* all Jews of tainted descent from Babylonia and brought them to Palestine: "Ezra did not go up from Babylonia [to Palestine] before he rendered it like fine sifted flour," that is, free from Jews of "impure" pedigree (bQid 69b). The result: "all countries are as dough in comparison to the Land of Israel, and the Land of Israel is as dough in comparison to Babylonia" (bQid 69b). In contrast to sifted flour, the "dough" implies the presence of impurities, hence the presence of Jews with tainted or questionable lineage.

Babylonian sages did not spare their Palestinian colleagues from the implications of this hierarchy. When the Babylonian Amora R. Zeira rebuffed the great Palestinian R. Yohanan's proposal that R. Zeira marry his daughter, R. Yohanan commented, "Our teaching is fit but our daughters are not fit?" (bQid 71b). Rav Yehuda took matters one step further. He balked at marrying off his daughter even to Babylonian families for fear of a hidden taint (bQid 71b). In this Babylonian twist on the comic paternal stereotype, "No one is good enough for my daughter," Rav Yehuda was paralyzed by the feeling that, "No one's lineage is good enough for my daughter." While most sages did not go to Rav Yehuda's extreme, they did take precautions to assure the genealogical purity of their marriages. The value of noble pedigree finds expression in a comment to mKet 1:5, which notes that a "court of priests" set the marriage payment (*ketuba*) of a virgin priest's daughter at 400 *zuz*, double the 200 *zuz* sum for a nonpriestly bride. The Babylonian Amora Shmuel comments that "families of noble birth" (*mishpehot meyuhasot*) have the same prerogative to demand 400 for their daughters' marriage payment. Pure lineage was literally worth more.

Babylonian families feared that they would be stigmatized by poor matches. The Bavli describes a ceremony called "breaking" (*qetsatsa*) that was performed when a brother married a woman who was not fit. Family members would bring a cask full of fruit, break it in the city square, and proclaim: "Hearken our brethren, the House of Israel: Our brother So-and-so married a woman who is not fit (*hogenet*) for him, and we fear lest our seed will mingle with their seed. Come and take for yourselves a sign for future generations that his seed did not mix with our seed" (bKet 28b). The brothers fear lest others assume that their descendants (seed) too are products of women with inferior pedigrees. The ceremony functions as a "sign," a memorable event, marking the fact that the adulterated lineage is restricted to one brother and not indicative of the family as a whole. Mention of "seed" and mixing seed makes it clear that the concern is a debasement of genealogical status, not that the woman is "unfit" in a characterological sense.[15]

An interesting manifestation of this concern was the effort to define the geographical boundaries of discrete regions. Because the rabbinic "Babylonia" was not coextensive with Sasanian Persia, the sages carefully delineated the area of "sifted flour" from which they could rely on the presumptive purity of prospective husbands and wives.[16] They rated the purity of the lineage of Jewish communities in Media, Elam, and other territories.[17] Several traditions identify cities whose residents are known to have genealogical taints (bQid 71a–b). The sages also claimed to have secret records of families with genealogical blemishes, sometimes threatened to reveal that information, and occasionally made public proclamations (bQid 70b). To impugn another's pedigree was therefore a blatant means of insult and apparently a common source of conflict: "When men feud with each other they feud about family lineage" (bQid 76a). Noble lineage was ultimately associated with holiness: "When God causes his presence to rest over Israel, it only rests over its families of high lineage" (*mishpehot meyuhasot*).[18]

Lineage in Sasanian Culture

The value of lineage is certainly an indigenous Jewish concept, found in both Palestine and Babylonia, among both Tannaim and Amoraim.[19] All ancient societies (almost all premodern societies for that matter) were divided into social classes based to some extent on lineage. Ancient and rabbinic Judaisms inherited from the Bible the basic division into priests, Levites, and Israelites, as well as the notion of tainted lineage (*mamzerut*) mentioned above. Tannaitic sources express a profound respect for priestly lineage and concern that it not be adulterated.[20] The Mishna rules that one who marries a priest's daughter must check the four preceding generations lest there be a taint (mQid 4:4). A Toseftan passage recalls that the high court that presided in a chamber of the temple checked the genealogy of priests and Levites (tHag 2:9). A few sources even extend the disadvantages of tainted genealogy beyond the framework of marriage. A Mishna restricts those eligible to judge capital cases to "priests, Levites, and Israelites who may marry into the priesthood," that is, those without tainted lineage (mSanh 4:2). A Toseftan passage recounts that the same restriction was "at first" applied to signatories on marriage documents, although here the specification "at first" implies that the limitation no longer obtained in Mishnaic times (tSanh 7:1).

Palestinian Amoraic sources provide essentially the same picture. As in the Mishna, we find respect for priestly lineage and concern that it remain pure. There are a few references to sages announcing in public a person's tainted genealogy.[21] But we do not find traditions similar to the Babylonian sources cited above: a deep fear of hidden taints, an awareness of extremely fine distinctions in the quality of lineage, threats to reveal blemished pedigrees, or assertions that families of noble lineage are somehow more holy. Palestinian and Babylonian traditions therefore differ to a significant degree in their estimation of the importance of lineage. As we shall see below, there also may be a subtle difference in the kind of prestige associated with high lineage: in Bavli traditions lineage is associated with rabbinic authority.[22] How are we to explain this discrepancy?

The heightened concern for lineage among Babylonian Jews should be understood partly in terms of the value placed on noble blood in Persian culture.[23] The ambient Persian society was divided into four classes: clergy, military, scribes and government bureaucrats, and finally farmers, laborers, and artisans.[24] In Sasanian times these classes had solidified almost to the point of castes. The underlying ideology held that the social order depended upon the three upper classes' preserving the purity of their lineage against corruption from men of inferior birth: "The theory was that men of low birth, even if they acquired the necessary skills, were not fit to handle the responsibilities of men of noble birth, and so it was incumbent upon kings to preserve the purity of the higher classes. Thus, it was invariably understood that the people must be kept to their own stations and might not aspire to cross the lines of social class."[25] The upper classes accordingly carefully guarded their lineage and placed great value on noble descent. Such values were considered the defining characteristic of the dynasty: "[T]he Founder of the Sasanian dynasty is quoted as having proclaimed that 'nothing needs such guarding as degree among men,' and is said to have established a 'visible and general distinction between men of noble birth and common people with regard to horses and clothes, houses and gardens, women and servants . . . so no commoner may share the sources of enjoyment of life with the nobles, and alliance and marriage between the two groups is forbidden.'"[26] Sasanian law thus prevented marriage between classes, leaving commoners little opportunity for social mobility into the privileged ranks.

The severity of this ethic is vividly illustrated by the folktale of the shoemaker who offered to provide the emperor Khusrau I with an enormous quantity of money to equip soldiers for war against the Byzantines. According to Yarshater, "All the shoemaker asks is that his son be allowed to enter the ranks of the bureaucrats (*dabiran*). The king, however, forgoes the money rather than allow such a corruption of the ranks."[27] Class was thus all but inviolable: the emperor considers the external threat of the destruction of his country in war less pernicious than the internal threat of the inferior classes debasing the purity of the social order. Positions of leadership were naturally reserved to those of upper-class pedigree, and even to be a heroic warrior required high birth. The accounts of battles between legendary kings begin with the rivals' ridiculing the low birth and lineage of their opponents.[28]

The importance of lineage among Babylonian sages can be profitably viewed against this background. My suggestion is not that Sasanian culture influenced the rabbis by imposing alien values, nor that the sages aspired to enter the Persian upper classes or acculturate to any significant extent. Rather, both the longstanding internal Jewish anxiety about tainted pedigree (*mamzerut*) and the value placed on priestly and other noble lineages were intensified in the Sasanian environment and ultimately manifested in a distinct idiom. While the Greco-Roman culture of Palestine also had social classes and aristocratic tendencies, late antiquity witnessed a weakening of class divisions.[29] The values of the ambient culture in Mesopotamia thus produced more exaggerated expressions of concern for genealogical purity among Babylonian sages than their Palestinian colleagues.

Lineage and the Academic Hierarchy

The most significant issue for our purposes is the extent to which lineage impacted the internal dynamics of rabbinic society. Was rabbinic society a pure meritocracy, as would be expected of an enterprise based upon knowledge, or did lineage play a role in determining rabbinic status? This question primarily applies to Stammaitic times after the rise of institutionalized academies; the disciple circles of the Amoraic period lacked the hierarchy and ranks which establish differences in status. Nevertheless, regarding Amoraic times the question can be framed in terms of the degree to which noble lineage was expected of students or advantageous in becoming a respected teacher.

We begin, then, with the Amoraic period.[30] One indication of the growing importance of lineage among Babylonian sages is the respect accorded priests (*kohanim*) and priestly genealogy. In an illuminating footnote in an article on the paintings found in the synagogue excavated in Dura Europos, Isaiah Sonne observed the comparatively high status granted priests in Babylonia:

> It may be noted in passing that priesthood seems to have retained much more of its dignity and prestige in the Babylonian than in the Palestinian center. In Babylonia, indeed, the priests, even during the Talmudic period, seem to have formed the majority of the learned nobility. Most of the famous Babylonian scholars were *Kohanim* (e.g.: Mar Samuel, R. Elazar ben Pedath, R. Ammi, R. Assi, R. Hisda, Rabba, Abayye, and Raba). It is also reflected in the following facts: a) There is a Babylonian Talmud on the fifth order of the Mishnah which deals mainly with matters concerning the sacrificial cult, but there is no Palestinian Talmud on this order; b) the Babylonian scholars were much more acquainted with the *Torah Ko-*

hanim (Sifra), the halakhic Midrash on Leviticus, than were the Palestinian scholars. . . . All of this indicates much more interest in the "priestly" world on the
Babylonian's side.[31]

While rabbinic sources, as we have noted, inherited the biblical world's
veneration of priests, the rabbis also competed with priests for religious
authority. Many rabbinic traditions polemicize against priests in an effort
to minimize priestly claims to leadership in the postdestruction era.[32] It is
therefore significant that Babylonian sages, in particular, should celebrate
priestly lineage, the defining characteristic of the priesthood.

Geoffrey Herman has pointed to additional evidence that priestly lineage
was highly regarded by Babylonian sages.[33] Numerous Babylonian Amoraim were priests: Shmuel, Rav Hisda, Rabbah, Abaye, Rav Huna b. Rav
Yehoshua, Rav Kahana, Rav Ashi, Mar Zutra — and many others.[34] Many
leading Amoraim also married daughters of priests, including Rava, Rav
Papa, Rav Mesharshia, and Rami bar Hama.[35] Moreover, Herman points
out, many of the sages whom the Geonim considered to be heads of academies were priests or married daughters of priests. Of the seven (purported)
heads of the Sura Academy whose lineage is known, one was a priest and
two married daughters of priests.[36] Of the nine heads of the Pumbedita
Academy whose lineage is known, five were priests and two married daughters of priests.[37] That these sages were heads of the academy is anachronistic. Rather, they were among the preeminent sages of their generation, the
leaders of disciple circles, and on that basis considered heads of the academy
by later sages.[38] In addition, many of the sages who left Babylonia for Palestine and rose to prominence there were of priestly descent, including Rabbis Eleazar b. Pedat, Ami, Asi, and Hiyya bar Hama. R. Ami and R. Asi in
fact were know as "the priests of Babylonia."[39]

Herman suggests that Babylonian sages may have embraced priestly lineage as part of their struggle with the Exilarch for prestige within the larger
Jewish community. The Exilarch's authority of course rested on Davidic lineage. To boast priestly lineage was therefore a means of competing with the
Exilarch on his own terms. In this way the sages were able to claim authority on the basis of both their knowledge of Torah and their lineage. It is well
known that many of the leading Geonic families claimed to be of priestly
descent and boasted (invented?) genealogical chains that reached back to
priests of the Second Temple Period.[40] Similar pressures that operated in
Geonic times may have influenced earlier sages. At all events, it appears that
already in Amoraic times, priestly blood, by birth or marriage, proved an advantage to becoming a prominent sage.[41]

The respect for both knowledge and lineage, and the complex relationship between the two, appears more explicitly in the following brief interchange:

> The rabbis said to R. Preda, "R. Ezra, the grandson of R. Avtulos, who is tenth [generation in descent] from R. Eleazar b. Azariah, who is tenth [generation in descent] from Ezra, stands at the door."

> He said to them, "What is all this? If he is a scholar — that is well. If he is the offspring of nobility (*bar avahan*) and a scholar (*bar orayan*) — that is even better. If he is the offspring of nobility but not a scholar — may fire consume him."

> They said to him, "He is a scholar." He said to them, "Let him enter" (bMen 53a).[42]

The rabbis are impressed with R. Ezra's lineage: they present him to R. Preda with a formal recitation of his pedigree. R. Preda, however, is not overwhelmed. His response, "What is this?" probably means "What is the point of all this lineage?" Why tell me about his ancestry? But he too concedes that "it is even better" if his visitor has distinguished lineage.[43] His final response, moreover, suggests that it was shameful for a man of high lineage to lack knowledge.

R. Ezra's eponymous ancestor, described by the Bible as both priest and scribe, embodied the combination of knowledge and priestly lineage that apparently garnered high esteem. Other aspects of lineage also concerned the Babylonian sages: "Rav Hamnuna sat before Ulla and they were discussing traditions. He [Ulla] said, 'What a great man, what a great man, if only he were not from Harpanya!' He [Hamnuna] was embarrassed. He [Ulla] said to him, 'Where to do you pay poll tax?' He said to him, "To Pum Nahara." He said to him, 'You are from Pum Nahara'" (bYev 17a).[44] The translation is somewhat uncertain, and perhaps should be: "What a great man and how much greater he would be were he not from Harpanya." In any case, why should Rav Hamnuna's birthplace concern Ulla or relate to his rabbinic potential? The Jews of Harpanya, the passage proceeds to inform us, had tainted genealogies, and that "defect," for Ulla, evidently impugned Rav Hamnuna's scholarly status. He considered it inappropriate that a great sage possess questionable lineage. To obviate the problem Ulla assigned Rav Hamnuna a false provenance.[45] As in so many cases, the source unfortunately tells us much less than we would like to know. Did Ulla think that Rav Hamnuna's rulings would not be heeded on account of his inferior pedigree, that to be perceived as a figure of authority required pure lineage? At all events, if these traditions are authentically Amoraic (which is by no means certain), they may indicate an emerging view, albeit tentative and ambivalent, that rabbinic status and pure pedigree are interdependent.

We turn now from the Amoraic to the Stammaitic period when we can speak of an academic hierarchy. A few tantalizing hints found in three lengthy narratives suggest that noble lineage was a prerequisite for the highest academic positions. While the three narratives ostensibly relate to the Palestinian Nasi, they are more profitably interpreted in terms of the late Babylonian reality.

First is the story of the attempted deposition of Rabban Shimon b. Gamaliel, discussed briefly in the previous chapter (bHor 13b–14a).[46] Recall that R. Natan and R. Meir, who hold the offices of "Head of the Court" and "Sage," the second and third positions in the academic hierarchy, attempt to depose the Nasi, Rabban Shimon b. Gamaliel, after he promotes his own honor at their expense. They justify their action on the grounds that they know more Torah than the Nasi, and they plan to accomplish their goal by challenging him to teach an obscure subject which he does not know, in an attempt to reavel his inferior knowledge to all. Their scheme fails when another sage tips off Rabban Shimon b. Gamaliel to the plot.

The "Nasi" in this story can be none other than the head of the academy (*rosh yeshiva*), despite the absence of the title.[47] He receives the highest honors within the academy, teaches the assembly of sages, and in a subsequent scene addresses questions and objections. It should therefore strike us as strange that this Nasi/head of the academy knows less Torah than other sages. The story explicitly concedes this point, both in the initial claim of R. Meir and R. Natan to superior knowledge and later when Rabban Shimon b. Gamaliel cannot solve the questions that his rivals send into the academy, which prompts the other sages to call for their return. The academy depicted in this story is no meritocracy.

What then is the basis of the authority of the Nasi/head of the academy? Lineage. When a dream vision directs R. Natan to apologize, Rabban Shimon b. Gamaliel tells him, "Perhaps the belt of your father benefited you in making you the Head of the Court. Shall it benefit you to make you Nasi?" The "belt" (*qamera*), a Persian word (part of the evidence of the Babylonian coloring of the story), was a decorative sash bestowed by the emperor as a sign of honor.[48] The ascription to R. Natan's father indicates hereditary prestige. In other words, R. Natan's high lineage suffices only to qualify him for the second rank within the academy; the head of the academy requires yet more exalted pedigree. Academic authority depends, at least in part, on lineage. In the final scene, moreover, R. Yehuda HaNasi (Rabban Shimon b.

Gamaliel's son) tells his son R. Shimon that R. Natan and R. Meir "tried to uproot your honor and the honor of your father's house." This unusual multigenerational perspective implies that the office of Nasi was essentially a dynasty. For this reason the challenge to Rabban Shimon b. Gamaliel simultaneously threatened the position of his descendants. If the Nasi achieved his position by proficiency in Torah, the conspiracy should not have impacted subsequent generations, who would have to earn their offices on their own merits.

The story stops short of endorsing lineage to the complete exclusion of knowledge as the basis for academic rank. Were it not for the fortuitous intervention of a colleague, the challenge would have exposed Rabban Shimon b. Gamaliel's inferior command of Torah and he would have lost his position. So the story assumes that the head of the academy requires some expertise in Torah in addition to his noble lineage. The three Nesiim mentioned in the story are not mere figureheads but teach Torah, answer questions, and study. Overall the story exhibits a tension between knowledge and lineage as the basis of authority. Ideally the head of the academy possesses both qualifications; in practice that is not always the case. But while we can readily understand why he should possess Torah, why lineage should be so important requires explanation.

The redactional context of the story is also significant. The story appears in the section of Talmud that comments on mHor 3:8:

(A) A priest precedes[49] a Levite. A Levite [precedes] an Israelite. An Israelite [precedes] a *mamzer*. A *mamzer* [precedes] a *natin*. A *natin* [precedes] a convert. A convert precedes a freed slave.

(B) When [is this the case]? When they are all equal. But if the *mamzer* is a sage and the high priest an ignoramus, then the *mamzer*-sage precedes the high-priest-ignoramus.

The first half of the Mishna determines precedence exclusively according to the status of lineage (A). But the second half of the Mishna abruptly undermines this genealogical hierarchy (B). It turns out that lineage never determines priority except in the unlikely event that two men possess exactly equal knowledge of Torah. Following the story appear several Amoraic discussions concerning two interrelated topics. First, what type of intellectual ability is optimal: excellent recall, analytical brilliance, sharpness, decisiveness, and so forth. Second, which of these qualities determines who should "rule" or be the "head," that is, lead the sages in the study-session.[50] The situation presented in the story contrasts with both the Mishna and the related Amoraic traditions. As opposed to the Mishna, lineage, not knowledge of Torah, determines rank (who is the Nasi / head of the academy) and prestige (who receives the greater honors). As opposed to the Amoraic discussions, lineage, rather than a particular intellectual ability, establishes leadership.

The story — which contains numerous indications of a late provenance — probably reflects the situation in Stammaitic times.[51] It appears that the high estimation of lineage among generations of Babylonian sages and the above-mentioned Amoraic (?) intimations that scholars should possess noble blood eventually caused exalted lineage to be considered a prerequisite for the highest positions in the academic hierarchy. True, the storytellers express ambivalence about this circumstance. They essentially warn the Nasi / head of the academy that his position stands in jeopardy as long as he is less proficient than others. But they nevertheless tell a story in which the Nasi prevails, heaven itself intervening on his behalf through the dream directing his opponents to apologize. The redactional context reinforces the bias in favor of the Nasi: the story functions as an admonition that sages should not attempt to enforce the policy of the Mishna in the contemporary academy lest they meet a fate similar to that of R. Natan and R. Meir.

The second story that correlates lineage and rabbinic leadership is the Bavli's version of the deathbed testament of Rabbi Yehuda HaNasi. This account originates in Palestinian sources but is substantially reworked and expanded by the Bavli.[52] The Yerushalmi relates that Rabbi made three requests upon his deathbed: that his widow not be moved from his house, that he not be eulogized in towns, and that those who cared for him during his life arrange the burial.[53] A separate story adds a fourth directive, recounting that Rabbi instructed his son (unnamed) to carry out a number of "appointments," namely the selection of judges within the patriarchal bureaucracy, and to appoint R. Hanina b. Hama first.[54] These judicial positions were not rabbinic offices but rather communal or municipal positions; other sources suggest that the patriarchs sometimes appointed nonsages on the basis of patronage relationships.[55] Hence the account contains nothing explicit about succession to the patriarchate or other rabbinic offices, nor any directive concerning academic affairs.[56]

In the Bavli's version Rabbi first summons his sons, whom he commands to honor his widow in several ways (bKet 103a–b). This behest corresponds to the order not to remove his widow from his house, found in the Yerushalmi's version. He then summons the "sages of Israel" and orders them: "Do not eulogize me in towns, and convene a study-session after thirty days.

My son Shimon will be the Sage. My son Gamaliel will be Nasi. Hanina bar Hama will sit at the Head (*yeshev barosh*)." The directive limiting eulogies corresponds to that in the Yerushalmi, but the address to the "sages of Israel" and the commissioning of a study-session are new. So too is the appointment of three sages — two of them his sons — to what seem to be rabbinic offices. The Bavli appears to have interpreted the Yerushalmi's instruction that R. Hanina b. Hama be appointed "first" (*berosha*) in terms of an academic office, "Head" (*yeshev barosh*).[57] A discrepancy in the image of the Nasi is readily apparent. The Yerushalmi depicts him as a wealthy aristocrat, powerful patron, and leader of the community. For the Bavli he is a rabbinic leader focused upon rabbinic matters: study-sessions and rabbinic offices.

The Bavli's rabbinized portrayal of the Nasi emerges even more clearly in the subsequent commentary to the deathbed testament. An extended *sugya* follows that intersperses other traditions, provides additional details, and even reports (invents) additional instructions. The salient portions are as follows:

(A) *Convene a study-session after thirty days.* (The Talmud interprets this as 'Resume the studies after thirty days.') [He meant that] 'I am not superior to Moses our Rabbi,' as it is written, *And the Israelites bewailed Moses in the steppes of Moab for thirty days (Deut 34:8).* (Therefore they desisted from their studies for only thirty days.) . . .

(B) *My son Shimon will be the Sage.* What did he mean? This is what he meant: even though my son Shimon is sage (= wise), my son Gamaliel will be the Nasi. Levi said, "Was it necessary to state this?" R. Shimon b. Rabbi said, "It is necessary for you and your limping."[58]

— What was difficult for him (R. Shimon b. Rabbi, that he belittled Levi's objection)? Does not Scripture state, *He gave the kingdom to Jehoram because he was first born (2 Chr 21:3)?*

— He [Jehoram] properly fulfilled the place of his ancestors. Rabban Gamaliel did not properly fulfill the place of his ancestors (and therefore would not have received the office were it not for a specific directive).

— Why then did Rabbi act in this way [and appoint Gamaliel]?

— Granted he did not properly fulfill the place of his ancestors in wisdom, he did properly fulfill the place of his ancestors in piety. . . .

(C) *Hanina bar Hama will sit at the Head (yeshev barosh).* R. Hanina did not accept [the position] since R. Efes was senior to him by two and one half years. . . .

(D) "He [Rabbi Yehuda HaNasi said] to them, 'Summon my younger son.'" R. Shimon went to him. He entrusted to him the protocols of [the office of] Sage (*sidrei hokhma*).[59]

(E) "He [Rabbi Yehuda HaNasi] said to them, 'Summon my elder son.'" Rabban Gamaliel went to him. He entrusted to him the protocols of the [office of] Nasi (*sidrei nesiut*). He said to him, "My son, conduct your [office of] Nasi high-handedly,[60] and cast bile upon the students."

These comments assume that the Nasi was the head of the academy, a point not lost on traditional commentators.[61] The interpretation of "convene a study-session," a standard ritual in honor of the deceased, in the sense of resuming a suspended course of studies, points to a formal academic setting (A). Rabbi instructs that his school return to its normal operation after the period of mourning. It is even possible that the Bavli's commentary has understood the term *yeshiva* ("session") in the sense of its later usage "academy": reconvene the academy after thirty days.[62] While Moses was a political and spiritual leader, for the sages he was first and foremost the highest rabbinic authority. The explanation analogizing Rabbi Yehuda HaNasi to Moses "Our Rabbi" thus implies that the Nasi too stands atop the rabbinic hierarchy. Rabbi's final instruction to his son Gamaliel, the future Nasi, pertains not to communal affairs but to relations with students, suggesting again that the Nasi is an academic officer or at least a teacher (E).

The other two titles "Sage" and "Head" also appear to be high offices within the academic hierarchy, presumably the second and third positions. While the first explanatory comment takes the term "sage" (*hakham*) as the adjective "wise" (B), the elaboration concerning the "protocols of the [office of] Sage" clarifies that the term refers to an office (D), parallel to the "protocols of the [office of] Nasi" (E).[63] That the "Head" refers to an office is clear from the comment that R. Hanina declined the position on account of lacking seniority (C). Moreover, yet another comment claims: "Since he [Rabbi Yehuda HaNasi] said, 'R. Hanina b. Hama will sit at the Head,' it was not possible that he should not rule (*malakh*)."[64] To "rule," as we have noted, refers to the head of the academy.[65] This comment points out that since R. Hanina b. Hama ascended to the office of "Head," he would eventually become head of the academy. Note that the triumvirate of Nasi, sage, and head (*rosh*) roughly corresponds to the three offices mentioned in the story of the deposition of Rabban Shimon b. Gamaliel discussed above: the Nasi, "Head of the Court," and sage. Goodblatt has pointed to evidence that the Babylonian academies were governed by three main positions in Geonic times.[66] While the titles are Palestinian in origin, Bavli storytellers seem to have used them to represent the top three positions in the contemporary academy.

It should be noted that all of these comments belong to the Stammaitic stratum. Even the dialogue between Levi and R. Shimon, which appears to be an Amoraic commentary to the story, is a fabrication.[67] With an ironic touch, R. Shimon rebukes a colleague who has suggested that Rabbi need not have bothered to appoint Gamaliel his successor, as no one would even have considered R. Shimon for the task! Now the Bavli's version of the testament, with its telling additions, itself appears to be a Stammaitic reworking of the Yerushalmi's story, notwithstanding the use of Tannaitic Hebrew. (The Tannaitic Hebrew does not point to an authentic Tannaitic tradition but comprises a type of pseudo-*baraita*.[68]) In all likelihood, we are dealing with a Stammaitic source (a Stammaitic reworking of the Yerushalmi's testament) with still later Stammaitic comments.

I am well aware that my interpretation of these sources is speculative. It is based on the assumption that the Bavli reworkings are Babylonian, not Palestinian, and reflect some Babylonian situation. When the Palestinian story says nothing about academic succession and almost nothing about the Nasi's involvement in rabbinic institutional life, and yet the Bavli portrays the Nasi appointing successors to academic offices and concerned with Torah study, I cannot read the Bavli passage at face value as a reliable historical source.[69] The question then becomes *what* Babylonian situation is represented. In light of the similar themes and tensions found in the story of the attempted deposition of the Nasi Rabban Shimon b. Gamaliel, I suggest that we are dealing with the late Babylonian academy here too.

Perhaps the fact that this interpretation was essentially anticipated by Shaye Cohen twenty years ago lends it some support. In a fascinating article entitled "Patriarchs and Scholarchs," Cohen observed striking parallels between Rabbi's deathbed testament and the testaments of "scholarchs," the leaders of philosophical academies, preserved in Hellenistic sources.[70] Scholarchs also made provisions for the care of their widows, for their burials and memorial services, and for succession to leadership of the academy.[71] Cohen even suggested that Rabbi's instructions concerning the "protocols" of office correspond to the "orders" that governed philosophical academies.[72] The Nasi transmits to his appointees directions about the conduct of the academy and the nature of the offices. Cohen noted, however, that directives relating to widows and funerals were not unique to scholarchs but were of potential concern to any aristocrat.[73] What distinguished the scholarch, hence what depicts Rabbi Yehuda HaNasi as a scholarch, are the directives appointing a successor and the transmission of the protocols. *Yet those provisions occur only in the Bavli.* In other words, the Bavli's Rabbi Yehuda HaNasi is a scholarch, an academic leader; the Yerushalmi's is not.[74] Cohen accordingly concluded the article with a caveat:

> Until this point I have assumed the fundamental historicity of the rabbinic accounts concerning the patriarchal school. . . . Yet it is obvious that the assumption is untenable. Our major text, B. *Ketubot* 103a–103b, is a complex document which presents a highly developed form of the material and which reached its present form long after the events it purports to describe. . . . We must admit too that the Babylonian Talmud has an unfortunate habit of transmitting fictional or highly embellished accounts of the internal affairs of the Palestinian patriarchate. Perhaps then the parallels between patriarchs and scholarchs tell us more about the Hellenization of Babylonian Jewry in the fourth and fifth centuries than about the Hellenization of Palestinian Jewry in the second.[75]

In the years since Cohen published the article (1981), scholars have increasingly accepted the fictional nature of rabbinic stories, the fact that stories inform us more about the storytellers than about the characters, and the propensity of the Bavli to rework its sources. We should therefore embrace Cohen's tentative conclusion with much greater confidence than Cohen was willing to venture: the parallels between patriarchs and scholarchs tell us about the academization of rabbinic society in fifth–sixth century Babylonia.

If this conclusion is correct, then the importance of lineage and the internal debate over its role deserve attention. Rabbi bequeaths the positions of Nasi and sage to his two sons, suggesting that a combination of heredity and testamentary designation determined succession to the highest academic offices.[76] However, the Bavli's discussion of this point reveals several different perspectives (B). The first voice strengthens the genealogical dimension by adding that the inferior scholar became Nasi / head of the academy. Were it not for this datum, we might have thought that Gamaliel knew more Torah or that the two sons possessed equal ability. So too the statement attributed to Levi takes for granted that the eldest sons should inherit the office, apparently regardless of his ability. Indeed, the scriptural prooftext referring to monarchic succession essentially views the Nasi / head of the academy as a royal dynasty (B).[77] The ensuing discussion, however, steps back from this perspective by suggesting that (1) an unworthy dynast may not succeed his father as Nasi without a specific appointment, and (2) a completely unworthy candidate is ineligible; Gamaliel's outstanding qualities compensated for his inferior knowledge. These comments insist that intellectual ability not be discounted completely when selecting a Nasi/head of academy. While one detects here competing ideologies contesting the importance of lineage, all consider it a prerequisite for succession to the leading positions within the academic hierarchy.

Let me briefly mention here another Bavli tradition that illustrates to what extent R. Yehuda HaNasi's death scene was reworked to reflect Babylonian concerns: "When Rabbi was dying he stated: there is a Humanya in Babylonia, which contains all Amonites; there is a Misgaria in Babylonia, which contains all *mamzerim;* there is a Birka in Babylonia . . ." (bQid 72a). That Rabbi should include in his testament information about the genealogical taints of remote villages in Babylonia obviously strains credulity.[78] Here too Bavli storytellers portray the Nasi in the image of a leading Babylonian sage who takes care to impart critical knowledge of blemished pedigrees so that his colleagues can avoid unfortunate matches.

The third story is the Bavli version of the deposition of Rabban Gamaliel. In Chapter 2 we noted that the Bavli changes the criteria that explain why the sages selected Eleazar b. Azariah to replace the Nasi Rabban Gamaliel.[79]

yBer 4:1, 7d	*bBer 27b*
They went and appointed R. Eleazar b. Azariah to the assembly.	Let us appoint R. Eleazar b. Azariah, for he is wise, and he is rich, and he is tenth in descent from Ezra.
R. Akiba sat and felt distressed. He said, "It is not that he is more learned in Torah than I, but that he is more the descendant of great men than I."	He is wise — so that if they object to him, he will solve it. He is rich — so that if he must pay honor at the court of the Emperor [he will be able to do so]. He is tenth in descent from Ezra and has ancestral merit — so that they cannot punish him.[80]
What was R. Eleazar b. Azariah's peg? He was tenth generation [in descent] from Ezra.	
	They went and said to him, "Will you consent to be the head of the academy?"[81]

In the Yerushalmi R. Eleazar is appointed Nasi solely on the basis of his lineage. R. Akiba accordingly laments that R. Eleazar is not his superior in Torah, but is "more the descendant of great men."[82] The Bavli adds to lineage both wealth and knowledge of Torah. Here too the Bavli understands the Nasi to be the head of the academy, an identification made explicitly in the sages' words to R. Eleazar b. Azariah: they ask him to accept that position.[83] What are the implications of this difference?

The Nasi of the Yerushalmi is the patriarch, primarily a political office within the Roman provincial system, and secondarily a rabbi who deployed his financial and political power to assist the sages.[84] The Nasi / patriarch was not a rabbinic office per se; it was the "property" of the family of Rabbi Yehuda HaNasi, passed down dynastically from father to son. In reality the rabbis had no control over the office and certainly could not depose a patriarch and appoint one of their own in his place. In the fictional story, however, they have this power (although even here they eventually restore the Nasi after he apologizes), and temporarily replace the Nasi with a sage boasting a similar status.[85] R. Eleazar b. Azariah is a scion of the dynasty of Ezra and therefore competes with Rabban Gamaliel on his own terms. The sages replace one political dynasty with another.

The Bavli, however, sets the story in the "study-house" (rather than "assembly-house" of the Yerushalmi)[86] and makes the Nasi into the head of the academy. Other additions in the Bavli's version relate to academic concerns such as the quality of students, access to the study-sessions, and criticism of the Nasi for "holding back Torah from Israel." As opposed to the Yerushalmi, where the Nasi is a political authority, in the Bavli he is concerned with the academy and Torah study.[87] Within this reworking, Bavli storytellers balk at accepting a purely dynastic claim to an academic office and therefore add that R. Eleazar is proficient in Torah. For the Bavli, the sages replace one head of the academy with another. They search for a candidate with the the same combination of lineage and knowledge that we have seen in the previous sources.[88] Once again, exalted lineage is a prerequisite for the highest academic positions.

In sum, we have three Bavli narratives extremely suggestive about the qualifications of the Nasi, two of which are reworkings of Palestinian sources.[89] The three Bavli narratives present a consistent image of the Nasi, an image that differs from that found in the Palestinian antecedents. In all three the Nasi appears to be the head of the academy, as the setting is the study-house or academy and academic concerns predominate. All three imply that the Nasi requires a combination of knowledge of Torah and noble lineage. While the demand for knowledge needs no explanation, the requirement of lineage seems surprising at first glance. In light of the high estimation of lineage in Babylonian rabbinic culture, it appears that exalted lineage was also seen as a prerequisite for the head of the academy and other high positions within the academic hierarchy. In contrast to Palestinian sources, these traditions suggest that in Babylonia lineage was a basis not only for social prestige but also for rabbinic authority. There also may be a hint that the position of head of the academy had become a dynasty, passed on from father to son or at least within the same family.

Dynastic Succession in the Geonic Era

The importance of priestly lineage in the Geonic period has been mentioned above. Here I would like to touch upon the principle of dynastic succession. In this respect too there may be continuity between Stammaitic and Geonic times. Sages in the Geonic academies were arranged in seven rows of ten according to the description found in the chronicle of Nathan the Babylonian, who visited them in the tenth century (see Chapter 1). The rows were theoretically ordered according to ability with an eminent sage leading each row. However, Nathan explains that heredity also played a significant role in the assignment of academic ranks:

> And the seven are called heads of rows. And it sometimes happens that others are greater than they in wisdom but are not appointed over them as heads of rows — not because of their intellect, but because they have inherited their father's rank. For if one of the heads of rows has died and left a son capable of filling his place, he is appointed to his father's place and occupies it. And if one of the fellows is slightly greater in wisdom than the child, he is neither promoted (over him) nor placed below the child (automatically), and it is the prerogative of the head of the academy to appoint as a head of the row whom he pleases. . . .
>
> And the father's place goes to the son unless he is seriously lacking in knowledge, in which case he is displaced; yet if there is something in him and he is worthy of sitting in one of the seven rows, he is placed there. And if he is not worthy of one of the rows, he is placed with the other members of the academy, the students. . . . And if one of the members of the seven rows is greater than another in wisdom, he is not seated in his place because he did not inherit it from his father, but he is given an increased allocation on account of his wisdom.[90]

Lineage essentially determines a sage's position as both head of a row and within the seven rows. As long as a son is "capable of filling" his father's place, he inherits it, regardless of whether a more knowledgeable sage exists.

We can almost hear in the background Rabban Gamaliel's rebuke of R. Natan that the belt of his father only entitles him to a certain rank but no higher. Yet one simultaneously senses a tension between lineage and knowledge of Torah ("wisdom"). If the son is "seriously lacking in wisdom" or "unworthy" he does not inherit his father's place but is relegated to the "students," apparently those without a set place among the seventy. Moreover, the head of the academy possesses a degree of discretion to evaluate the worthiness of a son and to appoint a more appropriate candidate. In this respect the tension between lineage and merit echoes the Bavli's comments concerning R. Yehuda HaNasi's appointment of his son Gamaliel noted above. Gamaliel's right to inherit the office of Nasi was both questioned and defended on the grounds of his "fulfilling the place of his ancestors."

The office of the Gaon (= the head of the academy) also became dynastic in the Geonic period.[91] An oligarchy of a few families boasting distinguished lineage controlled the Gaonate. At the death of the Gaon the office typically passed to another member of his family, and often subsequently passed to the Gaon's son. Yet the bitter struggles over the Gaonate suggest that the principle of dynastic succession was not accepted by all, or at least could be contested if the heir was "unworthy." Even an outsider like Saadia Gaon, of Egyptian origin and obviously not from the elite group of Babylonian families, could be appointed Gaon on the basis of his intellectual abilities when circumstances called for a strong leader.[92] Then again, the subsequent opposition to Saadia from leading Babylonian families indicates the fragility of claims to the office that did not involve a hereditary basis, despite the fact that Saadia invented a Davidic genealogy to legitimate his authority.[93]

Thus several of the cultural elements that appear in Babylonian reworkings of Palestinian traditions about the Nasi resemble those of Geonic times. I suggest that these point to significant continuity between the Stammaitic and Geonic eras in the criteria for academic rank and for positions of leadership. The prominence of noble lineage, dynastic succession, and heredity in Geonic times was anticipated to some extent in the Stammaitic era. Certainly, to draw connections between Talmudic narratives and later Geonic sources risks anachronism.[94] But I believe that danger to be less than the error of reading them in light of a second- or third-century Palestinian context.

In sum, esteem for lineage is a deeply rooted Jewish value, found in all rabbinic cultures. Despite our intuitive sense (and despite the claims of some scholars) that a society that made Torah study its central value should be a pure meritocracy, the truth is far more complex. To be sure, sages in both Palestine and Babylonia debated the significance of pedigree, and various circles seem to have attempted to minimize its influence. Nevertheless, noble lineage often exerted a substantial impact on status among the rabbis themselves. As a whole, Babylonian sages were much more concerned with ancestry than their Palestinian colleagues. Stammaitic sources suggest that lineage became an increasingly important factor in determining academic rank and perhaps a prerequisite for positions of leadership. The longstanding regard for lineage in Babylonian rabbinic culture ultimately became an important factor within the academic hierarchy.

Chapter 6

⌣∶⌢

Wives

Torah study, an activity pursued exclusively by men, inevitably created tensions for the sages in relation to their wives and families. Because women did not participate in the dominant aspects of rabbinic life — study, collegiality, master-disciple relationships — they could not share in the concerns most important to the sages. These social and intellectual gaps aside, to become a master of Torah required long hours of study each and every day, which naturally competed for attention with all other aspects of a sage's life. Moreover, in contrast to most other pursuits and careers that also caused men to neglect their families, the rabbinic ethic of Torah study made limitless demands. Pressure to study was magnified by numerous rabbinic maxims that upheld incessant study as an ideal, such as "You shall meditate over it day and night (Josh 1:8)," and "Torah is only established for those who kill themselves over it."[1] The obligations of domestic life were therefore a constant distraction from a sage's demanding vocation.

To eschew marriage and embrace celibacy — a remedy available to Greek and Roman philosophers and demanded of the Church Fathers — was not an option for the rabbis. Marital sex and procreation were *mitsvot*, consequently rabbis could not withdraw completely from female society out of singleminded devotion to Torah. Moreover, Babylonian sages believed that without a legitimate sexual outlet, men would inevitably transgress the law.[2] Marriage was the only way to avoid sin (illicit sex, adultery, masturbation) or "thoughts of sin" (lust, sexual fantasies).[3] Even widowers who had fulfilled the obligation to procreate were encouraged to remarry.[4] The sages therefore faced a fundamental systemic tension, in that competing commandments pulled them in opposite directions. For many, it was undoubtedly difficult to find the right balance.

An inherent aspect of the rabbinic value system, this tension appears in Palestinian sources to a limited extent. However, the conflict emerges more acutely in Bavli traditions, many of which bear signs of Stammaitic reworking. This resulted, in my opinion, from two factors. First, the extreme expressions of the value of Torah, discussed in Chapter 1, exacerbated the anxieties that prompted sages to devote all available time to study.[5] Second, the limited number of academies in Stammaitic times forced students of Torah to journey from their places of residence to the centralized institutions, a problem worsened by the much greater distances between cities in the vast territory of Persia.[6] Those who resided at a distance had to spend months or years away from home. In Palestine and in Amoraic Babylonia, students also may have had to travel to the home or school of a renowned master; but masters were found in numerous towns and villages, hence there was a greater chance that an aspiring student could study in relative proximity to his home.[7] And once a student achieved proficiency he could return to his hometown and gather disciples of his own, which was no longer possible when study took place in academic institutions. In Palestine, then, the tension never became a major cultural problem. As Michael Satlow has observed: "*the 'problem' itself is Babylonian.* The Palestinians did not attempt to solve the problem because they never problematized it."[8] The intrinsic rabbinic tensions between Torah study and domestic responsibilities, between love of Torah and devotion to the wife, were heightened in Stammaitic times.

Torah and Wives

This tension finds its clearest expression in a lengthy *sugya* found in bKet 62b and comprised of seven stories of rabbis who spend time away from home in order to study Torah (designated by numbers 1–7 on the pages below). The stories have been discussed by Yonah Fraenkel, Daniel Boyarin and Shulamit Valler, and my analysis owes much to their insights.[9] The *sugya* begins as follows:

(A1) *Students [of Torah] may depart for Torah study without permission [from their wives] for thirty days. Laborers—for one week.*

(A2) *The conjugal duty mentioned in the Torah [Exod 21:10]: Men at leisure—each day. Laborers—twice per week. Ass-Drivers—once per week. Camel-drivers—once per thirty days. Sailors—once per six months. These are the words of R. Eliezer (Mishna Ketubot 5:6).*

(B1) [Talmud:] Rav Beruna said Rav said: "The law follows R. Eliezer." Rav Ada b. Ahava said Rav said: "Those are the words of R. Eliezer [alone]. But the sages say, "Students [of Torah] may depart for Torah study for two or three years without the consent [of their wives]."

(B2) Rava said, "The rabbis relied on the words of Rav Ada b. Ahava and acted accordingly at the cost of their lives."

(1) For example: Rav Rahumei would frequent [the circle] of Rava in Mahoza. He would regularly come home every Yom Kippur eve. One day his studies captivated him. His wife was looking out [for him, thinking,] "He is coming now. He is coming now." He did not come. She became distressed and a tear fell (*ahit*) from her eye. He [Rav Rahumei] was sitting on a roof. The roof collapsed (*ifhit*) under him and he died."

(2A) When is the conjugal duty for scholars?[10] Rav Yehuda said Shmuel said, "Every Friday night."
Which yields its fruit in season (Ps 1:3): Rav Yehuda, and some say Rav Nahman, said: "This is one who has sex every Friday night."

(2B) Yehuda b. R. Hiyya, son-in-law of R. Yannai, went and sat in Rav's study-house. He would return home every Friday at twilight. Whenever he would come, people would see a pillar of fire [going] before him.[11] One day his studies captivated him and he did not come. Because they did not see that sign, R. Yannai said to them, "Overturn his bed,[12] for were Yehuda alive, he would not violate his conjugal duty." It was *As an error that goes forth from a ruler (Qoh 10:5),* and his [Yehuda's] soul departed.[13]

The Mishna defines the Torah's stipulation of a "conjugal duty," a protection in polygamous societies lest a husband neglect one of his wives in favor of others.[14] The frequency generally correlates with a man's occupation (A2). While the conjugal duty of scholars is not mentioned explicitly (unless they are assumed to be "men at leisure"), the Talmud fills the lacuna at 2A by specifying a weekly requirement. Now a daily or weekly obligation clearly would prevent a sage from traveling to study Torah for any length of time. The Mishna therefore grants a dispensation to "students of Torah" to depart for one month even against the wishes of their wives (A1). In this way the Mishna attempts to strike a balance between the two competing values. Though framed in legal terms, the awareness that the wife may oppose the husband's studies ("without permission") recognizes the danger of lengthy absences to her happiness. Two related though fundamentally distinct protections are thus juxtaposed. The basic guarantee of sexual rights deriving from biblical law protects a woman against neglect in favor of other wives. A second measure that stems from rabbinic concerns protects a woman from neglect in favor of Torah study. We sense a very nascent form of a notion that emerges more clearly in the Talmud, that Torah study competes with the wife for the erotic attention of her scholarly husband.

Although the Mishna is attributed to R. Eliezer (A2), the lack of an opposing position tends to indicate general agreement. We would expect the Amoraim to accept this ruling, and that is exactly what Rav Beruna citing Rav does (B1). The Yerushalmi too presents no alternative and apparently accepts the Mishna as law. Moreover, we find on the previous Bavli folio an earlier Amoraic discussion of the Mishna's ruling: "With permission, how long [can they go away]? For as long as they wish. What is the appropriate practice? Rav said, 'One month here [for study] and one month at home'. . . R. Yohanan said, 'One month here and two at home'" (bKet 62a). These Amoraim do not contest the limitation of one month without consent, and even attempt to restrict the length of absences where wives give permission. As Rashi explains, the concern is that husbands will coerce their wives to "permit" them extended leaves.[15] Even under the optimal conditions then, the early Amoraim instruct sages to return home frequently.

While it is by no means unprecedented for the Amoraim to reject the Mishna in favor of a dissenting view found in the Tosefta, it is somewhat unusual to introduce a new, otherwise undocumented Tannaitic opinion as the authoritative law, as does Rav Ada bar Ahava (B1). Given its complete lack of attestation in Tannaitic sources and the Amoraic discussion of the previous folio, the opinion would seem to be pseudepigraphic: the "sages" to which Rav Ada b. Ahava refers are really later Babylonian rabbis who found the one-month limitation inconvenient, not the colleagues of R. Eliezer. Extending the dispensation to leave home to several years can be seen as a necessary adjustment to a later (Babylonian?) situation in which sages had to travel greater distances to study Torah.[16] But it can also be seen as a self-serving invention that caters to the sages' interests. The next comment (B2), illustrated by the subsequent story of a sage's death (1), implies that the latter is the case.[17] Without entering into the legal debate, the comment undermines the dispensation by warning that sages who acted in accord with Rav Ada b. Ahava's tradition paid a heavy price. We have, then, an interesting example of the aggada and halakha in conflict: the halakha permits extended periods of Torah study, while the aggada cautions sages to think twice before putting the law into practice.

Fraenkel has noted the irony that makes the story of Rav Rahumei (1) so effective.[18] The sage "would frequent" his teacher's domain and would "regularly" return home — once a year. The name "Rahumei" derives from the root meaning "love," but the sage is no lover, at least not of his wife.[19] Torah is his true love, and its allure overpowers even that annual appointment. Were Rav Rahumei's real devotion not clear enough from the distribution of his time, the use of the verb "captivated" (*mashkheih*), with its erotic overtones, emphasizes that the rabbi's passion centers on Torah study. The focalization through the wife's eyes, somewhat unusual in rabbinic narratives, nicely illustrates the sage's thoughtlessness. She can hardly wait to see her husband after the long absence, only to be crushed when he fails to appear. A measure-for-measure theme, augmented by a wordplay, squarely places the blame on his head. *Because* a tear falls (*ahit*) from her eye, the roof falls (*ifhit*) from beneath Rav Rahumei.[20]

The similar story of Yehuda b. R. Hiyya deals with a sage who delays returning home at the appointed time of his conjugal duty (2B), which we know from the preceding paragraph (2A) is Friday night. He differs from Rav Rahumei, however, not only in the frequency of his visits home, but in his attitude. A pillar of fire in rabbinic sources indicates the presence of a holy man, and here it seems to symbolize the fervency of his passion as well.[21] He typically returns home full of joy to perform a *mitsvah,* a fact not lost on his neighbors. This portrait of a sage committed to both Torah study and his marital obligations suggests, at first glance, a happy resolution to the internal tension described above. However, like Rav Rahumei, Torah study once "captivated him," destroying the delicate balance of his obligations. Tragedy ensues. As Fraenkel points out, his father-in-law mistakenly takes the failure to perform his conjugal duty as the effect rather than the cause of his death.[22] In accord with a common folkloristic trope, the errant utterance takes effect and Yehuda dies. Again the measure-for-measure theme intimates his culpability: they overturn his bed (a sign of mourning) for neglecting the marital bed.

The two stories thus correlate with the two parts of the Mishna and with the two related halakhic comments in the Talmud. Rav Rahumei fails to return home after an extended period of Torah study (vs. A1, B1–B2), while Yehuda b. R. Hiyya violates his conjugal duty (vs. A2, 2A). The phrase "his studies captivated him" appears in both stories and links them together. The *sugya* therefore commences with a powerful warning against neglecting domestic responsibilities out of excessive zeal for Torah study. While Rav Rahumei's callous disregard for his wife seems to deserve punishment, even a sage such as Yehuda b. R. Hiyya, who normally fulfills his duties with enthusiasm, can meet an untimely end for one failure.

The next three stories are not as unambiguously critical of sages who depart to study Torah, although they certainly advise caution:

(3) Rabbi [Yehuda HaNasi][23] . . . went and planned for his son's [marriage] into the family of R. Yose b. Zimra. He [R. Yose] agreed [to support the son] so that he could go and study for twelve years in the study-house. They passed her before him [Rabbi's son]. He said, "Let it be six years." They passed her before him again. He said, "Let me consummate the marriage and then I will go." He was ashamed before his father. He said to him, "My son. You have your maker's inclination. At first it is written, *You will bring them and plant them in Your own Mountain, [the place You made to dwell in, O Lord, the sanctuary, O Lord, which Your hands established] (Exod 15:17)*. But then it is written, *Let them make me a sanctuary that I may dwell among them (Exod 25:8)*."[24]

He married her. He went and sat in the academy for twelve years. By the time he came back, his wife had become barren. Rabbi said, "What will we do? Should he divorce her? They will say, 'That poor woman waited in vain.' Should he marry another?[25] They will say, 'This one is his wife. That one is his whore.'"[26] He prayed for her and she recovered.

(4A) As R. Shimon bar Yohai's wedding celebration was winding down, R. Hananiah b. Hakhinai got ready to leave for the study-house. He [R. Shimon bar Yohai] said to him, "Wait for me and I will go with you." He did not wait for him.

(4B) He went and sat in Rav's study-house for twelve years. By the time he returned all the streets of his town had changed, and he did not know the way home. He went and sat on the bank of a river. He heard them calling to a certain girl, "Daughter of Hakhinai, Daughter of Hakhinai. Fill your pitcher and come along." He said, "That means this girl is ours." He followed after her. His wife was sitting and sifting flour. He attracted her eye. She saw him. Her heart rejoiced. Her spirit flew away [= she died]. He said before Him, "Master of the Universe. This poor woman—that is her reward?" He prayed for her and she revived.[27]

(5) R. Hama b. Bisa went and sat for twelve years in the academy. When he [prepared] to come [home] he said, "I won't do as did the Son of Hakhinai." He went and sat in the study-house [of his town], and sent [word] to his home.

R. Oshaya his son came and sat before him. He [R. Hama] asked him about his studies. He [R. Hama] saw that his studies were sharp. He became distressed, thinking, "If I had been here, I could have had a son like this one." He entered his house. His son entered [after him]. He [R. Hama] rose before him, because he thought that he [the son] wanted to question him about his studies. His wife said to him, "Was there ever a father who rises in front of his son?" Rami b. Hama applied to him the verse, *"The threefold cord is not readily broken (Qoh 4:12)* — this applies to R. Oshaya, son of R. Hama b. Bisa."[28]

Story 3 seems to poke fun at R. Yehuda HaNasi's son, whose passion for Torah initially paled in comparison to his desire for his betrothed. Yet this structuring of priorities is consistent with other Bavli sources that encourage early marriage and advise that Torah study be preceded by marriage, should "sinful thoughts" become a problem.[29] When the son feels ashamed at his apparent lack of fervor for study, R. Yehuda HaNasi consoles him with a midrashic tradition defending his priorities. The reluctance to depart hints at a downside to the practice of lengthy absences — sexual frustration — although that is not the principal focus of the story.[30]

In contrast to the previous stories, where disaster befalls the sages, here the lengthy absence has dire consequences for the wife, who ages to the point of losing her fertility. While the story expresses some sympathy for her predicament, its true concern is the difficulty this situation poses for her husband. In order to fulfill the commandment to procreate, he now will have to divorce her and remarry or take a second wife. Neither option is palatable because of what "people will say," a technical term employed in halakhic discussions to introduce mistaken and undesirable conclusions people will reach if certain rulings are promulgated or actions taken.[31] In this case the sage will be the object of criticism for causing his pitiable wife to wait until his return, only to divorce her on account of a condition for which he bears responsibility. Or he will be criticized for keeping a "whore," a wife with whom he exclusively engages in nonprocreative sex. Fortunately for the son, R. Yehuda HaNasi's prayers restore the wife's fertility, perhaps as a reward for the long years of study. Yet despite the happy ending, the story cautions its rabbinic audience against extended absences. Sages lacking an eminent father whose prayers effect miracles may want to obviate the situation by not spending years away from home.

The story of R. Hananiah b. Hakhinai (4) also contrasts with the first two stories in that the wife suffers harm. Whereas Rav Rahumei dies for failing to return home (1), here R. Hananiah's wife dies of shock when he returns home unexpectedly. His impulsiveness — and perhaps thoughtlessness — is adumbrated in the first scene (4A), which serves no other purpose than to portray this character trait. Consumed by a hunger for study, he cannot delay even a few days for his friend but sets out immediately. There may also be a hint of his low estimation of marriage, in his refusal to wait for R. Shimon b. Yohai to enjoy some time with his bride. At all events, the account of the arrival at home continues the previous story's interest in the impact of absence upon children. R. Hananiah does not know his own daughter, who has grown up during his absence. His lack of affinity is marked by her appellation "Daughter of Hakhinai," her grandfather, rather than "Daughter of Hananiah," and by Hananiah's following after her without any direct contact. The ending expresses more sympathy for the wife: the sage explicitly protests the injustice of her having waited so long, only to die upon his arrival. Yet the power to revive her seems again to derive from the merit of his Torah study or the miracle-working abilities Torah confers. If this is over-reading, at least it must be conceded that the merit accrued by waiting patiently while her husband studied Torah bestows divine reward. So this story too has a happy ending, in that R. Hananiah reunites with his wife and daughter, having enjoyed twelve[32] productive years of Torah study. However, it simultaneously raises for the audience concerns akin to those of the previous story. Sages who would rather not be strangers to their own daughters and do not wish to risk their wives' dying of shock should not disappear for so long.

The final story of this unit expresses still more optimism (5). R. Hama b. Bisa has learned from Hananiah b. Hakhinai not to arrive unexpectedly, thereby circumventing the danger to his wife. The story develops the theme of the sage's distance from his own children with the comic, if also poignant, portrayal of a father unwittingly discussing Torah with his own son and then mistakenly showing the very honor he ought to receive. Ironically, the local scholar with whom Hananiah speaks turns out to be the son, who has unexpectedly blossomed into a scholar despite his father's absence, perhaps due to the wife's upright childrearing. Torah fortunately runs deep in R. Hama's family, as the concluding comment notes. Again everything works out well for the sage. But the audience would once more absorb a cautionary lesson from R. Hama's reasonable concern: "If I had been there, I could have had a son like this one." Would a sage wish to risk his son's growing up without his guidance and potentially lacking knowledge of Torah? And would he want to be a complete stranger to his own sons, whether they turn out to be learned or not?

These three stories constitute a well-formed unit. In each a sage spends twelve years away from home in the study-house. Each centers on the encounter with the family upon returning home, as opposed to the first two stories in which the sage never makes it home. Each focuses on potential negative consequences to the sage's family due to his absence. Wives may lose their fertility or die of shock. The sage may not have children, not recognize children who have grown up in his absence, or have sons who do not know Torah. Yet each has a happy or at least relatively happy ending, as the most severe problems are ultimately avoided (although the fact that children grow up without knowing their fathers cannot be redressed). The stories portray to the sages the trade-offs they will experience by pursuing a life of Torah study at the leading academic centers. They will accrue great merit, engage in their beloved activity, and perhaps achieve glory. But their families and relationships may suffer unfortunate repercussions. While the stories warn sages against such extended absences, they are by no mean as unambiguously foreboding as the accounts of Rav Rahumei and Yehuda b. R. Hiyya. Indeed, the story of R. Hama b. Bisa suggests that with proper precautions everything may work out for the best.

The Bavli now presents the famous story of R. Akiba, which is often taken as a true account of the great sage's origins but should be seen as a rabbinic fantasy:

(6A) Akiba was the shepherd of Ben Kalba Savua. His daughter saw that he [Akiba] was modest and upright. She said, "If I become betrothed to you, will you go to the study-house?" He said to her, "Yes." She was betrothed to him in secret and sent him off. Her father heard. He threw her out of the house and swore that she should have no benefit from his property.

(6B) He went and sat for twelve years in the study-house. When he returned twelve thousand students came with him. He heard a certain old man say to her [Akiba's wife], "How long will you lead the life of a widow?" She said to him, "If he listened to me, he would stay another twelve years." He [R. Akiba] said, "Then I am doing this with her consent!" He went back and sat for twelve more years in the study-house.

(6C) When he returned twenty-four thousand students came with him. His wife heard and went forth to greet him. Her neighbors said to her, "Borrow something [nice] to wear and adorn yourself." She said, "*A righteous man knows the life of his beast (Prov 12:10).*" When she approached him she fell on her face and kissed his feet. His attendants pushed her away. He said to them, "Leave her be. What is mine and what is yours is hers."

(6D) Her father heard that a great man had come to town. He said, "I will go to him. Perhaps he can release me from my oath."[33] He came to him. He [Akiba] said to him, "Did you swear knowing that [your daughter would marry] a great man?" He said to him, "Had he known but one chapter or one law [I would not have sworn]." He said, "I am he." He fell on his face and kissed his feet and gave him half his money.

(6E) The daughter of R. Akiba did the same for Ben Azai. Thus runs the proverb, "Ewe follows ewe. As the ways of the mother so are the ways of the daughter."

This story differs from the others in imagining an ideal scenario. For R. Akiba there is no tension between his obligations to his wife and his drive to study Torah, since she not only permits but stipulates that he go. Nor is there the problem of the conjugal duty that tripped up R. Yehuda b. R. Hiyya (2), since the two do not marry until after his years of study. There is no expectation that he return home, as in the case of Rav Rahumei (1), for R. Akiba's wife actually does not want him to desist from his studies. Far from wishing for his return, she hopes that he will stay away! As opposed to the stories of sages who arrive home after twelve years only to encounter various problems (3–5), R. Akiba encounters no difficulties, because he does not actually arrive at his home. This is the force of the incredible scene where he journeys back to his hometown but upon overhearing his wife grant him permission for yet another twelve years departs without even greeting her. In this way R. Akiba becomes a great master of Torah accompanied by twenty-four thousand disciples, and ultimately acquires riches as well, thus guaranteeing him the opportunity to study Torah for the rest of his life. The story simultaneously addresses another difficulty inherent in the rabbinic vocation, that of earning a living. How would a sage support himself and his family while engaging in full-time Torah study? Note that the story of R. Yehuda HaNasi's son addresses this issue (3), as does the seventh story in the series (see below).

The addendum concerning R. Akiba's daughter (6E) serves two purposes. First, it informs us that his wife retained her fertility despite the twenty-four year delay in consummating the union and did not suffer the same fate as the daughter-in-law of R. Yehuda HaNasi (3). Second, as Boyarin has noted, the Bavli here resolves the problem represented by Ben Azai, a sage who refused to marry and procreate, explaining to his colleagues: "What can I do? My soul desires Torah. The world will be sustained by others."[34] Ben Azai's choice of celibacy obviates the central tension at the cost of violating rabbinic norms and perhaps constitutes a dangerous model for later sages. With a wife like R. Akiba's, Ben Azai can fulfill his desire for Torah while betrothed for decades, essentially celibate but simultaneously meeting the obligation to marry, at least *de jure* if not *de facto*.

This story portrays a fantasy wife. She encourages her husband to study, even at great personal sacrifice. She forgoes her right to limit her husband to a two- or three-year absence. She endures poverty and social ridicule. She even kisses his feet when he achieves greatness. Note the comparison to an animal in the verse she applies to herself (6C), reinforced by the proverbial analogy to a ewe (6E), and by R. Akiba's origin as a shepherd.[35] Even without pressing the imagery, the paternalistic attitude and message that she serves her husband like a faithful beast seems clear.[36] With such women the sages will gracefully share their merit by acknowledging, "What is mine and what is yours is hers." One wonders, however, whether many rabbinic wives would have been comforted by that recognition.

I consider the wife in this story a fantasy: she is "ideal" in the sense of "existing in fancy but unattainable in reality," not in the sense of an "ultimate object of endeavor." I make this distinction because I think it unlikely that the storyteller intended to instruct his audience to find wives like that of R. Akiba or to instruct women to emulate her. That such wives exist is belied by both the artificial and exaggerated plot and the more realistic depictions of the five previous stories. Those wives are neither negative models nor foils for the wife of R. Akiba. Indeed, they are portrayed in a neutral or favorable manner. The women in stories 3–5 do not stand in the way of Torah study; all have apparently given permission for their husbands to study for twelve years, far beyond the two or three years that the Bavli allows. Nor do they cause their husbands suffering. In stories 3 and 4 the wives bear the suffering; in story 2 the wife is never mentioned and the sage's death is caused by the neglect of conjugal duty combined with his father-in-law's errant conclusion. Only in story 1 can the wife be seen as the cause. But she is at most a very indirect cause, as it is not the absence of Rav Rahumei per se that causes disaster but his failure to appear at the designated time. The proximate stories, then, depict the potentially unfortunate consequences of extended absences *even* when sages marry pious, tolerant, and supportive women.

It is crucial to note that the story of R. Akiba sidesteps, more than resolves, the tensions. The tensions arise when the obligations of marriage conflict with the sage's devotion to Torah study. R. Akiba and his wife, however, do not marry until after his return. At the root of the fantasy is a contrivance, a pseudomarriage that really affords no solution for those sages actually married. The contrast between stories 1–5 and story 6 is not that of bad versus good wives, nor of types of wives to avoid versus types to marry, but of (relatively) realistic versus fantasy wives.[37] The tension is so intractable precisely because it cannot be avoided simply by marrying the right kind of woman: it inheres in the situation of marriage itself.[38]

What is the function of a fantasy such as this? I would argue that it functions in a manner similar to certain rituals as interpreted by Jonathan Z. Smith.[39] Smith seeks to account for the fact that some social processes are both described and enacted through ritual in idealized ways that clash with the manner in which the processes are carried out in real life. This puzzling discrepancy, he suggests, is actually central to the ritual function. We should not always expect the ritual or the descriptions of the actual social events to cohere with the reality:

> *Ritual is a means of performing the way things ought to be in conscious tension to the way things are in such a way that this ritualized perfection is recollected in the ordinary, uncontrolled course of things.* Ritual relies for its power on the fact that it is concerned with quite ordinary activities, that what it describes and displays is, in principle, possible for every occurrence of these acts. But it relies, as well, for its power on the perceived fact that, in actuality, such possibilities cannot be realized.
>
> There is a "gnostic" dimension to ritual. It provides the means for demonstrating that we know what ought to have been done, what ought to have taken place. But, by the fact that it is ritual action rather than everyday action, it demonstrates that we know "what is the case." Ritual provides an occasion for reflection and rationalization on the fact that what ought to have taken place was not done, what ought to have taken place did not occur.[40]

Ritual, then, does not always serve as a model for actual conduct but discloses how great is the distance between the real and the unattainable perfection. Indeed, the ritual enacts the perfect procedure in contradistinction to that which can be realized in reality, for only in ritual can all the factors — human, animal, and natural forces — be completely controlled.

The story of R. Akiba and his wife is not a ritual, except insofar as the Talmudic *sugya* may have been "ritually" recited in the academy. And of course one may question the relevance to a Talmudic text of Smith's anthropologically based observations.[41] Nonetheless, I wish to suggest that this fantasy of a rabbinic marriage may have served the same function as these idealized ritual enactments and counterfactual descriptions of social processes. The story expresses, as Smith says, "the way things ought to be in conscious tension to the way things are." In rabbinic fantasy a sage marries, so as to fulfill the requisite commandments, yet still spends years of uninterrupted study at an academy, and also has means of material support. In practice that cannot be done, for such women do not exist, such relationships cannot be sustained, and such material support usually will not be forthcoming. The fantasy provides a means of thinking about the disparity between the real and the utopian, a way of measuring to what extent each dimension of a sage's life compares with an unrealizable ideal. A story, even more than a ritual enactment, provides an environment in which all factors can be completely controlled. The storyteller can portray his characters however he wishes, and here he invents the perfect wife for R. Akiba. But real women and men will not play out the roles of the wife, R. Akiba, and the father-in-law. The story does not serve as a model for sages and wives to emulate but as means for sages to think about their marriages.[42]

Smith attributes the power of ritual to the fact "that what it describes and displays is, in principle, possible for every occurrence of these acts." Similarly, the power of R. Akiba's story lies in the fact that it lacks supernatural motifs. Unlike some of the proximate stories, no miracles occur. Yet the story as a whole is thoroughly unbelievable, and we should not expect that the storyteller intended it to be exemplary nor that the sages and their wives attempted to emulate it in practice. The story functions to stimulate thought, not behavior.

The *sugya* concludes with a final story:

(7) Rav Yosef b. Rava — his father sent him to the study-house [to study] before Rav Yosef [b. Hiyya]. They [the families] agreed [to support] him for six years. After three years, when the eve of Yom Kippur approached, he [Rav Yosef b. Rava] said, "I will go and see my family." His father heard. He took an axe and went forth to meet him. He said to him, "Did you remember your whore (*zonatkha*)?" Others say that he said, "Did you remember your dove (*yonatkha*)?" They quarreled and neither one ate the last meal before the fast.

This story recalls the first two stories in depicting a sage who fails to return home and posing the question of the appropriate object of love. Rava surprisingly refers to his son's wife as his "whore," implying of course that the Torah is the legitimate object of erotic attention. His comment seems to have been revised by a later voice offended by the crude language. Be that as it may, Rav Yosef evidently does consider his wife a "dove," or at least feels more devotion to her than his father deems appropriate. The textual confusion and wordplay nicely express the tension of love of wife versus love of Torah. The violent imagery, which signals how much is at stake, squares with the Bavli's propensity for hostile depictions (discussed in Chap. 3). That the two argue, though it is the eve of Yom Kippur, a time for reconciliation, and neglect to eat the final meal leaves us with a picture of stalemate. Just as the father and son could not resolve their quarrel and move ahead, so this fundamental cultural tension cannot be resolved completely. The intractable argument is a fitting conclusion to the cycle of stories that grapples with this issue.

Taken as a whole, the cycle of stories offers anything but a simple message. There is a certain amount of compassion for forsaken and neglected wives, expressed mainly in the first two stories and to a lesser extent in the accounts of unfortunate wives who become infertile or die (3 and 4). But the overall lesson is *not* that lengthy absences or long nights in the academy invite punishment, nor that commitments to wife and home should take priority.[43] Were that the point, the sages in stories 3–5 should experience misfortune like those in stories 1 and 2. But in those cases the wives suffer while ultimately everything turns out well for the sages: they enjoy twelve years of study and return to a normal family life. We might also have expected a different finale, showing unambiguously that domestic responsibilities deserve more attention. Rather, the stories manifest to sages the dangers of extended absences and the trade-offs entailed by that choice. The dangers: divine punishment for failing to return home at set times and for violating the conjugal duty, wives who become barren, uneducated sons. The cost: sexual abstinence, longing for wife and family, becoming a stranger to one's own children. The benefit: years of study with the beloved Torah. Those trade-offs cannot be avoided, except in the fantasy world of R. Akiba and his wife.

The tension is so acute, and so irresolvable, because certain trade-offs involve commandments: the conjugal duty, procreation, and teaching a son Torah are all *mitsvot*. To promote the emotional and psychological health of wives and to prevent their suffering, together with the suffering of all human beings, are important rabbinic values. Sages will not be able to satisfy these claims without reducing their Torah study. Yet the claim of Torah study is potentially infinite. To fulfill both sets of claims simultaneously requires a wife (and father-in-law) like that of R. Akiba, but she does not exist in the real world. I would say that the overall trajectory of the *sugya* warns sages that the dangers and trade-offs of spending years at the academy probably outweigh the benefits. Perhaps a sage should not exercise his legal right to spend two or three years away without permission, nor exercise his option to spend additional years if his wife allows him. But the message is hardly unambiguous. Ultimately the *sugya* manifests, but does not resolve, the tension.

An extended cycle of stories such as this is a product of the redactors, because they are responsible for the collection and arrangement of sources. In addition, there are specific indications of Stammaitic reworking and composition. First, the sequence of the stories, as we have seen, develops the themes in an effective way, which suggests that the Stammaim altered antecedent sources with purpose and design. Second, repeated phrases link the stories into units. The first two stories contain the phrase "his studies captivated him." In stories 3–5 the sage studies for twelve years in the studyhouse. In both 3 and 4 the wife suffers but recovers when the sage "prays for her." Stories 4 and 5 are connected through R. Hama b. Bisa's statement, "I won't do as did the Son of Hakhinai." Reference to a previous story marks redactional reworking, as the order of the stories is a function of their redactional setting. Story 6, the story of R. Akiba, again tells of a sage spending twelve years away, or actually two periods of twelve years. The final story connects to story 3 with the motifs of the families' agreeing to support the son while he studies, the six-year time span, and the reference to the wife as a whore. Third, different versions of several of the stories appear elsewhere, which suggests that Bavli storytellers introduced changes. A different version of story 2 appears in the Yerushalmi, but that story concerns a scholar who failed to meet his father-in-law on the Sabbath eve.[44] Story 3 (about R. Hananiah b. Hakhinai) also exhibits differences when compared with the Palestinian versions (see below). A version of the story of R. Akiba appears elsewhere in the Bavli, with a slightly different emphasis.[45] And a briefer allusion to this story appears in the Yerushalmi in which R. Akiba's wife sells her hair so that the sage can study, but does not send him away.[46] While several of the stories therefore originated in earlier periods, there is good evidence to attribute their current forms to the redactors.

The tension between Torah study and domestic responsibilities, as noted above, is found to a certain degree in earlier periods as well. Its prime expression appears in the Palestinian version of the story of Hananiah b. Hakhinai, cited here from *Leviticus Rabbah:*

> R. Hananiah b. Hakhinai and R. Shimon bar Yohai went to study Torah with R. Akiba in Bnei Barak, and stayed there thirteen years. R. Shimon bar Yohai corresponded and knew what was happening at home. R. Hananiah b. Hakhinai did not correspond and did not know what was happening at home. His wife sent to him saying, "Your daughter has grown up. Come and marry her off." Nevertheless, he did not go. R. Akiba saw by means of the holy spirit and said to them, "Whoever has a grown daughter at home, go and marry her off." He [R. Hananiah] paid attention to what he had heard, arose, asked permission [to take leave], and left. He went and sought his home, but he found that it had moved to another place. What did he do? He went and sat where women draw water. He heard the voice of some youths say, "Daughter of Hakhinai fill your pitcher and come up." What did he do? He walked after her until she entered her home. He

entered after her suddenly. His wife had hardly seen him and she died. He said, "Master of the Universe! This poor woman—that is her reward after thirteen years." At that time her soul returned to her body."[47]

Boyarin interprets the story as unmitigated condemnation of sages who leave home to study Torah.[48] R. Hananiah shows no interest at all in his wife and family; he even ignores his wife's behest and fails to return until prodded by R. Akiba. Punishment for his absolute indifference comes swiftly when his wife dies upon his arrival. According to Boyarin, her resurrection is not part of the original story but a later gloss influenced by the Bavli's version.[49] The parallel to the story in *Genesis Rabbah* concludes, "And some say her soul returned," which looks more like an addition. Thus the Palestinian story simply rejects extended absences from home, whereas the Bavli is conflicted. This interpretation is attractive to my thesis, as it coheres with what should be expected given the higher regard for Torah study and perhaps necessity of travel to academies in Babylonia. The difficulty with Boyarin's reading is that R. Shimon b. Yohai, with whom R. Hananiah is contrasted, apparently behaves appropriately simply by keeping in touch with his home. In addition, it is not certain that her revival is a later addition.[50] Finally, were the story a condemnation of sages who spend years away from home, R. Hananiah should be punished rather than his wife.

Ofra Meir, on the other hand, interprets the story as teaching the importance of proper order.[51] R. Hananiah deviates from proper protocol by not keeping in touch with home and by entering his house without advance notice. The description that he entered "suddenly" emphasizes his breach of conduct. The context in *Leviticus Rabbah* likewise stresses this theme. The story appears in the passage that comments on the death of Nadav and Avihu, who deviated from the proper sacrificial ritual order and died (Lev 10:1–10). Following the story appears a teaching attributed to R. Shimon b. Yohai listing four things that God hates, including "one who enters his house suddenly." If Meir's interpretation is correct, then the story teaches that to avoid misfortune one should observe proper etiquette, correspond with home, and not appear unannounced.

Common to both interpretations is the relative lack of tension manifested by the story. According to Boyarin, the story rejects lengthy absences; according to Meir, the problems created by absences easily can be avoided. I do not want to minimize the similarity of the conflict in this core plot to that of the Bavli version, namely a sage caught between dedication to Torah study and domestic responsibilities. But the Palestinian version certainly presents a much weaker expression of it. R. Shimon b. Yohai evidently discharged both *mitsvot* satisfactorily. And nothing suggests that the two demands are fundamentally irreconcilable.[52]

More significant is the different impression made by the collection of seven stories into an extended *sugya*. Here the whole is far greater than the sum of its parts. The progression of stories with varied circumstances and outcomes manifests the inevitability of trade-offs and the impossibility of completely resolving the tension. In this way the Stammaim created an elegant and complex story-cycle for succeeding generations of sages to ponder.

The Erotic Torah

Several locutions in these stories construe the Torah in erotic terms: the Torah "captivated" Rav Rahumei and R. Yehuda, while Rava calls the wife a "whore," implying that he regards Torah as the legitimate sexual object.[53] A similar conception underpins an exhortation not to study Torah in the presence of an *am ha'arets*: "R. Hiyya taught: He who engages in Torah [study] in the presence of an *am ha'arets*—it is as if he has sex with his bride in his [the *am ha'arets*'s] presence, as it is written, *Moses commanded us the Torah, the inheritance* (morasha) *of the congregation of Jacob (Deut 33:4)*. Do not read *morasha* (inheritance) but *meorasa* (betrothed) (bPes 49b)." Attitudes to the *am ha'arets* (the non-rabbinic Jew) will be explored in the next chapter. Here we should note that the analogies between study and sex, and between the Torah and a woman / bride, are explicit. Because a strict dualism of matter and spirit is alien to rabbinic thought, I would not suggest that the tradition points to a transfer of erotic focus from body to mind. Nevertheless, engagement with Torah apparently stimulated the sages with a powerful intellectual delight that competed with, or at least substituted for, bodily pleasure. The midrash on *morasha* (inheritance) and *meorasa* (betrothed) also appears in an interesting dream interpretation: "One who has intercourse with a betrothed (*meorasa*) maiden [in his dream] should expect [greatness] in Torah, as it says, *Moses commanded us* . . . [as above]."[54] This exegesis moves in a direction opposite to that of the previous source, from sex to Torah rather than Torah to sex. The vision of an erotic physical experience (sex with a betrothed maiden) has implications regarding the intellect (Torah), as opposed to an "erotic" intellectual experience (Torah) having implications regarding physical circumstances, that study should not be conducted in the presence of outsiders.

This and other sources hinting at normative consequences suggest that the erotic representation of Torah study should be considered more than mere rhetoric: "The school of Rav Anan taught: What is [the meaning of] the verse, *Your rounded thighs are like jewels, the work of a master's hand (Song 7:2)*? Why are words of Torah compared to the thigh? Just as a thigh is hidden, so words of Torah should be [studied] in private (bSuk 49b)." The sensual description of the maiden's body in the Song of Songs is applied to the experience of words of Torah. Because of its erotic nature, Torah study should be undertaken in private. It is also worth noting that both erotic symbolism and the demand for privacy characterize later Jewish mysticism (and mysticism in many religious traditions). In post-Talmudic times, Torah study itself was understood as a mystical praxis.[55]

A more graphic deployment of erotic imagery to capture the pleasures of Torah study appears in bEruv 54b:

> Rav Shmuel bar Nahmani said: What is written, *A loving doe, a graceful mountain goat. Let her breasts satisfy you at all times. Be infatuated with her love always (Prov 5:19)*. Why are words of Torah compared to a doe? Just as a doe has a tight vagina, and is beloved to her mate each time just like the first time, so words of Torah are beloved to those who study them each time just like the first time.

> *A graceful goat.* It bestows grace on those who study it.

> *Let her breasts satisfy you at all times.* Why are words of Torah compared to a breast? Just as a child finds milk in a breast whenever he fondles it, so a man finds meaning whenever he meditates on words of Torah (bEruv 54b).

Not only is the analogy between study and sex made explicit, but Torah study compares to the best type of sex (at least according to this common male fantasy). The Bavli invokes the same analogy to explain why King Ahasueros desired Esther above all the thousands of women he sampled before deciding on a queen: "R. Zeira said: Why is Esther compared to a doe? Just as a doe has a tight vagina, and is beloved to her mate each time just like the first time. So Esther was beloved to her mate each time just like the first time" (bYom 29a).[56] Whenever a sage probes the Torah he encounters "virgin" territory, as the Torah possesses an infinite capacity to yield new insights. The analogy to the breast shifts the figuration slightly from eroticism to fecundity by focusing on lactation, which points to the richness of the experience of study. Given Torah's eternal youth, fertility, and virginity, we can perhaps understand why sages tended to neglect their wives.

If a wife can be designated a "whore" in relation to the Torah (see story 7 above), then abandoning Torah study for other pursuits can be conceptualized as a sexual transgression. A tradition ascribed to Resh Laqish interprets

Prov 6:32, *He who commits adultery is devoid of understanding,* in terms of study: "This refers to one who studies Torah at intervals, as it says, *And that all of them be constantly on your lips (Prov 22:18)*."[57] The student betrays his rightful consort (Torah) by attending to her intermittently rather than at all times. This exegesis reverses the sense of the phrase "devoid of understanding" from the cause of adultery to the consequence. Physical adultery results from a dearth of understanding (of the severity of the sin), whereas metaphoric "adultery" vis-à-vis Torah *causes* a dearth of understanding, that is, inferior knowledge. The concluding verse is among those biblical prooftexts adduced by rabbinic sources to encourage dedication to Torah study which, when interpreted literally rather than figuratively, resulted in enormous psychological pressure on students.

In some respects this transforms the common biblical trope of idolatry as fornication into the spurning of Torah as adultery. Yet the rabbinic version raises the stakes considerably by comparing to sexual transgression not the study of other texts (the direct parallel to the worship of other gods) but attention to any other activity, causing the interruption of study. For the rabbis, then, not only active betrayal, but even *de facto* neglect, violates the incessant devotion demanded by Torah. This standard mirrors the sentiments expressed by such maxims as "They forsake eternal life and engage in temporal life," discussed in Chapter 1.[58] All pursuits, not only outright sins, are pejoratively classified as "temporal life" or "adultery" in comparison to Torah study.

Wives as Obstacles

While the stories discussed above focus on sages who neglect wives for the sake of Torah study, a number of sources move in the opposite direction, presenting wives as obstacles to their husbands' noble pursuit. This dynamic appears in Bavli additions to several stories attested in Palestinian works. In the account of the deposition of Rabban Gamaliel, for example, a scene is added in which R. Eleazar b. Azariah consults his wife as to whether he should accept the appointment to be head of the academy:

yBer 4:1, 7d	*bBer 27b–28a*
They went and appointed R. Eleazar b. Azariah to [lead the] session. . . .	They said . . . whom shall we appoint? . . . let us appoint Eleazar b. Azariah. . . . They went and said to him, "Will you consent to be head of the acad-

emy?"[59] He said to them, "Let me consult with the members of my household." He went and consulted with his wife.

She said to him, "Perhaps they will reconcile with him and depose you?" He said to her, "It has been taught: *One raises the level of holiness but does not diminish it (Mishna Menahot 11:7).*"[60] She said to him, "Perhaps he [Rabban Gamaliel] will harm you?" He said to her, "Let a man use a valuable cup for one day even if it breaks on the morrow." She said to him, "You have no white hair."

He was sixteen years old and his entire head was full of white hair.	That day he was eighteen years old. A miracle happened to him and he was crowned with eighteen rows of white hair.

The Yerushalmi story assumes R. Eleazar b. Azariah immediately accepted the appointment. In the Bavli he confers with his wife, who attempts to dissuade him by various arguments. Evidently she would prefer that he not accept a position that entails additional academic responsibility.[61] As a result of this interpolation, the description of R. Eleazar b. Azariah's premature gray hair in the Yerushalmi becomes a supernatural transformation in the Bavli. His hair miraculously turned white to parry one of his wife's objections.

In the lengthy biographical account of R. Eleazar b. R. Shimon, the wife even prevents the sage from going to the study-house (bBM 84b). After R. Eleazar voluntarily calls afflictions upon himself, "from that day onward she would not let him go to the study-house so that the rabbis would not trouble him." The sense of "trouble" is that the numerous questions the rabbis pose will wear him out given his already weakened state. When she subsequently learns that R. Eleazar caused his own sufferings, she "rebels" and leaves him. He then returns to the study-house and rules that many types of blood are clean, that is, not menstrual blood, so that in such cases the couples may resume sexual relations. Thus the wife has impeded rabbinic activity, and the

Bavli subsequently criticizes her on this account, "How much procreation did that wicked woman prevent in Israel." Even after his death the wife continues to oppose the rabbis by preventing them from burying R. Eleazar's corpse.[62] In the Palestinian version of the story, found in *Pesiqta deRav Kahana,* the relationship between R. Eleazar and his wife is completely harmonious.[63] She rejoices at having married such a holy man and explains to R. Yehuda HaNasi that her husband's greatness derives from his voluntarily undertaking sufferings. There is no mention of a study-house, let alone the wife's preventing R. Eleazar from going there.[64] In this account the residents of two towns quarrel over where the sage's body should be buried and the wife assists one side. Thus the Bavli presents the wife as an oppositional figure who prohibits a sage from attending the study-house and prevents him from adjudicating legal cases.

The problematic wife is not the focus of these stories, but only a minor aside. Yet the fact that two late Bavli stories add the motif to the Palestinian versions is significant. The Stammaim seem to have regarded their wives as impediments to their academic careers.

Chapter 7

⌣∴⌢

Elitism:
The Sages and the Amei ha'arets

Throughout Jewish history rabbis exhibited both elitist and populist tendencies. On the one hand, they saw themselves as the religious leaders of the entire Jewish people and perceived their role as, at least in part, to educate, inspire, and guide their fellow Jews. On the other, they naturally felt a sense of distance from their less learned and less pious brethren, and intermittently resentment and frustration. In antiquity, before rabbinic piety became the normative form of Judaism it would be in later times, these poles were exaggerated. The rabbis actively campaigned to become religious authorities such that the masses would treat them as spiritual leaders, appeal to rabbinic courts, and abide by rabbinic law. At the same time, that many Jews had not yet devoted themselves to rabbinic Judaism created a significant social and religious gap. These were not rabbinic Jews who, though lapsed or sinful, were ideologically committed; they were not rabbinic Jews at all.

All rabbinic works, including the Bavli, contain numerous traditions evincing both of these tendencies on the part of rabbis. As one would expect from collective literature compiled over the course of centuries, varying circumstances and personalities reflect the full spectrum of attitudes to nonrabbinic Jews. Yet among these diverse views there stands out a radical and hostile elitist streak unique to the Bavli. A number of Bavli traditions express a degree of contempt and disgust for nonrabbis that is completely absent from other rabbinic works. I suggest that these sources originate in the Stammaitic academy. The negative attitude should be understood as an expression of the internal discourse of the sages within the academy, intended for an audience of other sages. The invective functions mostly as a means of self-definition and self-justification, drawing a sharp contrast between the academic life of the rabbis and the outside world. These disparaging comments do not reflect real social relations; they constitute a hyperbolic expression of the core rabbinic ideology that places ultimate worth on Torah study.

Rabbinic sources use the term *am ha'arets,* literally "people of the land," to refer to nonrabbinic or uneducated Jews. This term derives from the biblical books of Ezra and Nehemiah, where it designates the Israelites who had remained in Judea when the aristocracy were deported to Babylonia during the first exile.[1] These people evidently formed a distinct social group in contrast to the exiles who returned along with Ezra and Nehemiah. In Tannaitic sources *am ha'arets* generally functions as a technical term referring to a Jew who does not observe laws of tithing and purity in a strict manner, as opposed to the *haver,* who observes such stringencies. This usage stems from an important aspect of Pharisaic piety, the practice of preparing food with the same standards of purity required of sacrifices and cultic offerings. The Tosefta accordingly defines the *am ha'arets* as: "Anyone who does not eat ordinary food in a state of purity, the words of R. Meir. But the sages say: anyone who does not tithe his produce (tAZ 3:10)." The transfer of priestly norms to lay practice made it difficult for Pharisees and early sages to associate with other Jews. Most Tannaitic law deals with how a *haver* eats with, borrows utensils from, or purchases the food of an *am ha'arets* without violating the higher standards.[2] Several Tannaitic sources, however, go beyond this narrow focus on purities and tithes to caution against close social relations. Dosa B. Harkinas warns that "sitting in the meeting houses of the *am ha'arets* drives a man out of this world" (mAvot 3:10).[3] The picture does not change much in the Yerushalmi and Palestinian midrashim.[4] While there is certainly no deep respect for the *am ha'arets,* there is little opprobrium either. The sources expect that sages and *amei ha'arets* associate in a variety of contexts; they provide rules to govern interactions, but they frown on too much intimacy.[5] This also is the dominant view of the Bavli, which cites and comments on many of the Tannaitic traditions.

A different conception of the *am ha'arets* begins to emerge in the Bavli in Amoraic times. A Bavli *baraita* defines the *am ha'arets* in more general terms.

Our sages taught: Who is an *am ha'arets?* Anyone who does not recite the *Shema* evening and morning, these are the words of R. Eliezer. R. Yehoshua says: Anyone who does not put on *tefilin.* Ben Azai says: Anyone who does not have fringes on his garments. R. Natan says: Anyone who does not put a mezuza on his door. R. Natan bar Yosef says: Anyone who does not devote his sons to Torah study.

Others say: Even if he has studied Scripture and Mishna but does not attend upon the sages — behold, this one is an *am ha'arets* (bBer 47b).[6]

This is one of those problematic *baraitot* found only in the Bavli and therefore of doubtful authenticity. Like many such *baraitot*, it attributes views to Tannaim that are not attested in any Palestinian source. Since Babylonian Amoraim comment on the *baraita*, it should probably be dated to early Amoraic times. The views represented here conceive of *amei ha'arets* as Jews who do not observe common commandments. These Jews seem to be not heretics or ideologically opposed to the rabbis so much as lax in their religious commitments. The last two opinions go an additional step by extending the definition to all those who do not dedicate themselves to a rabbinic way of life. To include men who raise sons who observe the commandments but do not study Torah in the same manner as sages, or who study Torah and Mishna (!) but do not serve the sages, broadens the category considerably. It comes close to regarding all Jews who are not sages or their apprentices — all "Others" — as *amei ha'arets*.

The Stammaitic stratum contains a more extreme perspective on the *am ha'arets,* a perspective that differs dramatically from all earlier sources in its expressions of unabashed contempt. The negative views are concentrated in a long *sugya* found at bPes 49a–b which has been comprehensively studied by Stephen Wald in his critical commentary to the third chapter of Tractate Pesahim.[7] Although most of these traditions are attributed to Palestinian sages, generally to Tannaim, no comparable traditions appear in either Tannaitic or Amoraic Palestinian compilations.[8] These are Stammaitic creations pseudepigraphically attributed to Tannaim. Wald has even identified specific signs of Stammaitic reworking.[9] My discussion is indebted to Wald's superb analysis.

Marriage

The Bavli's contempt for the *am ha'arets* emerges in the vehemence with which it discourages marriages between rabbinic and nonrabbinic families. The Stammaitic *sugya* at bPes 49a–b begins with two *baraitot* that all but forbid such unions:[10]

Our rabbis taught: Let a man always sell all his possessions and marry the daughter of a scholar, *for if he dies or is exiled, his sons will be scholars. But [let him not marry] the daughter of an* am ha'arets, *for if he dies or is exiled, his sons will be* amei ha'arets. And let a man sell all his possessions and marry his daughter to a scholar. A parable: [This may be compared with] grapes of a vine among grapes of a vine, which is a comely and appropriate thing. *[But let him not marry] an* am ha'arets. *A parable: [This may be compared with] grapes of the vine with berries of a thorn bush, which is an ugly and inappropriate thing.*

Let a man always sell everything he has and marry the daughter of a scholar. If he does not find the daughter of a scholar, let him marry the daughter of the leaders of the generation. If he does not find the daughter of the leaders of the generation, let him marry the daughter of the heads of synagogues. If he did not marry the daughter of heads of synagogues, let him marry the daughter of supervisors of charities. If he does not find the daughter of supervisors of charities, let him marry the daughter of teachers of schoolchildren. *But [let him] not [marry] the daughter of an* am ha'arets, *for they are repulsive, and their wives are vermin, and concerning their daughters it is said, "Cursed be he who lies with any beast" (Deut 27:21).*

The italicized portions represent the Stammaitic reworking of the original sources, as reconstructed by Wald.[11] Without the Stammaitic additions these traditions simply encourage marriage with scholarly families. If one cannot marry off one's daughter to a sage, he should seek out as pious a groom as possible. Such exhortations are typical of the high regard for Torah study and those associated with it. The Stammaim contribute negative exhortations to the otherwise positive guidelines. It is not enough to aspire to marry into a rabbinic family, but one must not marry an *am ha'arets* or his daughter. These matches are prohibited in almost the same way as marriages between Jews and non-Jews.

More significant than the discouragement of marriages is the imagery and language employed. The metaphor of the vine and thorn bush gives the impression of two distinct species, reminiscent of biblical prohibitions against mixing different kinds (*sheatnez;* Lev 19:19; Deut 22:11). The thorn as opposed to the vine obviously carries a negative valence, made abundantly clear by the adjectives "ugly" and "inappropriate." The Stammaitic addition to the second *baraita* intensifies the imagery by describing the wives of the *amei ha'arets* as "repulsive," rather than condemning the act of marriage. Again the notion of mixed kinds is suggested, this time of humans and animals. The verse quoted implies that *amei ha'arets* are subhuman, as does the comparison to "vermin"—a theme to which the *sugya* will return—and suggests that such marriages are not only improper but sinful.

In Palestinian sources one occasionally finds negative views of marriages with *amei ha'arets* but never outright expressions of contempt. In tAZ 3:9–10 the Tannaim dispute as follows:

One does not give them [*amei ha'arets*] daughters [in marriage], neither adults nor minors; these are the words of R. Meir. But the sages say: One may give him an adult daughter [in marriage] and stipulate with him that she not rely on him to prepare foods in a state of purity.[12] It happened that Rabban Gamaliel the Elder married his daughter to the priest Shimon b. Netanel, and he stipulated with him that she not rely on him to prepare foods in a state of purity. (tAZ 3:9)

The stipulation clarifies the issue. R. Meir and the sages agree that minors, who are not proficient in the laws of purities, should not be married to *amei ha'arets,* as they will violate the regulations. The sages believe that an adult woman, who already knows how to prepare food according to rabbinic strictures, will not transgress, provided her husband agree that she need not rely on his authority. R. Meir believes that this arrangement is not tenable; even an adult woman will inevitably break the law. The concern is exclusively about purity. Nothing implies that there is anything wrong with the *am ha'arets* or his character per se. No less a figure than Rabban Gamaliel the Elder, an early rabbinic hero, married his daughter to an *am ha'arets.* Another Tannaitic source quoted in the Bavli is even more permissive.[13] The sages debate whether daughters and widows of *haverim* married to *amei ha'arets,* and daughters and widows of *amei ha'arets* married to *haverim,* must explicitly commit themselves to the higher standards of purity. All parties envision the possibility in principle of these unions; the problem is how to ensure that no laws will be transgressed. Many Tannaitic sources accordingly describe a variety of social relations, such as borrowing utensils, performing domestic work together, purchasing articles, and dwelling in close proximity.[14]

The same picture emerges from the Yerushalmi. The only gesture at a restriction on marriage is a tradition attributed to the Amora R. Yose, who draws an inference based on a discussion of Samaritan food, that R. Eliezer would also prohibit marriage with the daughter of an *am ha'arets* (yShev 8:10, 38b). But the basis for this inference is rejected. No other source, to the best of my knowledge, prohibits such marriages.

The different metaphors used in Palestinian sources provide a good sense of the contrast in perspectives. Foliar and vegetable images that in the Bavli indicated inappropriate mixtures are mobilized to a much different effect:

> *The fruit of goodly trees (Lev 23:40).* These are Israel. Just as an etrog has taste and fragrance, so Israel has men who are learned in Torah and perform good deeds.
> *Palm branches (Lev 23:40).* These are Israel. Just as the date tree has taste but no fragrance, so Israel has men who are learned in Torah but do not perform good deeds.

Branches of leafy trees (Lev 23:40). These are Israel. Just as the myrtle has fragrance but no taste, so Israel has men who perform good deeds but are not learned in Torah.

And willows of the brook (Lev 23:40). These are Israel. Just as the willow has neither fragrance nor taste, so Israel has men who are neither learned in Torah nor perform good deeds.

What does the Holy One do with them? To destroy them is unthinkable. Rather the Holy One says, Let them all form one band and atone for each other (*Leviticus Rabbah* 30:12 [709]).[15]

Just as the leaves of the vine protect the clusters, so it is with Israel that the *amei ha'arets* protect the scholars (*Leviticus Rabbah* 36:2 [839]).

R. Shimon b. Laqish said: "This nation [= Israel] may be compared to a vine. Its branches — these are the wealthy. The clusters — these are the scholars. The leaves — these are the *amei ha'arets*. The shoots — these are the ignorant." This explains that which they sent from there [= Palestine]: "Let the clusters pray for the leaves, for were it not for the leaves, the clusters could not exist" (bHul 92a).

The first citation from *Leviticus Rabbah* interprets the four components of the lulav in terms of four types of Jews. While the term *am ha'arets* does not appear explicitly, "men who are neither learned in Torah nor perform good deeds" would certainly qualify by the Bavli's definition. The comparison to the lulav's species, however, teaches the importance of unity. Joining the different kinds of plants / humans is not "ugly and inappropriate" but essential: the vicarious merit of the pious atones for the sins of the transgressors. Granted that the homily does not speak specifically of marriage, the inclusive floral imagery functions in a manner opposite to that of the Stammaitic traditions above.

The second and third traditions employ the simile of a vine. Yet here we find no opposition to "thorns," but a comparison of its parts to different types of men. Rather than emphasize the fundamental dissimilarity of sages and *amei ha'arets,* the figure stresses their affinity: both are of the same vine species, interrelated and interdependent. Rather than curse the *am ha'arets* and his family, the tradition ascribed to R. Shimon b. Laqish encourages sages to pray for them. Indeed, the sages depend on the *am ha'arets* just as the clusters of grapes depend on the vine leaves for protection. The point seems to be that the *amei ha'arets* work to provide food and other necessities, allowing the sages to spend their time engaged in the study of Torah.[16] Here too the codependence of the different types of Jews is stressed, albeit in the opposite fashion. Where the metaphor in *Leviticus Rabbah* 30:12 emphasizes that the *amei ha'arets* depend vicariously on the merits of the pious to avoid death, the vine metaphors suggest that scholars depend on the material support of the *amei ha'arets* to survive. Although the third tradition appears in the Bavli, the explicit assignment to Palestine ("the West"), the attribution to the Palestinian R. Shimon b. Laqish, and the correlation with the *Leviticus Rabbah* tradition suggests that it accurately expresses Palestinian ideas.

The Subhuman *Am ha'arets*

The Stammaitic traditions against marriage essentially equate female *amei ha'arets* with animals, referring to such wives as vermin and applying a biblical verse about beasts to daughters. This notion emerges in a more striking fashion in the succeeding traditions of the same *sugya* (bPes 49a–b):

(A) R. Eleazar said, "It is permitted to stab an *am ha'arets* on Yom Kippur that falls on the Sabbath." His students said to him, "Master! Say 'to slaughter him.'" He said to them, "The one [slaughtering] requires a blessing; the other [stabbing] does not require a blessing."

(B) R. Shmuel b. Nahmani said in the name of R. Yonatan, "It is permitted to tear an *am ha'arets* like a fish." R. Shmuel b. Yizhaq said, "[This means to tear] along his back."

(C) It was taught: R. Akiba said, "When I was an *am ha'arets* I used to say, 'Would that they put a scholar before me, for I would bite him like an ass.'" His students said to him, "Master! Rather say, 'Like a dog.'" He said to them, "The one [an ass] breaks bones; the other [the dog] does not break bones."

(D) It was taught: R. Meir used to say, "He who marries his daughter to an *am ha'arets*, it is as if he bound her before a lion. Just as a lion mauls and eats and has no shame, so an *am ha'arets* strikes and copulates and has no shame."

(E) It was taught: R. Eliezer b. Yaakov says, "If we did not need them for business we would kill them."[17]

(F) Greater is the hatred with which the *amei ha'arets* hate the sages than the hatred with which the nations of the world hate the Jews. And their wives [hate] even more than they do. It was taught: One who studied and then abandoned [his studies] hates the most.

As noted above, while mostly attributed to Tannaim, these traditions are Stammaitic pseudepigraphs. The equation to animals is most explicit in (B) and (D), which liken the *am ha'arets* to fish and lions. On this basis, we should note, (D) adds another reason against "intermarriage" to the sources discussed above, now discouraging a sage from marrying his daughter to an *am ha'arets* as opposed to rejecting marriage to an *am ha'arets's* daughter.[18] The savage mores of the *am ha'arets* are more suited to beasts than human mates. R. Akiba's confession of his former attitude as an *am ha'arets* implies that the perspective was mutual: the *amei ha'arets* treated the sages as animals just as the sages viewed the *amei ha'arets* (C). Furthermore, Wald observes that the verbs employed in these traditions apply to actions done by humans to animals and *vice versa*.[19] The term "stab" (from the root *n-ḥ-r*) in R. Eliezer's tradition (A) typically pertains to killing animals.[20] The point of his students' response is that he should at least use the term "slaughter" (*shehita*), which refers to ritual slaughter, a less cruel and brutal act. Conversely, R. Akiba claims that as an *am ha'arets* he aspired to "bite" sages and break their bones "like an ass." That several of the traditions use similes (*like* a fish / dog / ass; *as if* he bound her) hardly mitigates the imagery. The sources portray the *am ha'arets* as not fully human, neither behaving in a human manner nor deserving humane treatment.[21] Similarly, bSot 22a applies the scriptural verse, "I will sow the House of Israel and the House of Judah with seed of men and seed of cattle (Jer 31:27)," to men who know neither Scripture nor Mishna.[22] In other words, such men are accounted the "cattle" among the Israelite people. Elsewhere Rav Ashi reportedly commented that sages are punished for calling people asses (bNed 81a). As in the sources about marriage, sages and *amei ha'arets* appear to be two distinct species.

These traditions bear a certain affinity to earlier sources, both Palestinian and Babylonian, that compare slaves and gentiles to animals.[23] Various laws are not applied to slaves or gentiles on the grounds that scriptural exegesis connects them to animals. We find, for example, "Rav said: All agree that a slave has no relatives, as it says, *Thus Abraham said to his servants, 'You stay here with the ass' (Gen 22:5)* — a people similar to an ass" (bYev 62a).[24] For this reason, Rav suggests, the standard prohibitions against marriage to close relatives do not apply to slaves. Or again, "One does not accept condolences for [the death] of a slave because slaves are as animals."[25] Both halakhic and aggadic traditions describe gentiles — or idolators, to be more precise — as violent and sexually depraved. For instance, mAZ 2:1 considers idolators suspect of committing bestiality, rape, and murder, and prohibits Jewish men and women to be alone with them on those grounds. The Bavli claims that an idolator prefers to commit bestiality than to have sex with his own wife.[26] That an *am ha'arets* lacks any sexual self-control or propriety, but will strike his wife and copulate at will, fits well with the Bavli's image of the sexual habits of idolators (E). The comparison of the hatred between sages and *amei ha'arets* with the hostility between Jews and idolators almost makes this analogy explicit (F): sages vis-à-vis *amei ha'arets* = Jews vis-à-vis gentiles = humans vis-à-vis animals.[27]

Yet the Babylonian *am ha'arets* traditions differ from these perspectives on slaves and gentiles in important respects. No appeal is made to Scripture, nor is any law at issue. The animal imagery rather functions as an explanation for mutual hatred and as a justification for violence. Sages may tear an *am ha'arets* "like a fish" or stab and slaughter him in the manner of beasts *because* of his subhuman, bestial nature. Just as vermin and insects can be killed without cause, so R. Eliezer asserts that sages would kill *amei ha'arets* were it not for their commercial utility. No rabbinic source comes close to suggesting that Jews are permitted to kill idolators or slaves.[28] The characterization of idolators as violent and predatory serves as justification for laws that prohibit contact and create social distance, thereby protecting the Jews. Similar directives appear among Amoraic traditions regarding the *am ha'arets:* a tradition attributed to Resh Laqish, for example, warns against living near the domicile of an *am ha'arets* (bShab 63a).[29] In contrast to these prohibitions, the negative characterization of the *am ha'arets* in the Stammaitic *sugya* at bPes 49a–b comes close to advocating murder.

It goes without saying that these injunctions are hyperbolic and should not be taken literally.[30] Bavli narratives and exegeses frequently include vivid, exaggerated, graphic, and macabre imagery. The Romans did not just stab R. Yehuda b. Bava to death; they "impaled him with three hundred iron lances and made his body like a sieve" (bSanh 14a). Kozvi and Zimri do not just fornicate; they have sex 424 times until "she became like a trench filled with water" (bSahh 82b). The Bavli does not just discourage gazing at women, it states, "whoever crosses a river behind a woman has no portion in the world to come" (bEruv 18b). (We have noted the Bavli's predilection for violent and hostile expressions in Chapter 3). Nevertheless, when this tendency is channeled into hateful invective — murder on Yom Kippur that coincides with the Sabbath, splitting a human being into two halves "like a fish," binding a daughter before a lion — the intensity of the rhetoric is astonishing.[31]

Depictions of the *am ha'arets* as an animal are almost completely absent in Palestinian sources. Where they seem to appear, comparison to Bavli traditions only underscores the difference between the conceptions. Consider the following stories:

Leviticus Rabbah *9:3 (176–78)*	*bBB 8a*
Once R. Yannai was walking on his way when he encountered a certain man who was finely dressed.[32] He [Yannai] said to him, "Will it please my master to dine with us?" He said to him, "If it pleases you." He brought him to his house. He examined him in Scripture and found that he knew nothing. He examined him in Mishna and found that he knew nothing. He examined him in *haggada* and found that he knew nothing. He said to him, "Recite the blessing." He said to him, "Let Yannai recite the blessing in his own home." He said to him, "Can you repeat what I say?" He said to him, "Yes." He said, "Say, 'A dog ate Yannai's bread.'" He [the guest] stood up and grabbed him. He said to him, "Is my inheritance then in your possession that you insult me in this way?" He said to him, "And what inheritance of yours is in my possession?" He said to him, "Children say [the verse], *Moses commanded us the Torah, the inheritance . . . (Deut 33:4)*. It is not written, 'of the congregation of Yannai' but *of the congregation of Jacob (Deut 33:4)*." After they appeased one another, he [Yannai] said to him, "Why did you merit eating at my table?" He said to him, "Never in my life did I hear an evil word and	Rabbi [Yehuda HaNasi] opened his storehouses [of food] in a time of famine. He said, "Let all those enter who have studied Scripture, studied Mishna, or studied Talmud. But let the *am ha'arets* not enter." R. Yohanan b. Amram forced his way in. He said, "My Master, give me food." He said to him, "My son, have you studied Scripture." He said to him, "No." "Have you studied Mishna?" He said to him, "No." "If that is so, how can I give you food?" He said to him, "Feed me like a dog or a raven." He gave him food. After he departed Rabbi sat down distressed. He said, "Woe is me, for I have given bread to an *am ha'arets*." R. Shimon b. Rabbi said to him, "Perhaps it was Yohanan b. Amram, for throughout his life he never consented to derive benefit from the honor of the Torah." They checked and found that it was as he had spoken. Rabbi said, "Let all enter." And Rabbi acted in accordance with his own dictum. For Rabbi said, "Suffering comes to the world exclusively on account of the *amei ha'arets*."

relate it to the man (about whom it
was said). And I never saw two men
quarreling with one another without making peace between them."
He said to him, "You have such
good conduct and yet I called you a
dog?!" He applied to him the verse,
*To him who improves his conduct I will
show the salvation of God (Ps 50:23).*

While the two stories differ too much to be considered versions of a single
narrative, they share several elements. In both a sage feeds a man who lacks
(or appears to lack) knowledge of Torah, in both the man is equated with a
dog for that reason, and in both the sage initially regrets feeding the man.
Yet the stories move in opposite directions. In the Palestinian story the uneducated man partakes of the sages' food due to an innocent mistake:
R. Yannai erroneously takes the man's fine clothes as the mark of a sage and
invites him to sup. The Bavli story begins on a more chilling note: during a
time of famine Rabbi announces that he will only sustain the learned and
specifically disinvites the *amei ha'arets*. That they may starve to death does
not seem to trouble the Nasi (although it distressed several medieval commentators).[33] The concluding dictum clarifies Rabbi's reason for banning
the *amei ha'arets* and perhaps provides a measure-for-measure justification:
the famine (=suffering) was ultimately caused by the sins of the *amei ha'arets*,
so they do not deserve to be sustained.[34] In *Leviticus Rabbah* the rabbi subsequently feels remorse that he insulted the man despite his ignorance. He
is consoled that the man's high moral character makes him a worthy guest
after all. In the Bavli story the sage does not feel subsequent remorse. He is
consoled only upon discovering that he has not actually supported an *am
ha'arets*. Hence the crucial inversion: in *Leviticus Rabbah* a man who appears
to be learned turns out to be ignorant, but nevertheless possesses merit,
while in the Bavli a man who appears to be ignorant turns out to be learned,
and therefore possesses merit. Note that in the Palestinian source the man's
exemplary morals contrast sharply with the depraved sexual morality of the
am ha'arets pictured in the Bavli tradition above (D). Here his benevolent
humanity establishes that he should not be called a dog, while the Bavli's
view of the *am ha'arets*'s brutality elicits the leonine analogy. The Palestinian
story teaches that sages should not deride the unlearned; even those who do
not know elementary aspects of Torah may possess excellent character. Far

from being equivalent to animals, some of the uneducated truly merit eating at the table of the sages and deserve salvation, as foretold by the final scriptural citation. The Bavli story never recognizes the merit of an *am ha'arets*. The sage only offers to feed them on account of masquerading scholars who scruple at deriving material benefit from their Torah knowledge. In principle the *am ha'arets* requires no better treatment than a dog or raven: he can be sacrificed so that humans (= sages) should live. Thus the Bavli story is consistent with the idea that an *am ha'arets* rates no higher than an animal, while the Palestinian story explicitly rejects that view and cautions sages against disparaging their fellow Jews.

No Palestinian source entertains the possibility of perpetrating violence against *amei ha'arets*. However, Wald has identified a source that possibly comprises the literary kernel of the Bavli's hostile expressions:[35]

> R. Akiba said: This was how I began attending upon the sages. Once I was walking on my way and I came upon an abandoned corpse.[36] I carried it four miles until I brought it to a cemetery and buried it. When I came to R. Eliezer and R. Yehoshua, I told them about it. They said to me, "For each and every step you took, it was as if you shed blood."[37] And I thought: If I incurred guilt when I intended to earn merit, how much the more so [am I incurring guilt] when I don't intend to earn merit? From then on I never ceased attending upon the sages. He [Akiba] used to say, "Whoever does not attend upon the sages is worthy of death (*qatla hayyav*)" (yNaz 7:1, 56a–b).

The concluding line is a rabbinic maxim, which probably generated the fictional anecdote; it appears in Aramaic, whereas the story appears in Hebrew.[38] The maxim is meant figuratively: Akiba did not really shed blood, nor does the principle he violated entail punishment. In its strongest form the maxim warns that those who do not know rabbinic teachings will transgress laws and commit sins the theoretical punishment for which is death. The Stammaim, however, seem to have literalized the maxim and applied it to the *am ha'arets* based on the opinion cited above that defines the *am ha'arets* as one who "does not attend upon the sages" (bBer 47b). Ergo, an *am ha'arets* is worthy of, or deserves, death. (The Aramaic *qatla hayyav* sustains both meanings.) Such literalizations of figures and idioms are not uncommon in rabbinic literature, especially in exegetical traditions that play on scriptural metaphors.[39] Here the literalization produces a powerful effect: in sharp contrast to the Palestinian story, which illustrates how lack of knowledge of Torah can lead to sin, the Stammaitic revision baldly states that *amei ha'arets* may be killed.[40]

Other Palestinian sources are more favorable towards the *am ha'arets.* An anecdote in the Yerushalmi relates that R. Meir showed respect by standing up before an elderly *am ha'arets* on the grounds that his longevity must be for good reason, that is, reward for piety or fine character (yBik 3:3, 65c).[41] A midrashic tradition in *Leviticus Rabbah* interprets a verse in terms of scholars who "enter the houses of *amei ha'arets* and sustain them with words of Torah."[42] More significantly, according to a story found in *Genesis Rabbah,* an *am ha'arets* tells R. Hoshaya a midrash that so pleases the sage that he promises to repeat it in the name of the *am ha'arets* in public.[43] These favorably inclined traditions stand at odds with the Stammaitic expressions of contempt.

Lack of Torah

To understand the foundation of the Stammaitic view of the *am ha'arets,* it will help to revisit the Bavli version of the story of R. Shimon b. Yohai and the cave, discussed briefly in Chapter 1.[44] Recall that R. Shimon b. Yohai begins with criticism of the Romans and their preoccupations but subsequently burns up Jewish peasants on the grounds that they "forsake eternal life and busy themselves with temporal life." This story, also a Stammaitic reworking of an earlier source,[45] shares in common with the *am ha'arets* traditions an extremely negative view of unlearned Jews, represented here by the peasants. The sages actually murder them, just as the sources in bPes 49a–b advocate. That the story begins with antipathy for gentiles but quickly shifts to attacks on Jews coheres with the implicit association between the *am ha'arets* and gentiles noted above. The two groups share a fundamental defect in rabbinic eyes, namely, lack of engagement with Torah. In this radical perspective, any Jew who fails to occupy himself with the study of Torah, the means to eternal life, and engages in "temporal life," even the ostensibly legitimate task of providing food for his family, deserves death. While the story rejects this extreme view, the fact that it is imputed to a leading sage is significant. It provides a fairly explicit representation of the ideology that underpins traditions hostile to the *am ha'arets.*

Several sources not only identify lack of Torah study as the defining characteristic of the *am ha'arets* but link this problem to specific impairments and limitations. Two traditions from the *sugya* at bPes 49a–b are apposite:

> It was taught: Rabbi [Yehuda HaNasi says], "An *am ha'arets* is forbidden to eat meat, as it says, *This is the torah of animals, birds . . . (Lev 11:46).* He who engages in Torah [study] is permitted to eat the flesh of animals and birds, but he who does not engage in Torah [study] is forbidden to eat the flesh of animals and birds."

And R. Eleazar said, "It is forbidden to accompany him [= an *am ha'arets*] on a journey, as it says, *For with it (Torah) you shall have life and long endure (Deut 30:20)*. If he takes no care for his own life [by neglecting Torah], how much the more so [will he have no care] for the life of his fellow."

The first tradition forbids an *am ha'arets* to eat meat on the grounds that he does not study Torah, since Scripture uses the term "Torah" (law) in connection with the instructions about permitted foods. Contributing to this limitation may be the conception of the *am ha'arets* as subhuman. Genesis 9:3–5 establishes a hierarchy in which humans may kill animals and eat their flesh, but animals may not kill humans. If an *am ha'arets* has subhuman status, it stands to reason that he lacks the covenantal dispensation to eat animal flesh.[46] The technical midrashic prooftext in turn points to the reason the *am ha'arets* lacks human status: the nonengagement in Torah study. For the same reason the tradition attributed to R. Eleazar considers the *am ha'arets* to be a source of danger. Lacking the supernatural protection that Torah confers, the *am ha'arets*—and his companions—will be vulnerable on journeys, which inevitably involve peril. That he "takes no care for his own life" echoes the maxim "they forsake eternal life." We have here another variation on the theme of the devalued life of the *am ha'arets*.

The basic meaning of "they forsake eternal life" obviously pertains to posthumous reward. As expected, the Bavli denies the *am ha'arets* "eternal life" for his neglect of Torah study: "R. Eleazar said, 'The *amei ha'arets* will not live [again], as it says . . . *For Your dew is like the dew on fresh growth, You make the land of "the loose" come to life (Isa 26:19)*. Whoever makes use of the dew of Torah, the dew of Torah makes him live [again]. But whoever does not make use of the dew of Torah, the dew of Torah will not make him live'" (bKet 111b). This tradition appears in a long *sugya,* concerning the merits accrued by dwelling in the Land of Israel, that substantially reworks an earlier Palestinian passage.[47] Like the *am ha'arets* traditions from bPes 49a–b, it lacks any parallel in Palestinian sources and should be considered a Stammaitic fiction. Despite the ominous pronouncement, the ensuing discussion is less pessimistic. R. Yohanan disagrees with R. Eleazar, arguing that the verse pertains to Jews who practice idolatry, and even (pseudo-)R. Eleazar finds a "solution," advocating that the *am ha'arets* marry his daughter to a sage and benefact scholars from his property.[48] In this respect the *sugya* disagrees with that of bPes 49a–b and resembles the Palestinian traditions suggesting that the *am ha'arets* derive merit vicariously by cleaving to the sages. In any case, even the proposed solution points to Torah study as the determinative factor. But for a connection to the sages through kinship or commerce, an *am ha'arets* will not be resurrected. A well-known Mishna promises, "All Israel has a share in the world to come," with few exceptions (mSanh 10:1).[49] In Stammaitic theology, all those who engage in Torah study have a share in the world to come or resurrection. Thus the Bavli's depiction of the inauguration of "the next world" begins with God taking a Torah scroll and announcing "whoever busied himself with this, let him come and take his reward."[50]

The Reclusive Academy

I have suggested that the expressions of contempt toward the *am ha'arets* surveyed above derive from the scholastic worldview of the academy and its internal discourse. If this is correct, one wonders to what extent the sages considered the academy a space closed to outsiders. Were nonrabbis discouraged from entering the academy or rabbinic circles in general? In the previous chapter we noted that the representation of Torah study in erotic terms carried with it a demand for privacy. A tradition based on the description of the maiden's body in Song of Songs concluded: "Just as a thigh is hidden, so words of Torah should be [studied] in private" (bSuk 49b).[51] More germane to our topic was the tradition analogizing study in the presence of an *am ha'arets* to one who "has sex with his bride in his [the *am ha'arets's*] presence," also found in our Stammaitic *sugya* (bPes 49b).[52] The specific exclusion of the *am ha'arets* suggests that the Stammaim considered Torah study and perhaps the academies where it was conducted to be private rabbinic domains. The graphic simile implies that to let nonrabbis (or at least whatever component of nonrabbis the *amei ha'arets* comprised, if not all nonrabbis) witness or participate in rabbinic activity was considered a gross transgression of boundaries. These sentiments diverge from the vast majority of rabbinic traditions, which encourage all Jews to study and rabbis to teach those who desire to learn.[53] It should also be noted that the basis for the exclusion of the *am ha'arets* is the midrash on Deut 33:4, "the inheritance (*morasha*) of the congregation of Jacob" as the "betrothed" (*meorasa*). This interpretation undermines the contextual meaning of the verse which presents Torah as the heritage of all Israel.[54] The same biblical verse was cited by the uneducated man mistakenly invited to R. Yannai's table in the Palestinian source discussed above, to precisely the opposite effect: the man insists that the Torah belongs to "the congregation of Jacob" not "the congregation of Yannai." In contrast, the Stammaim transform the Torah from the heritage of all Jews to their betrothed maiden, off limits to others. Within the walls of the academy the sages are intimate with their beloved Torah; to take Torah outside smacks of exhibitionism.[55]

A similar sentiment is expressed in a brief story of Rabbi Yehuda HaNasi's prohibition against teaching Torah in public:

> Once Rabbi [Yehuda HaNasi] decreed that they should not teach disciples in the marketplace.
>   — What did he expound [as the basis for this decree]? *Your rounded thighs are like jewels, the work of a master's hand (Song 7:2).* Just as the thigh is hidden, so words of Torah should be hidden. —
> R. Hiyya went out to the marketplace and taught his two nephews, Rav and Rabbah bar bar Hannah. Rabbi heard about it and became angry. . . . (bMQ 16a–b)[56]

The parallel Yerushalmi story attributes this conflict between Rabbi and R. Hiyya to an entirely different matter (yKil 9:4, 32b). The decree, moreover, has no parallel in Palestinian sources, which routinely describe sages studying Torah in markets and other public places, much like philosophers throughout the Hellenistic world.[57] Babylonian Amoraim also seem to have studied in a variety of locations, as small disciple circles can meet almost anywhere.[58] The story also bears signs of redactional composition, namely the parenthetic explanation of Rabbi's motivation, so we are most likely dealing with a late Babylonian reworking of an earlier Palestinian tradition.[59] The purported exegesis in fact involves the same application of feminine imagery from the Song of Songs as the tradition from bSuk 49b mentioned above, and it may well have been borrowed from that source. The Stammaim seem to have explained Rabbi's curious ban on public teaching in terms of their view of Torah study as an erotic, hence private, activity that should not be observed by others. While the *am ha'arets* is not mentioned specifically, the source essentially forbids study in the presence of all nonrabbis. (The "marketplace" is paradigmatic of public places in general.) That the story mentions R. Hiyya's opposing perspective may point to an internal debate among the Stammaim.[60] Some sages evidently opposed any attempt to sequester Torah study.

Several highly suggestive Bavli stories intimate that some sages attempted to keep outsiders away from rabbinic institutions. The Bavli version of the deposition of Rabban Gamaliel, for example, superimposes on the Palestinian story the theme of restricting and allowing access to the academy.[61] Both stories relate that the rabbis deposed Rabban Gamaliel from his position as Nasi due to his mistreatment of R. Yehoshua and appointed R. Eleazar b. Azariah to replace him. At this point Bavli additions change the slant of the story:

yBer 4:1, 7d	*bBer 28a*
	(a) It was taught: On that day they removed the guard at the door and gave permission to students to enter. For Rabban Gamaliel had proclaimed: Let any student whose inside is not like his outside not enter the study-house.
(B) How many benches were there?	(b) That day they added many benches.
(C) R. Yaakov b. Sisi said: Eighty benches of scholars were there, apart from those standing behind the fence. R. Yose b. R. Avun said: There were three hundred there, apart from those standing behind the fence.	(c) R. Yohanan said: Abba Yosef b. Dosthenai and the sages disagreed. One said that 400 benches were added, and one said 700 benches.
	(d) Rabban Gamaliel became distressed. He thought, "Perhaps, God forbid, I held back Torah from Israel." In a dream he was shown white casks filled with ashes. (e) But this was not so. He was shown this only to settle his mind.
(F) As we learned there. *On that day they seated R. Eleazar b. Azariah in the session (mYad 4:2).* It was taught there: *R. Eleazar b. Azariah taught the following midrash before the sages in the vineyard at Yavneh (mKet 4:6).* But was there a vineyard	(f) It was taught: [Tractate] Eduyyot was taught on that day. And wherever it is taught [in the Mishna] "On that day" refers to that very day. There was not one law that had been left hanging in the study-house that was not explained. Even Rab-

there? Rather this refers to the scholars who formed rows like a vineyard.

ban Gamaliel did not hold himself back from the study-house for even one hour, as we learned: *On that day Yehuda, an Ammonite convert came before them [the sages] in the study-house. He said, "Am I permitted to enter the congregation." Rabban Gamaliel said, "You are forbidden to enter the congregation." R. Yehoshua said, "You are permitted to enter the congregation."... Immediately they permitted him to enter the congregation. (= mYad 4:4).*

In both stories Rabban Gamaliel then apologizes to R. Yehoshua and is restored to his position. But the Bavli contains another addition: before the apology R. Akiba says, "Bolt the door [of the academy] so that the servants of Rabban Gamaliel do not come and trouble the rabbis."

The focus of the Yerushalmi is the conflict between the two sages and Rabban Gamaliel's abuse of his colleague. To this conflict the Bavli adds that Rabban Gamaliel had prevented prospective students from entering the academy by placing a guard there (a). A consequence of Rabban Gamaliel's removal was increased access to the academy, marked by the *addition* of benches of students (b) and echoed by the theme of entry to the congregation in the Mishna cited as the debate held "on that day" (f).[62] The Yerushalmi, by contrast, describes benches that were already there (B), not that were added, and cites a different Mishna (F).

Most telling is the story's own ambivalence toward Rabban Gamaliel's policy (d–e). At the influx of students the sage wonders whether he made a mistake by restricting access, only to be informed through a dream vision that he should not fret: the white casks filled with ashes indicate that the new students are unworthy, their insides in fact unlike their outsides. What seems to be a different voice immediately counters that that dream was false, provided only to console Rabban Gamaliel.[63] He had in fact "restricted Torah from Israel" as he first thought. The story thus contains an internal debate concerning the merits of limiting access to the academy. While the storytellers ultimately reject Rabban Gamaliel's restrictive policy, the internal debate and the motivation for the story suggest that some sages — perhaps the leadership of the academy itself — thought that the academy should be closed to outsiders.

The mention of R. Akiba's bolting the doors to prevent entry may even reflect some contemporary practice.

The figure of the "guard" also occurs in the famous story of Hillel at bYom 35b, found exclusively in the Bavli. A poor man, Hillel usually gave half his earnings to the "guard of the study-house" and used the other half to support his family. One day he failed to earn sufficient money "and the guard of the study-house would not allow him to enter." He therefore climbed to the roof in order to listen in on the discussions and almost froze to death. The story insists that poverty is no excuse for failure to study and portrays Hillel as a model of the zeal with which Torah should be pursued. Here too a guard purportedly restricts entry to the study-house, although he does not keep out ignorant or unworthy students but impoverished ones.[64]

Several Bavli stories contain the potentially related motif of sages removed from the study-house / academy.[65] After Rabban Shimon b. Gamaliel foils R. Meir and R. Natan's plot to depose him, he orders that the two sages be removed from the academy (bHor 13b–14a). According to this late story (discussed at length in Chapter 5), the sages write objections and responses on pieces of paper and send them to the academy until they are readmitted.[66] A brief tradition relates that R. Yirmiah was "removed from the study-house" for asking a silly question.[67] R. Ami reportedly removed a certain disciple from the study-house for revealing a secret confided to him twenty-two years previously (bSanh 31a). While R. Yirmiah and R. Ami are Palestinians, these anecdotes have no parallels in Palestinian sources, nor do Palestinian sources, to the best of my knowledge, ever tell of sages' being removed from a rabbinic institution. The Bavli traditions, though opaque, may point to the difficulty of gaining entry to the Stammaitic academy.

These traditions are suggestive, not probative. They may shed light on the powerfully negative rhetoric against the *am ha'arets* by pointing to a growing sense of detachment that prevailed within the academy. The sages perhaps perceived their academic world of Torah study as increasingly professionalized, elitist, and isolated from the general population. As a result, nonrabbis outside of the academy were viewed as "Others" and even included with other categories of "Others"—slaves, gentiles, and animals.

Let me close by emphasizing that I am very hesitant to draw conclusions about real social relations that prevailed between rabbis and other Jews *outside of the academy* based on the hatred of the *am ha'arets* shown in these traditions.[68] It is quite possible, even likely, that relations between rabbis and nonrabbis in the Stammaitic period were no different from those of earlier periods or those of Palestine.[69] The sources, in my opinion, express the self-promoting snobbery of the private discussions of the rabbis, intended solely for an audience of other rabbis, not unlike ethnic jokes today.[70] When framed in the Bavli's hyperbolic rhetorical style, this attitude produced shocking expressions of contempt. My point is not to dismiss their significance, for they surely tell us something important. But they tell us about Stammaitic attitudes and beliefs, not necessarily social life. In the rarefied walls of the academy, where sages esteemed dialectical Torah study to an unprecedented degree, they simultaneously minimized the significance of all other religious practices. Nonrabbis were ultimately categorized with others who did not engage in Torah study and who consequently had almost no redeeming virtue. Traditions reviling the *am ha'arets,* then, are ultimately an expression of the Torah-centered theology of the Stammaim.

Chapter 8

Conclusion:
The Legacy of the Stammaim

The legacy of the Stammaim was the Bavli: they created a document that became the basis of the rabbinic curriculum, the foundation of Jewish law, and a source of biblical interpretation, customs, theology, and ethics. The following pages briefly discuss how the themes explored in the chapters of this book left their imprint in succeeding centuries. The treatment is cursory rather than comprehensive. My goal is to point out some of the main lines of development in which the legacy of the Stammaim can be perceived and to note a few areas of significant change.[1]

The Academy

The academy became the dominant form of rabbinic study and education and remains so to the present day. The immediate descendants of the Stammaitic academies were the great Geonic academies of the Islamic era. After the Islamic conquest, at some point in the ninth century, the academies of the Stammaim, initially located in the cities of Sura and Pumbedita, relocated to Baghdad, the seat of the Abassid Caliphate.[2] For the next three hundred years they exerted tremendous influence on the Jewish communities throughout the Mediterranean basin, answering legal queries, sending out emissaries, playing a role in community politics, and collecting contributions to support their scholars. During this time a rabbinic academy formed in the Land of Israel and attracted a sphere of influence of its own. The efforts of the Geonim to disseminate the Babylonian Talmud spawned the organization of rabbinic academies in North Africa and Spain in the ninth and tenth centuries, and slightly later in Egypt. In the eleventh through thirteenth centuries academies were founded in German regions, such as Mainz, Speyer and Worms; in southern France (Provence), in Narbonne, Lunel, and Carcasonne; and in various cities in northern France.

Rabbinic academies perhaps attained their acme of cultural prominence in Poland and Lithuania during the sixteenth through nineteenth centuries, despite the Chmielnicki massacres of 1648–49. The academy of this period can no longer be considered the province of an intellectual and spiritual elite. Such a high value was placed on Talmud study that almost every male spent several years, if not more, studying in an academy. Communities extended a great deal of financial support to the local academy and took great pride in the stature of its scholars. Many of the great eastern European academies relocated to Israel and North America after the Holocaust. Study in the academy remains a cultural ideal for most of Orthodox and Hasidic Judaism today.

Dialectics

The dialectical questioning thematized in Stammaitic narratives appears to be related to reports of the dialectical methods with which the assembly of scholars studied in the Geonic academies. Nathan the Babylonian describes the manner of answering responsa as follows:

> And this was their custom regarding responsa to questions: on each day of Adar he [the head of the academy] brings out to them all the questions which have arrived and gives them permission to respond (*sheyashivu teshuva*). . . . Then each one speaks according to his understanding and wisdom, and they raise objections and solve them and discuss each matter (*maqshin umefarkin venosim venotnim*) and analyze it thoroughly. And the head of the academy listens to their words and understands everything that they say and that they object one to another.[3]

Here the dialectic has a practical function, namely to answer the legal query through analysis of the different sides of the issue. The Talmudic sources suggest a more hypothetical exercise not necessarily related to practical law, but the procedure and terminology are identical. In one of his letters, Sherira Gaon refers to a related manner of instructing students: "Also our young man Hayya is diligent in teaching them and putting (the texts) in their mouths; and whoever does not know how to ask, he teaches him the method of objection (*derekh qushya*) and endears this method to him."[4] Training for even elementary students, those who do "not know how to ask," involved dialectics. That Sherira refers to a "method" of objections suggests a formalized practice and indicates that such ability was expected of all sages at this time.

Written Geonic commentaries and responsa, however, generally do not evince a dialectical structure, nor do they expand lines of Talmudic argumentation to any great extent. In the High Middle Ages the Tosafists returned to dialectics as a mode of creative intellectual and spiritual expression. Beginning in the Franco-German academies in the twelfth century, the Tosafistic commentorial tradition spread throughout the Sephardic world to Spain, Egypt, and North Africa. The Tosafists were primarily dialecticians. They typically pointed out a contradiction (or a purported contradiction) that emerged from the juxtaposition of two Talmudic passages and solved the problem by drawing a distinction. The rhetorical form of the Tosafot is dialogical, replicating the questions and answers of an oral debate: "If you should say. . . . I will answer . . . and it could also be objected . . . but I would respond." These series of questions and answers are sometimes multiplied at great length, nested with subquestions and answers, and spawn digressions and tangents.

In many ways the Tosafists complete the unfinished project of the Stammaim. The Stammaim frequently juxtaposed two potentially conflicting Tannaitic sources or Amoraic dicta and resolved the apparent contradiction. In some cases, however, the Stammaim either failed to point out the conflict or did not perceive there to be a conflict. The Tosafists routinely took up these cases and resolved the contradiction with many of the techniques commonly used by the Stammaim. There are also a number of *sugyot* that stand in tension with one another in that they make different legal assumptions or arrive at conflicting decisions. The Tosafists identified these contradictions and attempted to reconcile them. Where the Stammaim attempt to harmonize contradictory Tannaitic and Amoraic opinions, the Tosafists took it upon themselves to harmonize the entire Talmud, including contradictions in the Stammaitic layer of disparate passages. They extended, completed, and developed the contribution of the Stammaim. Thus Ephraim Urbach comments: "Rabenu Tam and the other Tosafot added new issues to the Talmud, continuing in its path and completing it. This is evident from the many passages of the Tosafot which could be inserted into the body of the Talmudic *sugya,* such that one would not know that they entered its midst, nor could one detect that they can be separated from it."[5] The Tosafists, for example, will ask why "the Talmud" (we would say the Stammaim) does not pursue a line of questioning in a certain passage that it advances elsewhere. Often they also formulate the potential argumentation and provide theoretical answers. While the Tosafists' motivation was to make the Talmud consistent, their efforts resulted in a proliferation of questions and answers. Like the Stammaim, the Tosafot address theoretical issues and minority opinions which have no connection to practical law.[6]

The result of the three centuries of Tosafistic activity (12th–14th centuries) was a tremendous increase in rabbinic halakha and, in a more general sense, in Torah. Haym Soloveitchik compares the nondialectical codification of Maimonides, the *Mishneh torah* or *Yad*, with the dialectical labors of the Tosafists:

> Anyone who comes to the *Yad* from studying a *sugya* with the writings of the Tosafists, with their vast collection of data, their discovery of hidden problems and proffer of multiple solutions, will find Maimonides' presentation thin and simplistic. Valid, at best, but far from the final word. On a practical level, moreover, the *Yad* had ceased to sum up the state of Halakhic affairs. By dint of the Tosafist method thousands of inferences were being drawn from the Talmud of which Maimonides (and the Geonim) had never dreamt. How skeletal and inadequate a code the *Yad* had become by the first quarter of the thirteenth century can be seen by comparing the several laws regulating the purging of vessels (*Hag'alat kelim*) given by Maimonides in *hilkhot hames u-masah* (V:21–26) with the extensive section 464 in the *Rabyah*. Or compare what is probably the most comprehensive set of rules in the *Yad*, *hilkhot malveh ve-loveh*, with the massive *Sefer ha-Terumot* of R. Samuel Ha-Sardi, the joint product of French, Provençal and Spanish thought around the year 1255.[7]

This comparison incidentally sheds light on the appeal of dialectical approaches, the possibilities of deriving new insights and creating new Torah. It helps us understand R. Yohanan's lament at the replacement of his study-partner Resh Laqish, with whom he had engaged in dialectics such that their "discussions expanded," by R. Eleazar b. Pedat, who simply supported his conclusions.[8]

Pilpul, another dialectical method of study, developed in the fifteenth and sixteenth centuries in Ashkenazic academies.[9] This designation, as we have seen, derives from Bavli passages that glorify sharpness and erudition.[10] Medieval *pilpul* subjected the Talmudic text to rigorous casuistic analysis, making extremely fine distinctions to resolve tensions and apparent conflicts. "Pilpulists" assumed that no Talmudic phrase could be redundant or devoid of significance, so they teased meaning out of almost every single word by subtle differentiations. The purpose of *pilpul*, to some extent, was didactic, to train students' minds through complex arguments and applications of logic. In the sixteenth and seventeenth centuries the mark of an outstanding rabbinic student was to excel in pilpulistic disputation.

Dialectical approaches to Talmud study were by no means an inevitable or natural development. The Geonim did not write explanations or responsa in a dialectical manner. Rashi's commentary is largely free of dialectics. Before the Tosafist method spread to the Sephardic world, Spanish and North African scholars generally did not engage in dialectical analysis or extending the argumentative portions of the Talmud. They focused on determining practical law and explicating the extant text. Even in Ashkenaz the Tosafists faced opposition and criticism in their time, especially from Pietist circles (*hasidim*).[11] As pilpulistic discourses became increasingly convoluted, hypothetical, and pretentious, a means by which scholars showed off their erudition, a backlash developed that bestowed on the term *pilpul* a pejorative sense.

From the late Middle Ages until the present day, study of the Tosafot has become an intrinsic component of the study of the Bavli. For this reason the printers of the Talmud decided to flank the text with the commentaries of Rashi and Tosafists. The Tosafistic tradition and other modes of dialectical study are among the most enduring legacies of the Stammaim.

Violence and Shame

The prevalence of verbal "violence" and shame in the medieval academies is difficult to assess in post-Talmudic times. We generally lack literature that reflects the conditions of medieval or even early modern rabbinic academies in the same way that the Talmud depicts the Stammaitic academies.[12] Stories analogous to Talmudic tales of the conflicts of sages within the academy, the richest source of insight into academic life, are rare. Post-Talmudic commentaries, codes, and responsa mostly explicate the Talmud, not the situation of the authors. Our main sources of descriptions of life within the academies are personal memoirs and journals, which are scarce in premodern times. Even where such memoirs are available, we must take into account that an individual sage writing his own text is a vastly different social setting for the production of literature than a group memorizing traditions and transmitting them orally.

The few extant descriptions suggest that an "agonistic" ethos akin to that of Talmudic times characterized many medieval and early modern academies. R. Yehuda HaHasid (d. 1217) contrasts those who are motivated by the "fear of heaven" to understand "the objections and solutions" of Talmudic debate with those who "learn for the sake of victory" and cautions, "if two argue in order to defeat one another, do not teach them."[13] These students apparently seek dialectical expertise so as to triumph in debate and outshine their rivals. R. Isaac Profiat Duran (d. 1410) likewise notes the relationship between dialectics and competition for status: "Many of them [students] aim at understanding the depth of the give-and-take, at making objections and solving solutions in thousands and myriads, not for the purpose of understanding the laws of the Torah that emerge from the *sugyot,* but to exalt themselves over one another."[14]

A few centuries later R. Yaakov b. Yehezqel Zlatovi protests against this type of mean-spirited competition because of its deplorable consequences:

> When engaging in Torah study they spar like rams, one against the other, to swallow each other. They lord themselves over one another with insults: "You are an ox, not a man; a jackass, worth nothing." Each wants to be superior, as if [to say], "I am the best one, and there is none besides me." Is this type of *pilpul* agreeable to God? What benefit and pleasure does our Father in Heaven obtain from this Torah? They will not separate from one another until they tear the Torah to shreds.[15]

Here we have a rare account of the actual insults articulated to demean a fellow student and explicit testimony regarding the motivation, namely to be perceived as the most erudite. The author again links the propensity for verbal violence to the dialectical mode of study (*pilpul*) that foments competition.

Such insults, as we might expect, resulted in feelings of shame. R. Zelig Margoliot (late 17th century) reports the following:

> A certain scholar bitterly told me what another scholar had done to him. Once he taught a "distinction" before the sages and scholars, and the scholars were very pleased with his words and with his novellae. When the other scholar heard this, he sent for him to tell him what he had taught. . . . When he told him the "distinction," he began to rebuke him with vain and trivial words, with forced explanations, and to humiliate him. Jealousy had entered his heart because he had also stated a "distinction" on that same law, lest others say that his colleague was as learned as he.[16]

A "distinction" (*hiluq*) is a standard Tosafistic technique that explains why two apparently similar entities differ and should be subject to different laws. The rival felt jealous of the status attained by the first scholar by virtue of the "distinction" and wished to demonstrate his own, superior, ability. He objected to the teaching so as to manifest its weaknesses and establish his superior prowess. The first scholar, to be sure, dismissed the quality of these objections, but the fact that he felt ashamed suggests that he was unable to parry them and therefore lost status in the eyes of the other sages. In this way, competition for prestige breeds feelings of jealousy and ill-will. Note again that the embarrassment results in part from the fact that status is achieved through dialectical skill. As in the Talmudic sources, the ability to object and respond both confers and undermines status.

Two anecdotes attributed to R. Isaac Luria provide a rare medieval parallel to the Talmudic stories about shame within the academy:

> Once a certain sage acted this way toward his colleague — that one day a certain member of their fellowship stated a certain discourse of Torah. When he came to a certain word, this sage knew that he would make a mistake. He said to the entire fellowship, "Be quiet, do not say anything." Because the colleagues kept quiet, he made a mistake with that word and was ashamed. Later that sage who shamed his colleague died. He stood at the entrance of the Garden of Eden, but the Cherubim held him back and would not let him enter there. . . . He (Luria) also reported the case of a child who would embarrass his teacher with objections and received a severe punishment.[17]

The crucial datum that the offending sage was denied posthumous reward of course marks the story as fictional, but there is every reason to believe the scenario draws on contemporary academic experience. A spiteful sage essentially ambushed a colleague, creating the conditions that caused him to be embarrassed. Had the sage not cautioned his colleagues to remain silent they presumably would have helped the speaker through the difficult matter before his ineptitude became clear. The account actually bears some affinities to the Talmudic story of R. Meir and R. Natan planning to ask Rabban Shimon b. Gamaliel to teach a subject he did not know, fully aware that his failure would cause him to be shamed.[18] Similarly, the brief anecdote about the child echoes the Talmudic warnings that questions should be suppressed if the master will not be able to answer, lest he feel ashamed.[19]

Responsa literature also bears signs of the competitive and violent climate of Talmud study. To "fight in the war of Torah" becomes a stock accolade praising the virtue of another rabbi. Thus Shmuel b. Moshe de Medina (d. 1589) describes a colleague as "a mighty man, a soldier in the war of Torah, who debates in Mishna and Gemara, learned and wise in Sifre and Sifra."[20] The editor of Aharon b. Joseph Sasson's (d. 1626) responsa extols the rabbi as "a lion in our camp, who fights in the war of Torah, an everflowing spring."[21] Abraham Gombiner (author of the *Magen avraham*) is described as "uprooting mountains and grinding them with his sharpness (*pilpulo*), his hands strive for him with power and might in the war of Torah."[22] Yehezqel Landau (d. 1793) addresses his interlocutor as a man "great and powerful, clothed with weapons in the war of Torah."[23] It is also significant that Nahmanides called his work responding to R. Zerahia Halevi's criticisms against the *Halakhot* of R. Yitzhaq Alfasi the "Book of Wars of the Lord" (*Sefer milhamot hashem*) and that the commentators to Maimonides's *Mishneh torah* are known as his "armor bearers."

Authors of responsa frequently use military imagery when asked to settle complicated issues about which other rabbis disagree. R. Yaakov Berab (d. 1546) writes that he has heard of "quarrels in the gates, war in the camp of the Hebrews, the sound of the war of Torah to bring this law to light."[24] R. Levi ibn Haviv (16th century) notes, "I have seen lions roaring at each other, each clings to his fellow, they array themselves — behold they are the mighty warriors, who wage battles in the war of Torah."[25] R. Moses b. Yosef of Trani (d. 1580) resolves to try to adjudicate a disputed law because, "I have seen scholars goring each other, fighting the war of Torah, and pitting army against army."[26] Israel Isserlein remonstrates that he cannot address a certain case: "you have troubled me at an inappropriate time to enter the war of Torah when I lack my weapons," explaining that the books at his disposal are insufficient.[27] The imagery of books as weapons underscores the difference between the situation of the Stammaim, where oral arguments constituted the mode of war, and that of post-Talmudic times, when such "battles" were conducted by consulting sources and writing.[28]

Despite the indirectness of the medium of writing vis-à-vis the face-to-face confrontations of oral debate, some responsa and medieval halakhic writings indicate that the authors felt acutely insulted by the way other rabbis objected to their rulings. A spectacular example is the aptly titled "Matters of Controversy" (*Divrei harivot*), an exchange of seven letters between R. Zerahia Halevi and R. Avraham b. David of Posquieres.[29] In these letters the two great twelfth-century jurists debate a minor point of civil law. The tone of the first two letters is relatively cordial, with numerous stock phrases of honor and admiration mixed with a smattering of harsh locutions of exasperation at the other's obstinacy. R. Zerahia concludes the third letter with a complaint against R. Avraham's insults, and the subsequent letters become increasingly acrimonious. R. Avraham responds in the fourth letter that in fact he is the aggrieved party:

> I did not deserve the heavy blows with which you struck me with your words. You humiliated me, you embarrassed me, you cursed me. You made me out to be a

heretic, one who disrespects the Torah, and one who disparages his teachers. You called me a fox who thinks himself to be wise. Worse than that, you made me out to be a woman, as if I were exempt from reciting the Shema, and [exempt] from study of Torah, as if I were unable to speak. And as to the matter of the disparaging insults that you think I was wrong [to direct at you], and that you think I engaged in more than you did — I swear that I would have forgiven them and I would have attributed them all to the custom of the Spanish sages (*sephardim*) and their way of speaking harshly, were it not that you portrayed me as an angry sinner, and that you thought I was your enemy, and you said that you would wipe out the friendly name from my book which I wrote. Therefore I knew that your heart comes from the roots of the dead, and that you vented your strong anger, and that you opened your mouth wide against me to destroy me.[30]

The anger and insults in this passage pretty much speak for themselves. This text is unusual in that we possess the entire series of letters and can trace the debate as it unfolds. In the course of an argument comprised of objections and responses focused for the most part on the legal issue, an occasional harsh word was answered in kind, then misconstrued, then directed at the author rather than his claims, then interpreted as an insult, and then escalated into a full-blown attack. One can imagine that were the two debating face to face their animosity and the mutual sense of insult would only be magnified.

R. Avraham's allusion to the custom of Spanish sages to use harsh expressions in their disputes is suggestive, even though R. Zerahia professes in his next letter that he does not know to what R. Abraham refers.[31] The comment indicates a perception that violent rhetoric characterized certain rabbinic cultures while the rabbis of Provence generally adopted a more friendly and respectful tone. This perspective is reminiscent of the Bavli tradition that the sages of the Land of Israel are "pleasant to one another" in legal debate, whereas the Babylonians "damage one another" in their competitive encounters.[32] In medieval times we see the same awareness that some rabbis routinely engage in harsh exchanges, although here R. Abraham feels that R. Zerahia overstepped the bounds of this expressive style.

Lineage

Because the significance of noble lineage (*yihus*) in rabbinic culture is an extremely vast topic, I will focus here on lineage and dynastic succession as factors in appointment to leadership positions. In this respect we noted several instances of continuity between Stammaitic and Geonic times: the concentration of the Babylonian Gaonate in a few aristocratic families, claims of priestly descent, and the inheritance of positions within the academic hierarchy.[33] While the Arab conquests and spread of Islam placed the Geonim in a cultural climate different from the Sasanian environment of the Stammaim, Islamic society also prized noble lineage, especially Mohammedean descent.[34] Thus the same combination of traditional Jewish esteem for pure pedigree and respect for noble birth in the ambient society operated in both periods.

A remark by Sherira Gaon in his Epistle nicely illuminates the role of lineage in the Gaon's self conception: "Our ancestors were from the family of the Exilarchs, but they abandoned the ways of the Exilarchate and joined the sages of the academy, preferring meekness and humility. But we are not from the descendants of Bustanay; rather, before that our ancestors joined the sages of the academy."[35] By asserting Exilarchate ancestry Sherira simultaneously claims Davidic descent, as the Exilarch's authority rested exclusively on this basis. Sherira takes pains to point out that he does not descend from Bustanay, the Exilarch who married a Persian princess but failed to convert her before she bore his children, at least according to rabbinic polemics. As a result, all descendants of Bustanay have tainted genealogies. In this way Sherira asserts that the lineage of the Geonim surpasses even that of the Exilarch. Sherira's pedigree combines Davidic descent, outstanding character (meekness and humility), and the wisdom of the academy. This combination resembles the mix of knowledge and lineage idealized in late Bavli sources.

By the ninth century, the earliest time for which information is available, the Palestinian Gaonate, then in an Islamic rather than Byzantine cultural sphere, had also become a dynastic institution. The leading positions in the academy were controlled by three families, two of which claimed priestly descent.[36]

Avraham Grossman argues that lineage was of paramount importance in the selection of heads of academies and other positions of religious authority in medieval Italy, Germany, and France until the end of eleventh century. Most of the heads of academies came from a few leading families, and the office often passed from father to son as if by a principle of dynastic succession. In Ashkenazic communities noble lineage continued to be an advantage in attaining religious leadership well into the fourteenth century.[37] While in Spain and North Africa the position of head of the academy generally did not pass directly from father to son, it was frequently occupied by members of a few leading families.[38] Grossman considers the role of lineage in the medieval academies to be a deviation from the Talmudic period, related to the specific character of the Ashkenazic communities and paralleled by the prestige of noble blood throughout Europe at this time. However, if we understand the stories discussed in Chapter 5 as pointing to the Babylonian, rather than Palestinian, situation, then we should conclude that this trend began in Stammaitic times.

The trend toward dynastic succession received a more formal grounding in medieval law codes. In the *Mishneh torah* Maimonides formulates the principle thus: "Not only the monarchy, but all positions of authority and all appointments in Israel are passed on by inheritance to the son and the grandson forever. This is the case when the son fulfills the place of his ancestors in wisdom and in fear of God."[39] The scope of "positions of authority" and "appointments" is admittedly vague and need not necessarily include the head of academy or a rabbinate. Nonetheless, many subsequent authors of responsa interpreted Maimonides to refer to these offices. In his glosses to Yosef Caro's *Shulhan arukh*, R. Moses Isserles is more explicit: "A rabbi who has attained a position in a city, even if he attained it by virtue of his own merit, is not to be relieved of his office, even if a rabbi greater than he comes to that place. Even his son and descendants take precedence over others, as long as they fulfill the place of their ancestors in fear of God and are somewhat knowledgeable."[40] Note that both jurists add the proviso that the candidate must "fulfill the place" of his ancestors. They adopt this language from the Bavli's story of R. Yehuda HaNasi's testament, namely the Talmud's explanation of why the dying sage appointed his son Rabban Gamaliel to be Nasi even though his other son, Shimon, was more knowledgeable.[41]

Late medieval and early modern responsa take up in greater detail the issue addressed by Isserles's ruling, especially whether a rabbi may "inherit" the post of his father. As the rabbinate became professionalized, cities and villages appointed rabbis to be the religious and spiritual authority for the entire community, which in many cases involved heading the local academy as well. This structural change reduced the importance of lineage to some extent, as the community in theory retained the privilege of appointing whomever it pleased. In practice, however, sons or sons-in-law often put in a claim to succeed their fathers, a claim sometimes opposed by other factions. When the community turned to other rabbis to help settle the dispute, authors of responsa frequently ruled that the son should inherit his father's office even if his rival was more knowledgeable. The responsa regularly invoke as precedents the late Bavli stories we have discussed: that R. Yehuda HaNasi appointed his son Gamaliel to be Nasi despite the fact that his other son was wiser (bKet 103b), that R. Eleazar b. Azariah was appointed to replace Rabban Gamaliel by virtue of his "ancestral merit" despite the fact that R. Akiba was his superior in Torah (bBer 27b–28a), that Rabban Shimon b.

Gamaliel retained his position as head of the academy despite the fact that R. Meir and R. Natan were more knowledgeable (bHor 13b–14a).[42]

Particularly prominent use of a Talmudic precedent is made by Raphael Shmuel Laniado (d. 1793), who was involved in a bitter battle when he tried to bequeath his rabbinic office as head of the Aleppo community to his son.[43] In a lengthy responsum Laniado cites the entire story of R. Meir and R. Natan, focusing on Rabban Shimon b. Gamaliel's statement to R. Natan that "the belt of your father benefited you in making you the Head of the Court."[44] This explanation demonstrates, for Laniado, that R. Natan merited the office "solely on account of his father," which provides "absolute proof" that his son should inherit his office. He also points out that R. Meir and R. Natan were "greater in knowledge than R. Shimon b. Gamaliel, and even so R. Shimon b. Gamaliel was the Nasi because he had inherited the crown from his father Rabban Gamaliel." These gestures toward dynastic succession resulted from the circumstances and pressures of the times, not from the direct influence of the Bavli. Yet, given the general understanding of the rabbinate as a meritocracy—a point repeatedly emphasized by these same responsa—the Stammaitic narratives served as important precedents. One wonders whether without these sources the jurists would have approved of a less knowledgeable rabbi, his ties of kinship notwithstanding.

Dynastic succession of course resurfaced in a new way in Hasidism and to a certain extent in modern non-Hasidic orthodoxy.[45]

Wives

The proliferation of academies in medieval times seems to have attenuated the problem of students' leaving home for many years to pursue their studies. Still, not every scholar lived in a location that hosted an academy, while the best scholars endeavored to travel to the largest and most prestigious academies. Elijah Capsalli (d. 1555) reports of academic life in Venice that twice each year, during the months of Nisan (for Passover) and Tishrei (for Rosh Hashana and Yom Kippur), "a few of the rabbis and students who came from distant lands on account of the academy, and who left their wives and children—for the holidays they would march their feet, make a pilgrimage with their steps, and return to their lands, to their tongues, to their peoples, to rejoice in their homes with their children and wives."[46]

Opposition to these absences by wives seems to have been rare—or at least rarely reported in the extant literature. One example appears in a responsum of Jacob b. Moses Moellin (MaHarIL; d. 1427) concerning a wife who refused to give her husband permission to leave home to study Torah elsewhere.[47] She argued that an academy was located in their vicinity, adding that her husband was "neither sharp nor astute." Moellin nevertheless rules that the aspiring student may depart without her permission for up to eighteen months, adducing the opinion of the sages in bKet 62b.[48] He dismisses her objections on the grounds that the Talmudic sages journeyed great distances to study where and with whom they believed they would make the best progress, and that the intelligence of a student does not reduce the value of Torah study.[49]

Erotic representations of Torah study, also discussed in Chapter 6, become an explicit and important dimension of Kabbalistic mysticism, as has been described in detail by Elliot Wolfson.[50] The Zohar presents Torah study as a means of uniting with the feminine elements of God:

> Similarly, when scholars are separated from their wives on weekdays in order to study Torah, celestial intercourse is granted them and does not desert them, so that male and female may exist together. . . . Similarly, when a man's wife has her menstrual period and he has proper respect for her, celestial intercourse is granted him during those days, so that male and female may exist together. When his wife has become purified he must give his wife the joy of the commandment, exalted joy.[51]

According to the Talmudic tradition cited in Chapter 6, the conjugal duty of sages is once a week on the Sabbath.[52] The Zohar claims that although a sage abstains from physical intercourse during the week, he engages in "celestial" intercourse with the *Shekhinah,* namely the mystical experience of "cleaving" to or uniting with God.[53] Likewise, when he refrains from sex with his wife due to her ritual impurity, he is compensated by celestial intercourse achieved through passionate Torah study. Torah study and marital sex are presented as complementary and even interdependent activities in that celestial intercourse is a reward for satisfying the wife's sexual needs at the proper time. This interpretation is ultimately grounded on the mystical view of marital sex, like other commandments and rituals, as a symbolic act that influences the life of divine potencies. But that Torah study is analogized to intercourse rather than some other ritual underscores the eroticism of the experience.

The parallel erotic experience of the intellectual and physical emerges even more clearly in the following Zoharic passage that discusses the sanctity of midnight:

> The comrades who are engaged in [study of] Torah join the community of Israel in praising the holy King as they are occupied with the Torah. For the rest of the

[Jewish] males this is the acceptable time to be sanctified in the sanctity of the Holy One, blessed be he, and to direct their intention to be conjoined to him. With respect to the comrades who are engaged in [study of] Torah, the time for their sexual intercourse is the time that another intercourse takes place, and this is on the eve of Sabbath.[54]

Wolfson's analysis of the passage is worth quoting in full:

The mystics rise at midnight to study Torah at precisely the time that other Jewish males should ideally engage in sexual intercourse. The hermeneutical activity of the kabbalist is viewed as distinct from yet isomorphic to the conjugal sex of the layman: Just as the latter is conjoined to God through the proper intention in sexual intercourse, so the former attains the state of conjunction by means of textual exegesis. The phenomenological structure of the two experiences is identical: by uniting with the female (in the case of the ordinary male his wife and in the case of the mystic the *Shekhinah*) the male gains access to the masculine potency of the divine.[55]

Wolfson also notes that in a later Kabbalistic ethical work, Elijah de Vidas (16th century) describes Torah study of sages as "spiritual intercourse" (*zivug ruhani*) that corresponds to the "physical intercourse" (*zivug gashmi*) of laymen.[56]

Hasidic writings continue to present Torah study in erotic terms. For Moses Hayyim Ephraim of Sudlikov (c. 1737–1800), study functions as a means of uniting with the (feminine) Torah herself: "When a person is occupied with Torah for its own sake . . . He and the Torah become one in unity and perfect oneness like the unification of a man and his wife . . . if with respect to physical unification [it says] "And they will be of one flesh" (Gen. 2:24), *a fortiori* with respect to spiritual matters he becomes a perfect unity with the Torah."[57] Clearly the notion of uniting with the Torah must be understood metaphorically. That the author analogizes this unification to sexual unity again points to the erotic nature of study.

To be sure, Kabbalistic mysticism is a religious system that differs from classical rabbinic Judaism in significant ways. Yet the influence of the Bavli can be seen in that many of these passages from Kabbalistic and Hasidic texts quote the Talmudic midrash from bPes 49b cited in Chapter 6 that plays on Deut 33:4, reading "inheritance" (*morasha*) as "betrothed" (*meorasa*).[58] Here, as in many cases, the Kabbalistic developments can be seen in part as a midrashic interpretation of earlier rabbinic sources.

The *am ha'arets*

Geonic sources adopt an apologetic attitude toward the passages contemptuous of the *am ha'arets*. Rav Sherira Gaon, for example, limits the tradition permitting one to kill an *am ha'arets* even on a Sabbath that falls on Yom Kippur to the case in which an *am ha'arets* pursues another man in order to murder him or pursues a betrothed maiden so as to rape her.[59] Of course one may also kill a sage in such circumstances, so Sherira explains why the tradition singles out an *am ha'arets* as follows: *because* an *am ha'arets* has not studied the law, he does not realize that anyone can kill him when he attempts to murder another, and may therefore suffer a horrid death such as being split apart like a fish. Sherira also insists that the Talmudic tradition cannot be taken at face value, as it contradicts such rabbinic norms as the need for a trial, witnesses, and standard judicial protocols. This apologetic perspective is exactly what we would expect given the shift in the tradition's audience. When the Talmud became a written text and was disseminated throughout the Jewish world, the potential audience came to include rabbis and non-rabbis alike. Moreover, as the Geonim promoted the Bavli as the authoritative source of law, it gained a wide following. The *am ha'arets* traditions were no longer the private discourse of the sages but public statements. Sherira's apologetic interpretations are intended to neutralize any normative or legal impact.

Kabbalistic texts, on the other hand, take up the negative *am ha'arets* traditions and adapt them in service of aspects of mystical theology. In several places the Zohar equates sages with human beings and the *amei ha'arets* with subhumans, such as this portrait of messianic times: "But they [*amei ha'arets*] will be despised by scholars, like darkness before light, for the mixed multitude, the *amei ha'arets*, are darkened. And they are not called "Israel," but slaves sold to Israel, since they are like beasts, and they have already explained this, while Israel are called 'human.' "[60] "They have already explained this" refers to the Bavli traditions from bPes 49b that compare the *amei ha'arets* to animals. Because the *amei ha'arets* do not study Torah, the Zohar deprives them of the status of "Israel," meaning that they are not fully Jewish, and consequently not fully human.[61] The Zohar assigns them second-class status as slaves of the scholars, and the continuation of the passage relates that those who do not accept their status will be killed. In this way the Zohar perpetuates the Bavli's debasement of the *amei ha'arets* and projects it to the eschaton: those who do not study Torah have no right to exist except insofar as they serve the sages.

Similarly, the Zohar essentially endorses the Talmudic tradition advocating violence against the *amei ha'arets:* "It is true that the world really consists of none but the companions who study the Torah and understand its mysteries. The companions rightly issued decrees against the *amei ha'arets,* who corrupt their ways and cannot distinguish between right and left, for they are like beasts, who deserve to be punished, even on Yom Kippur. Concerning their children it is said: 'They are children of harlotry' (Hosea 2:6)—real harlotry."[62] The subhuman nature of the *amei ha'arets* deprives them of any claim to be a part of the world, reading them out of the Jewish people. And because they (and their parents) do not possess mystical knowledge of sexual law, they have sex at the wrong times, causing their children to have the status of those conceived from sinful unions. The "decrees" alludes to Talmudic traditions disqualifying *amei ha'arets* from testifying in court and suchlike.[63] While the Zohar somewhat ameliorates the tradition granting a dispensation to slay *amei ha'arets* by the formulation that they "deserve to be punished," the attitude remains contemptuous. Most important for our purposes is that the Zohar incorporates these Talmudic traditions into its worldview rather than reinterpreting or repudiating them, as do the Geonic sources. This contrast tends to support the understanding of the Talmudic traditions as the inner discourse of the academy intended only for an audience of likeminded sages. Mystical literature, also intended for an elite and limited audience, embraces the negative traditions, whereas the Geonim, engaged in the project of disseminating the Bavli and establishing it as the authoritative source of law, neutralize them.

Epilogue: The Triumph of the Bavli

The story of the Bavli's dissemination outside of Babylonia and its establishment as the authoritative source of law belongs to the post-Talmudic era. These processes were part of the campaign of the Babylonian Geonim to promote themselves as the legal authorities for the entire Jewish world, consequently to champion the Bavli—of which they were the expert interpreters—as the foundational halakhic text. Their ultimate success was due primarily to political and economic factors, including the move of the academies of Sura and Pumbedita to Baghdad, the seat of the Abassid Caliphate and center of the Islamic empire, which enhanced their prestige and ability to influence distant Jewish communities. At the same time, the characteristics of the Bavli should not be discounted. As the Babylonian academies were eclipsed by other centers of learning, and as the authority of the Geonim was supplanted by that of other scholars, nothing guaranteed that the Bavli should retain its centrality. Part of the Bavli's enduring power should be attributed to the nature of the text itself. The depth of the Bavli's argumentation, the intricately textured *sugyot*, the richness of its dialectical debate, and the complexity of its narratives captured the imaginations of succeeding generations of sages.[64] The *sugyot* of the Yerushalmi, by contrast, are for the most part terse and poorly developed. As noted in the Introduction, this difference is due to the Stammaim, who wove earlier apodictic traditions into complex *sugyot*, adding layers of argumentation and debate.

The leading competitors of the Babylonian Geonim were their Palestinian counterparts.[65] Besides possessing the rival Talmud Yerushalmi, the Palestinian Geonim based strong claims to authority on their location within the Holy Land and their continuity with early rabbinic tradition. To justify the primacy of the Bavli and Babylonian halakhic tradition over the Yerushalmi and Palestinian tradition the Babylonian Geonim and their intellectual descendants advanced two polemical arguments. A ninth-century tract authored by a certain Pirqoy b. Baboy addressed to Jewish communities of North Africa and Spain claimed that persecutions in the Byzantine era had disrupted the continuity of Palestinian tradition and corrupted its halakha.[66] Pirqoy charges that Palestinian practices are "the customs of persecution" (*minhag shemad*), the results of the inability of communities to observe the law properly. Babylonian tradition, on the other hand, was passed down without interruption or discontinuity. When Babylonian and Palestinian practices conflict, one should follow the pure, unadulterated Babylonian tradition. A second influential argument, advanced by R. Yitzhaq Alfasi (1013–1103) in his *Halakhot*, one of the first comprehensive legal codes, is that the sages in Babylonia had access to the Yerushalmi and took its rulings into account.[67] The Bavli is the posterior, more complete statement of Jewish law. Therefore, when the Bavli and Yerushalmi conflict, the law should follow the Bavli. While the Bavli certainly postdates the Yerushalmi, modern scholars almost universally reject Alfasi's claim.[68] Nevertheless, it served as a compelling legal justification for subsequent jurists to accept the Bavli as canonical.[69]

The *Tanhuma*, a post-Talmudic midrash, offers a variation of this ideology, promoting Babylonian tradition by retrojecting the academies (*yeshivot*) to the time of the first temple:

> Therefore the Holy One, blessed be He, established two *yeshivot* for Israel, so that they would be discussing Torah day and night, and would come together from all their localities twice a year — in Adar and Elul — and engage in the "wars of Torah" until they determine the correct law. . . . Those two *yeshivot* have seen neither captivity nor persecution nor despoilment. Neither Greece nor Edom [Rome] has

ruled over them. For twelve years before the destruction of Jerusalem [by the Babylonians] the Holy One, blessed be He, removed them from Jerusalem with their Torah and learning. . . . [He] acted righteously with Israel in that He had the exile of Yekhonyah precede the exile of Sidqiyah — in order that the Oral Torah not be forgotten by them. And they [the *yeshivot*] have dwelt in Babylonia with their Torah from that time until now; neither Greece nor Edom has ruled over them, nor have they been persecuted. And they will not even suffer "the pangs of the Messiah."[70]

The midrash locates the founding of the academies in the "exile of Yekhonyah" (Jehoiachin) who became king during his father's rebellion against Nebuchadnezzar and was taken in chains to Babylonia in 597 B.C.E. (2 Kgs 24:8–17). Their founding antedates by about ten years the exile of the bulk of the people following Zedekiah's failed revolt in 587/6 B.C.E. (2 Kgs 25:1–7). The traditions of the Babylonian academies, that is, the Bavli, therefore stand in direct continuity with the biblical transmitters of Oral Torah. The insistence that the academies suffered neither persecution under the Greeks or Romans nor despoilment nor captivity, rehearses Pirqoy b. Baboy's polemic that the Palestinian tradition was corrupted. Ancient security is complemented by a guarantee of future protection. Paraphrasing a tradition found in the Bavli, the midrash asserts that the academies will remain undamaged by eschatological upheavals.[71] Although this account makes no explicit comparison to the Palestinian situation, the message is clear: Babylonian tradition is more ancient, original, reliable, and secure than that of Palestine.

The struggle by Babylonian Geonim for supremacy over the Palestinian sages has roots in the Stammaitic period, if not before.[72] We have mentioned two manifestations of the conflict. Both Talmuds contain a story in which the Babylonians attempt to usurp the Palestinian prerogative to determine the calendar.[73] In both versions the Babylonians claim that they are superior in knowledge of Torah and consequently should possess calendrical authority, but they ultimately yield to Palestinian pressure. The Bavli account, however, contains a brief but significant dialogue not paralleled in the Yerushalmi account, as has been noted by I. Gafni.[74]When first confronted by the Palestinian delegation, the Babylonian sage Hananiah adduces a precedent for his actions, "Did not Akiba b. Yosef intercalate years and determine new moons outside of Israel?"[75] To this the Palestinians reply, "Leave aside R. Akiba, as he left behind no equal [in knowledge] in the Land of Israel." The Palestinian sages essentially concede that Akiba justifiably intercalated the year in the diaspora. They argue, however, that at the present time their knowledge of Torah is superior, or at least equal, to that of Hananiah. This interchange, which the Yerushalmi version lacks, leaves open the possibility that at such a time when the Babylonians surpass the Palestinians in knowledge, they may justifiably assume this traditional Palestinian prerogative, just as Akiba did. Legal authority, the storyteller suggests, devolves on those most proficient in Torah. In the early tenth century this issue resurfaced when the Babylonians challenged the calendar proclaimed by the Palestinian authorities. A furious conflict erupted and for three years Jewish communities observed the festivals on different days.[76] While we do not know the specific contours of the debate, it seems reasonable to assume that the Babylonians believed their knowledge of Torah in general, and their mastery of the laws of intercalation in particular, to be superior to that of the Palestinian sages, and may well have found a precedent in the Talmudic story.

A second source by which Babylonians claim superior knowledge is the story of Rav Kahana's travel to the Land of Israel and encounter with R. Yohanan, discussed in Chapters 1 and 2 (bBQ 117a–b). This story portrays the Babylonian sage as vastly superior to his Palestinian colleague in dialectical ability.[77] At the end of the story, after inadvertently causing Rav Kahana's death, R. Yohanan goes to his burial cave but is refused admission until he petitions, "Let the student approach his teacher." R. Yohanan thereupon resurrects Rav Kahana and for thirty days asks every legal question on which he has doubts. After Rav Kahana resolves them all, R. Yohanan — in a scene that would have made any Palestinian cringe — admits: "What I thought was yours, was actually theirs," that is, "I thought that expertise in Torah was yours, O Palestinians; but now I see that it belongs to the Babylonians."[78] The story claims not only that the prowess of a Babylonian sage far outstripped that of the greatest Palestinians, but that the Palestinians learned authoritative law from the Babylonians.

This claim to have been the source of the Palestinian Torah comprises a reversal of one marker of Palestinian prestige: continuity with the earliest rabbinic masters. Rabbinic tradition in fact arose in Palestine; it was exported to Babylonia when the first generation Amoraim Rav and Shmuel brought R. Yehuda HaNasi's Mishna to Babylonian commmunities and campaigned to establish it as the basis for Jewish law. While proficiency need not in theory align with point of origin, to the ancient mind sources and foundations carried enormous prestige. It could only enhance the status of the Babylonians to allege that Palestinian tradition derived from their own. Indeed, the Babylonians presented themselves as a constant fount of Palestinian Torah from earliest times: "When Torah was first forgotten from Israel, Ezra came up from Babylonia and reestablished it. Again it was forgotten — Hillel the Babylonian came up and reestablished it. Again it was forgotten—R. Hiyya and his sons came up and reestablished it (bSuk 20a)."[79] The biblical hero Ezra, a Babylonian sage of priestly descent, becomes the model for successive waves of Babylonians who restored Torah to their Palestinian brethren. Palestinian sages therefore owe what knowledge of Torah they possess to the far more proficient Babylonians. This charge that "Torah was forgotten in Israel" seems to lurk in the background of the *Tanhuma*'s concern that "the Oral Torah not be forgotten by them." The Babylonians, unlike the Palestinians, preserved their tradition without interruption and therefore were able to restore Torah to the Palestinians when needed. We thus find Stammaitic traditions adumbrating the post-Talmudic polemics: Babylonian tradition is superior, more exact, continuous, and complete, while that of the Palestinians is discontinuous, dependent, and indebted to the Babylonian academies.

That the Stammaim chose to express themselves in an anonymous voice is an interesting historical irony. They saw themselves as living in a post-classical age, as being inferior to their predecessors, the Amoraim. They set about justifying and explicating inherited traditions, not producing new legislation or legal innovations. Yet through their halakhic practice of dialectical argumentation, to which they subjected those previous traditions, and through reworking narrative traditions, where their voice came through more prominently, they stamped the Bavli with the values, worldview, and ethos of their own culture. The Bavli having become the foundational rabbinic text, these anonymous sages have made an enduring contribution to Jewish societies in succeeding centuries even to the present day.

~•~

Notes

Introduction

1. On the neglect of study of Scripture in favor of study of Talmud, see Frank Talmage, "Keep Your Sons from Scripture: The Bible in Medieval Jewish Scholarship and Spirituality," *Understanding Scripture,* ed. C. Thoma and M. Wyschogrod (Mahwah, N.J.: Paulist Press, 1987), 81–101; Mordechai Breuer, "Keep Your Children from *Higgayon*," *Religion in a Religious Age,* ed. S. D. Goitein (Cambridge, Mass.: Association for Jewish Studies, 1974), 247–61 (Hebrew).

2. Yaakov Sussmann, "Veshuv lirushalmi neziqin," *Mehqerei talmud I,* ed. Y. Sussmann and D. Rosenthal (Jerusalem: Magnes, 1990), 132–33 n. 187.

3. bSanh 43a, according to the reading of Sherira Gaon and R. Hananel. See *Iggeret rav sherira gaon,* ed. B. M. Lewin (Berlin, 1921), 70–71.

4. See Leib Moscovitz, *From Casuistics to Conceptualization* (Leiden: Brill, 2002), on the difference in legal science (abstraction, generalization, conceptualization) between the two Talmuds.

5. See Yaakov Elman, "Orality and the Redaction of the Babylonian Talmud," *Oral Tradition* 14/1 (1999), 70, for these estimates.

6. Sussmann, "Veshuv lirushalmi neziqin," 98–99.

7. David Weiss Halivni and Shamma Friedman reached this conclusion independently. See Halivni, *Meqorot umesorot,* 5 vols. (Tel-Aviv: Devir, and Jerusalem: Jewish Theological Seminary, 1968–94), 3:5–27, 5:7–21; Friedman, "Pereq ha'isha rabba babavli," *Mehqarim umeqorot,* ed. H. Dimitrovksi (New York: Jewish Theological Seminary, 1977), 283–321. Halivni summarizes his views in his English book, *Midrash, Mishnah, and Gemara: The Jewish Predilection for Justified Law* (Cambridge: Harvard University Press, 1986), 76–104.

8. Note that the Stammaitic policy is the exception, not the rule. The founding fathers of America, for example, preserved the Constitution, the results of the lengthy

debates of the Constitutional Convention, but not the debates themselves. The various opinions, arguments, and discussions that led up to the final document were not considered of sufficient importance to record for posterity.

9. There were actually two Ravinas: one lived during the fifth generation, one at the end of the sixth and into the seventh. The latter Ravina is intended here. According to Sherira Gaon, Ravina died in 499 c.e., Rav Ashi in 427 c.e.. On the matter of Ravina, see now Avinoam Cohen, *Ravina and Contemporary Sages* (Ramat-Gan: Bar Ilan University Press, 2001), 256–74 (Hebrew).

10. See Jeffrey L. Rubenstein, *Talmudic Stories: Narrative Art, Composition, and Culture* (Baltimore: Johns Hopkins University Press, 1999), 48–60, 255–67. See too Shamma Friedman, "La'aggada hahistorit batalmud habavli," *Saul Lieberman Memorial Volume,* ed. Shamma Friedman (New York: Jewish Theological Seminary, 1993), 119–63; Louis Jacobs, *Structure and Form in the Babylonian Talmud* (Cambridge: Cambridge University Press, 1991), 100–106; Sussmann, "Veshuv lirushalmi neziqin," 100–101 n. 186.

11. See Rubenstein, *Talmudic Stories,* 48–60, 255–67.

12. See Jacobs, *Structure and Form,* 105: "In the light of our investigation, it is necessary to go much further than Halivni to see the Stammaim as far more than mere editors of earlier material. They were, in fact, creative authors who shaped the material they had to provide the new literary form evident in the passages we have examined and, indeed, on practically every page of the Babylonian Talmud."

13. See Rubenstein, *Talmudic Stories,* 3–8, for a review of the scholarly literature.

14. See nn. 10–12.

15. See Yaakov Elman's judicious discussion "How Should a Talmudic Intellectual History be Written? A Response to David Kraemer's *Responses,*" *JQR* 89 (1999), 361–86.

16. The discussion of methodology is rather detailed and is intended primarily for specialists. It can be skipped or skimmed without loss.

17. The Bavli did not necessarily receive the *exact* versions now extant in Palestinian documents but versions similar to those that circulated in Palestine. See Rubenstein, *Talmudic Stories,* 244, 255–67.

18. A *baraita* (plural: *baraitot*) is a Tannaitic source that is not found in the Mishna.

19. bPes 49b; for full discussion, see Chap. 7.

20. Shraga Abramson, "Min peh lefeh," *Mehqerei lashon* 2–3 (1987), 23–50, shows that Amoraim occasionally incorporate phrases from Tannaitic sources and earlier Amoraic dicta into their statements. But these quotations never amount to the type of transference and adaptation that characterize Stammaitic reworking.

21. I consider stories about Babylonian Amoraim to be distinct from Amoraic dicta. Within stories, all sages function as fictional characters. At issue are traditions attributed to Amoraim.

22. This point is discussed in Chap. 1.

23. Although I assume that the ambient culture had some impact in all cases. Sasanian culture presumably influenced the rise of the rabbinic academy in some way, if only such that the general climate made the development of the institution a possibility in that time and place. I address this issue in Chap. 1, under "The Christian Academy at Nisibis." But for this and most other topics, it is hard to point to clear and direct influences (granted that this is a slippery distinction.)

24. Jacob Neusner, *The Bavli and Its Sources: The Question of Tradition in the Case of Tractate Sukkah* (Atlanta: Scholars Press, 1987); *Judaism: The Classic Statement: The Evidence of the Bavli* (Chicago: University of Chicago Press, 1986); *The Documentary Foundation of Rabbinic Culture* (Atlanta: Scholars Press, 1995), etc.

25. See most recently Richard Kalmin, *The Sage in Jewish Society of Late Antiquity* (London: Routledge, 1999).

26. See Shamma Freidman, *Talmud arukh: pereq hasokher et ha'omanin* (Jerusalem: Jewish Theological Seminary, 1990–96), 2:8–23. See too David Kraemer, "On the Reliability of Attributions in the Babylonian Talmud," *HUCA* 60 (1989), 175–90.

27. In recent studies, Shamma Friedman has shown that Babylonian redactors reworked *baraitot* to a significant extent. See Friedman, "Uncovering Literary Dependencies in the Talmudic Corpus," *The Synoptic Problem in Rabbinic Literature,* ed. Shaye J. D. Cohen (Providence: Brown Judaica Series, 2000), 35–57, for additional literature see p. 43 n. 34. See too Friedman, "Habaraitot shebatalmud habavli veyihasan latosefta" (forthcoming), and Yaakov Elman, *Authority and Tradition: Toseftan Baraitot in Talmudic Babylonia* (Hoboken, N.J.: Ktav, 1994), 44–46, 145–64.

28. See Rubenstein, *Talmudic Stories,* 261–62.

29. For criticism of Neusner's method, see too Daniel Boyarin, "On the Status of the Tannaitic Midrashim," *Journal of the American Oriental Society* 112 (1993), 455–64; Eliezer Segal, "Anthological Dimensions of the Babylonian Talmud," *Prooftexts* 17 (1997), 35–37; Robert Goldenberg, "Is 'The Talmud' a Document?" *The Synoptic Problem in Rabbinic Literature,* ed. Shaye J. D. Cohen (Providence: Brown Judaica Series, 2000), 3–10.

30. See the previous note.

31. See Rubenstein, *Talmudic Stories,* 255–67. And see Chap. 5, n. 66, for a case of fabrication. Occasionally even halakhic statements were fictionalized: see Menahem Kahane, "Intimation of Intention and Compulsion of Divorce: Towards the Transmission of Contradictory Traditions in Late Talmudic Passages," *Tarbiz* 62 (1993), 230–31, 248–50, 260–62 (Hebrew); Jay Rovner, "Pseudepigraphic Invention and Diachronic Stratification in the Stammaitic Component of the Bavli: The case of Sukka 28," *HUCA* 68 (1997), 11–62.

32. Clifford Geertz, "Thick Description: Towards an Interpretive Theory of Culture," *The Interpretation of Cultures* (New York: Basic Books, 1973), 4–5.

33. The rabbinic attitude to the *am ha'arets,* I will argue in Chap. 7, does not tell us much about real social relations.

34. Peter Brown, "The Rise and Function of the Holy Man in Late Antiquity," *Journal of Roman Studies* 61 (1971), 80–101; reprinted with other of Brown's articles in *Society and the Holy in Late Antiquity* (Berkeley: University of Califronia Press, 1989). On the impact of Brown's work, see J. Howard-Johnston, "Introduction," *The Cult of Saints in Late Antiquity and the Middle Ages,* ed. J. Howard-Johnston and P. A. Hayward (Oxford: Oxford University Press, 1999), 1–27.

35. See the critical assessment of Brown's conclusions by Averil Cameron in "On Defining the Holy Man" and by Phillip Rousseau in "Ascetics as Mediators and as Teachers," both in *The Cult of Saints in Late Antiquity and the Middle Ages,* ed. J. Howard-Johnston and P. A. Hayward (Oxford: Oxford University Press, 1999), 27–43 and 45–62. Cameron writes: "But I still believe that Byzantinists, like scholars of early Christianity, should be trying to understand discourse, the rhetorical strategies which combine to produce sets of ideas and practices, which in turn determine the nature of culture. This is the element which I find most wanting in the otherwise enormously stimulating work of Peter Brown" (p. 42). Rousseau observes concerning one of Brown's claims: "It is difficult to know how we might know that. In spite of the phrase 'in reality', the 'spiritual landscape' is also in the text. Indeed, Brown later admitted that it was *the function of the literature* to make things seem less complicated; 'to bring order to a supernatural world shot through with acute ambiguity'. Texts are now behaving in the argument as holy men did in its previous stages. Where are we left, then, when we read that 'holy men themselves were frequently less tidy, in practice, in their choice of explanatory systems than were their biographers, in retrospect'? What evidence is being appealed to?" (pp. 50–51).

36. See Daniel Boyarin, *Carnal Israel: Reading Sex in Talmudic Culture* (Berkeley: University of California Press, 1993), 13–16.

Chapter 1. *The Rabbinic Academy*

1. David Goodblatt, *Rabbinic Instruction in Sasanian Babylonia* (Leiden: Brill, 1975).

2. Goodblatt, *Rabbinic Instruction,* 267, defines an academy as: "an institution which transcends its principles. It has a staff, a curriculum, and, most important, a life of its own, a corporate identity. Students come and go, teachers leave and are replaced, the head of the school dies and a new one is appointed — the institution goes on."

3. For manuscript variants see *Diqduqei Sofrim Hashalem: The Babylonian Talmud with Variant Readings. Tractates Yebamot, Ketubot, Nedarim, Sotah,* ed. M. Hershler and A. Liss (Jerusalem: Institute for the Complete Israeli Talmud, 1977–91), ad loc., and I. Gafni, *The Jews of Babylonia in the Talmudic Era: A Social and Cultural History* (Jerusalem: Shazar Center, 1990), 221. Some mss add "R. Hiyya b. Abba said, 'I am

among the leaders of the smaller Kallah-sessions (*reshe kallah*) of Rav Huna, and six hundred rabbis used to attend.'"

4. See the summary of scholarship on this topic in Goodblatt, *Rabbinic Instruction*, 55–56. Some scholars suggest that the departing rabbis went home at the end of each day.

5. Cf. Goodblatt, *Rabbinic Instruction*, 56–57.

6. I refer to the perspective known as "the decline of the generations." See below at n. 62.

7. So read the mss. Printed texts read "eight rows." This story is attributed to Rav Yehuda in the name of Rav. But the length of the story does not fit the terse traditions of early Amoraim.

8. *Resh sidra*. The precise sense of this term is unclear. It may be synonymous with "head of the academy."

9. See too bTa 21b. When Rav Nahman b. Yizhaq made an insightful comment, Rav Nahman b. Rav Hisda said to him, "Let the master arise and come closer to us," i.e., relocate to a seat of greater honor.

10. The exception is the story of the deposition of Rabban Gamaliel found in yBer 4:1, 7c–d; yTa 4:1, 67d: "How many benches were there? R. Yaakov b. Sisi said, 'There were 80 benches there of students, besides those standing behind the fence. R. Yosi b. R. Abun said, 'There were 300, besides those standing behind the fence'. . . . There we learned, *R. Eleazar b. Azariah expounded this homily before the sages at the vineyard at Yavneh (mKet 4:6)*. But was there a vineyard there? Rather, these are the disciples who sat in rows like a vineyard." Here then we do have a Palestinian description of a large gathering of sages, including benches and rows of students. Yet it is called an assembly-house, while the mention of a fence implies that the gathering was outdoors. Interestingly, the parallel in *Shir HaShirim Rabbah* 8:11 reads: "But was there a vineyard there? Rather, this was the *sanhedrin* which was organized in rows like a vineyard." This reading is consistent with Tannaitic sources that describe the Sanhedrin arranged with rows of judges and their students. Moreover, the mention of benches in the Yerushalmi's version comes as a non sequitur, as the preceding narrative has nothing to do with the nature of the assembly. In the Bavli, however, the parallel section about benches fits perfectly: the story relates that Rabban Gamaliel had restricted access to the study-house but after his deposition they allowed students to enter and added a number of benches. (See Chap. 7, under "The Reclusive Academy" for synoptic presentation of these passages, and S. Krauss, "Outdoor Teaching in Talmudic Times," *JJS* 1 [1948–49], 82.) I would not be surprised if the Yerushalmi has been contaminated by the Bavli's version in this case, although I realize that it is methodologically suspect to explain away a source that contradicts one's theory. For examples of Babylonian contamination in the Yerushalmi see Leib Moscovitz, "Double Readings in the Yerushalmi," *The Talmud Yerushalmi*

and Greco-Roman Culture, ed. P. Schäfer (Tübingen: J. C. B. Mohr, 1997), 100–101. And see Yonah Fraenkel, "Remarkable Phenomena in the Text-History of the Aggadic Stories," *Proceedings of the Seventh World Congress of Jewish Studies—1977* (Jerusalem, 1981), 3:51–69 (Hebrew).

11. Catherine Hezser, *The Social Structure of the Rabbinic Movement in Roman Palestine* (Tübingen: J. C. B. Mohr, 1997), 214. See her survey of all the evidence, pp. 195–214, and see pp. 202–4 on the "great hall" (*sudra rabba*).

12. See Rubenstein, *Talmudic Stories,* 3–10.

13. For comprehensive argument of this point, see Jeffrey L. Rubenstein, "The Rise of the Babylonian Talmudic Academy: A Reexamination of the Talmudic Evidence," *Jewish Studies, an Internet Journal* (www.biu.ac.il/JS/JSU) (2002).

14. Daniel Sperber, "On the Unfortunate Adventures of Rav Kahana: A Passage of Saboraic Polemic from Sasanian Persia," *Irano-Judaica,* ed. S. Shaked (Jerusalem: Yad Izhaq Ben-Zvi, 1982), 83–100.

15. Isaiah Gafni, "The Babylonian *Yeshiva* as Reflected in Bava Qama 117a," *Tarbiz* 49 (1980), 192–201 (Hebrew); Adiel Schremer, "'He Posed Him a Difficulty and Placed Him'—A Study in the Evolution of the Text of TB Bava Qama 117a," *Tarbiz* 66 (1997), 403–16 (Hebrew).

16. Israel Ben-Shalom, "'And I Took Unto me Two Staves: the One I Called Beauty and the Other I Called Bands' (*Zach. 11:7*)," *Dor-Le-Dor: From the End of Biblical Times up to the Redaction of the Talmud. Studies in Honor of Joshua Efron,* ed. A. Oppenheimer and A. Kasher (Jerusalem: Bialik, 1995), 242–44 (Hebrew). The issue of verbal violence is discussed in Chap. 3.

17. See the discussion of this story in Chap. 7, under "The Reclusive Academy," and especially n. 63.

18. On this question see Goodblatt, *Rabbinic Instruction;* Isaiah Gafni, "'Yeshiva' and 'Metivta'," *Zion* 43 (1978), 12–37 (Hebrew); and Goodblatt's response to Gafni, "New Developments in the Study of the Babylonian *Yeshivot,*" *Zion* 46 (1981), 14–38 (Hebrew). I reexamine all the evidence in the article mentioned in n. 13.

19. See Robert Brody, *The Geonim of Babylonia and the Shaping of Medieval Jewish Culture* (New Haven: Yale University Press, 1988), 26–29 on Nathan the Babylonian, and 35–53 on the Geonic academy.

20. Brody, *Geonim,* 46 n. 48 suggests that "reads" (*qore*) need not point to a written text here.

21. The translation is based on Goodblatt, *Rabbinic Instruction,* 161–62; cf. Brody, *Geonim,* 46–47 for a slightly different translation and commentary. The original text can be found in A. Neubauer, ed., *Mediaeval Jewish Chronicles and Chronological Notes* (Oxford: Clarendon Press, 1887–95), 87–88.

22. For discussion of this issue see Chap. 5, under "Dynastic Succession in the Geonic Era."

23. See Brody, *Geonim*, 44.

24. See p. 5.

25. See e.g. Julius Kaplan, *The Redaction of the Babylonian Talmud* (New York: Bloch, 1933), 293–96, 315. In this they relied on the Epistle of Rav Sherira Gaon; see *Iggeret rav sherira gaon*, ed. Lewin, 94–97 ("Spanish" rescension). Sherira mentions persecutions in 455 C.E. and 470–74 C.E. and dates the "closing of the Talmud" to the time of R. Asi or R. Yosi, who presided after 476 C.E. For discussion of Sherira's dating, which is based on his interpretation of bBM 86a, see Halivni, *Midrash, Mishnah, and Gemara*, 76–77, 83–84, 99–100, and 140 n. 1. Cf. Zecharia Frankel, *Mavo hayerushalmi* (Breslau: Schletter, 1870), 48a, who offers a similar explanation for the redaction of the Yerushalmi.

26. Salo Baron, *Freedom and Reason, Studies in Philosophy and Jewish Culture in Memory of Morris Raphael Cohen*, ed. S. Baron, E. Nagel, and K. Pinson (Glencoe, Ill.: Free Press, 1951), 340–44.

27. Richard Kalmin, *Post Rav-Ashi Amoraim: Transition or Continuity?* (Ph.D. diss., Jewish Theological Seminary, 1985), 272–73 n. 11.

28. See Jack N. Lightstone, *The Rhetoric of the Babylonian Talmud, Its Social Meaning and Context* (Waterloo, Ont.: Wilfred Laurier University Press, 1994), especially 264–81. Lightstone argues that the rhetorical traits of the Bavli shed light on the institutional and social setting of the editors and also legitimate the newly emerged academies of the fifth–sixth century.

29. I will return to this point in the next chapter. As noted in the Introduction, the Tannaim and Amoraim engaged in dialectical argumentation but did not consider it worthy of preservation. I am suggesting here that more weight is placed on argumentation in a large academy than in a small disciple circle.

30. Brody, *Geonim*, 60–62, 185–201.

31. Ibid., 61. Cf. Louis Ginzberg, *Geonica* (New York: Jewish Theological Seminary, 1909), 6: "Any Talmudic treatise selected at random will reveal dozens of authorities on every folio. . . . On the other hand, if we examine the Geonic Responsa for a period of about 400 years, we shall find that the name of hardly a single authority who is not a Gaon has come down to us."

32. Brody, *Geonim*, 60–62, 185–201.

33. Rav Revai is mentioned once, bSanh 43a (according to the reading of Rav Sherira and R. Hananel). Rav Ahai of Be Hatim is mentioned in bGit 7a (printings of the Talmud read "Be Hozai") and elsewhere. Rav Eina is mentioned in bSuk 50b and several other places. See *Iggeret rav sherira gaon*, ed. Lewin, 70–71, 99.

34. J. N. Epstein, *Mavo lenusah hamishna*, 2nd ed. (Jerusalem: Magnes, 1964), 488–89.

35. For sources see Dan Urman, "The House of Assembly and House of Study: Are They One and the Same?" *JJS* 44 (1993), 236–57.

36. The translation of R. Yizhaq's reply is uncertain. The sense is: You follow Hananiah's intercalation, as if your Torah reads, "These are the set times of Hananiah." But the verse says, "of the Lord," and we inhabit his Holy Land.

37. Earlier in the story Hananiah honored the emissaries. They argue now that since he built them up with his first proclamation, he can no longer discredit them.

38. Hananiah's place of residence, a city in Babylonia.

39. See Aharon Oppenheimer, "The attempt of Hananiah, son of Rabbi Joshua's brother, to intercalate the year in Babylonia," *The Talmud Yerushalmi and Greco-Roman Culture II,* ed. P. Schäfer (Tübingen: J. C. B. Mohr, 2000), 255–64; Isaiah Gafni, *Land, Center and Diaspora: Jewish Constructs of Antiquity* (Sheffield: Sheffield Academic Press, 1997), 109–10.

40. That they "went *up*" does not necessarily imply elevation. The Talmuds routinely use "go up" (*slq*) and "go down" (*nht*) as synonymns that simply mean "go."

41. bYev 16a; yYev 1:6, 3a.

42. The Bavli spells this out explicitly ("he was a man great in Torah"); in the Yerushalmi it is implied.

43. For additional sources, see Gafni, "Yeshiva and Metivta," 31; Goodblatt, *Rabbinic Instruction,* 68.

44. For the variants, see Goodblatt, *Rabbinic Instruction,* 78.

45. bMak 11b, bBQ 92a, bSot 7b. See Chap. 2, under "Objections and Solutions."

46. See Lev 13:1–3.

47. P. S. Alexander, "Bavli Berakhot 55a–57b: The Talmudic Dreambook in Context," *JJS* 46 (1995), 233 and nn. 6–7.

48. yMS 4:9, 55b–c.

49. See Patricia Cox Miller, *Dreams in Late Antiquity* (Princeton: Princeton University Press, 1998). This passage in fact cites a dictum of Rav Hisda: "A dream which is not interpreted is like a letter which is not read" (bBer 55b).

50. "Head of a Study-session" = *rosh livnei kallah.* There are a great many textual variants to both of these citations, and many manuscripts do not read "will become head of an academy." Ms M, for example, reads "will rise to greatness" in place of "will become head of an academy" (in the first citation). See Gafni, "Yeshiva and Metivta," 26 and nn. 70–71. So these attestations must be treated with caution. On the other hand, that the references to the "head of an academy" entered the text at a late date supports the claim that academies developed only in the post-Amoraic era.

51. Attributed to R. Shmuel b. Nahmani in the name of R. Yonatan; bBer 55b.

52. Or perhaps: "His position as head of the academy will be offered to you."

53. See Moshe Idel, *Kabbala: New Perspectives* (New Haven: Yale University Press, 1988), 156–57; 170–72. The term "universe maintaining activity" derives from Peter Berger and Thomas Luckman, *The Social Construction of Reality* (New York: Double-

day, 1966). On the development of the concept of Torah, see Jacob Neusner, *Torah: From Scroll to Symbol in Formative Judaism* (Atlanta: Scholars Press, 1988).

54. bPes 68b; bNed 32a; bAZ 3a. The verse means something quite different in context. See also the related concepts in bShab 88a (= bAZ 3a, 5a) and bTa 27b (= bMeg 31b).

55. *GenR* 1:1 (2) and 3:5 (20); *SifDeut* §37 (70) and §48 (114); mAvot 3:14; *ARNA* §39 (59b). See Louis Ginzberg, *Legends of the Jews* (Philadelphia: Jewish Publication Society, 1909–38), 5:5–6.

56. The traditions from bSanh 99b are not paralleled in Palestinian sources. The Palestinian version of the tradition from bMak 10a reads "More precious to me is the justice and righteousness that you (King David) do than sacrifices . . ." (yMQ 3:7, 83d and parallels). This difference again points to the Bavli's greater emphasis on Torah study. The traditions from bMeg 16b are attributed to Babylonians (Rav, Rabbah, Rav Gidel; see *DQS* ad loc.). There are no Palestinian parallels.

57. For comprehensive analysis, see Rubenstein, *Talmudic Stories*, 106–38.

58. yShev 9:1, 38d; *GenR* 79:6 (941–45); *PRK* §11 (191–94); *QohR* 10:8 (26b).

59. A different version of the tradition appears in *PRK* 4:7 (72): "R. Aha said: Matters that were not revealed to Moses were revealed to R. Akiba and his colleagues." There is no intimation that Moses would not have understood the discussions of R. Akiba and his students, no picture of an academy, and no paradoxical assertion that the same laws in fact have their source in the original revelation. The point is simply that there was an additional, later revelation.

60. Rashi, ad loc., s.v. *beneziqin,* explains that the earlier sages only studied the three *Bavot* tractates, not the entire Mishnaic Order.

61. Following Rashi, ad loc., s.v. *havayot.* The sense of this idiom is not completely clear.

62. See bShab 112b; bYom 9b; bEruv 53a; yDem 1:3, 21d; yTa 3:8, 66d. See Menachem Kellner, *Maimonides on the "Decline of the Generations" and the Nature of Rabbinic Authority* (Albany: State University of New York Press, 1996); Michael Berger, *Rabbinic Authority* (New York: Oxford University Press, 1998), 78–79.

63. Cf. bEruv 53a: "R. Yohanan stated: The heart of the ancients was like the entrance to the hall [of the temple]; that of the later [scholars] like the entrance to the sanctuary; and ours like the eye of a fine needle."

64. bTa 24a–b. The reference to Rav Yehuda makes more sense here, as the people tell Rabbah after the fruitless fast that Rav Yehuda's fasts worked. Yet here too the section interrupts Rabbah's direct response to the question. So the section may first have been added to this tradition and then transferred to the similar tradition of Rav Pappa and Abaye. The section also appears, with minor variations, in Rava's explanation as to why propounding legal problems, as did the great sages Doeg and

Ahitofel, is not necessarily a sign of moral excellence (bSanh 106b). Here too it has been interpolated before Rava's conclusion that "the Holy One requires the heart," i.e., God values those who are pious and God-fearing, not merely clever.

65. S. Brock, "From Antagonism to Assimilation: Syriac Attitudes to Greek Learning," *East of Byzantium: Syria and Armenia in the Formative Period*, ed. N. Garsoïan et al. (Washington, D.C.: Dumbarton Oaks, 1982), 17. I do not mean to create an artificial distinction between the "Hellenized" West and the non-Hellenized, Semitic East. All of the Near East was Hellenized to a certain degree. According to Brock, a great many Greek texts were translated into Syriac at this time.

66. Most scholars assume that the school had been founded by members of the school of Nisibis that had been closed when the city was ceded to the Persians by the Emperor Jovian in 363 C.E. If so, then the move to Nisibis was a return to its original location. See H. J. W. Drijvers, "The School of Edessa," *Centres of Learning: Learning and Location in Pre-Modern Europe and the Near East,* ed. H. J. W. Drijvers and A. MacDonald (Leiden: Brill, 1995), 50–51. On the debate concerning the exact date of the exodus from Edessa and the founding of the school, see Arthur Vööbus, *History of the School of Nisibis* (Louvain: Secretariat du CorpuSCO, 1965), 33–56.

67. A. Vööbus, *History of Asceticism in the Syrian Orient* (Louvain: Secretariat du CorpuSCO, 1960), 1:319–22.

68. G. J. Reinink, "'Edessa Grew Dim and Nisibis Shone Forth': The School of Nisibis at the Transition of the Sixth–Seventh Century," *Centres of Learning: Learning and Location in Pre-Modern Europe and the Near East,* ed. H. J. W. Drijvers and A. MacDonald (Leiden: Brill, 1995), 77–78. R. Macina, "Cassiodore et l'ecole de Nisibe," *Le Muséon* (1982), 131–66, traces the influence of the school's exegetical methods. See too George Foot Moore, "The Theological School at Nisibis," *Studies in the History of Religions presented to Crawford Howell Toy,* ed. D. G. Lyon and G. F. Moore (New York, 1912), 259: "Other schools were established, at Selucia for example, but none of them rivalled Nisibis, which was for two centuries or more the principal institution for the training of the clergy of Persia. . . . Its decline is coincident with the general decay of Christianity in the East, but only in the ninth century did it yield the preeminence to the school at Bagdad, the capital of the Califate."

69. Vööbus, *History of the School of Nisibis,* 60, 143; idem, "Abraham De-Bet Rabban and His Role in the Hermeneutic Traditions of the School of Nisibis," *Harvard Theological Review* 58 (1965), 204.

70. See Brock, "From Antagonism to Assimilation," 21 and n. 42. In Edessa the school had been a center of translation of Greek works into Syriac. See Drijvers, "The School of Edessa," 50–51. Most of this literature is unfortunately not extant.

71. Arthur Vööbus, *The Statutes of the School of Nisibis* (Stockholm, 1962).

72. Mar Barhadbeshabba Arbaya, "Cause de la fondation des écoles," ed. A. Scher, *Patrologia Orientalis* 4, no. 4 (Paris: Lefebvre, 1907), 327–97. There is some debate as

to exactly how the title should be translated. The Syriac is *'elta da-syam mawtba d-'eskule*. See Reinink, "The School of Nisibis," 82 n. 17 and Vööbus, *History of the School of Nisibis*, 142.

73. I. Gafni, "Nestorian Literature as a Source for the History of the Babylonian *Yeshivot*," *Tarbiz* 51 (1981–82), 571 (Hebrew); Goodblatt, *Rabbinic Instruction*, 79 n. 34 and 164 n. 16; Vööbus, *Statutes of the School of Nisibis*, 79 n. 30.

74. Gafni, "Nestorian Literature," 571; Goodblatt, *Rabbinic Instruction*, 164 n. 16; Vööbus, *History of the School of Nisibis*, 186–87; Vööbus, *Statutes of the School of Nisibis*, 77 and n. 20.

75. Gafni, "Nestorian Literature," 571–72 and n. 31. Some text witnesses read "do not appear at the school" or at the "study-house."

76. Gafni, "Nestorian Literature," 572–73, and references in n. 40. For example, bBB 22a relates, "Rav Nahman b. Yizhaq was a *resh kallah*." Geonic sources apply the title to a position within the academic hierarchy. See the excerpt from R. Nathan the Babylonian cited above.

77. Vööbus, *Statutes of the School of Nisibis*, 79; Gafni, "Nestorian Literature," 573.

78. Adam Becker, "Bringing the Heavenly Academy Down to Earth: Divine Pedagogy in the East-Syrian Tradition," *In Heaven as it is on Earth: Imagined Realms and Earthly Realities in Late Antique Religions*, ed. R. Abusch and Y. Reed (forthcoming); Reinink, "The School of Nisibis," 83–87. On the heavenly academy in the Bavli, see above in this chapter.

79. Shaye J. D. Cohen, "Patriarchs and Scholarchs," *Proceedings of the American Academy for Jewish Research* 48 (1981), 79–80. I discuss this story in Chap. 5, under "Lineage and the Academic Hierarchy."

80. Adam Becker, " 'The Cause of the Foundation of the Schools': The Development of Scholastic Culture in Late Antique Mesopotamia," (Ph.D. dissertation; Princeton: Princeton University, forthcoming); José I. Cabézon, "Introduction," *Scholasticism: Cross-cultural and Comparative Perspectives*, ed. José I. Cabézon (Albany: State University of New York Press, 1998, 4–8. See too L. Van Rompay, "The Christian Syriac Tradition of Interpretation," *Hebrew Bible / Old Testament* 1/1, ed. Magne Sabeo (Göttingen: Vandenhoeck & Ruprecht, 1996), 635–41.

81. See e.g. "The Story of the Wonderful and Divine Struggles of the Holy Mar Aba," *Histoire de Jabalaha et trois autres Patriarches*, ed. P. Bedjan (Paris, 1895), 211; John of Ephesus, *Lives of the Eastern Saints*, ed. E. W. Brooks (*Patrologia Orientalis* 18, no. 3; Paris: Firmin-Didot, 1923–25), 41.

82. For references see Aharon Oppenheimer, *Babylonia Judaica in the Talmudic Period* (Wiesbaden: Ludwig Reichert, 1983), 319 34. Some Patristics scholars have hazarded to suggest that the Christian academy was influenced by and patterned after this (putative) Jewish academy. See Macina, "Cassiodore," 151–52; J. B. Segal, *Edessa, the Blessed City* (Oxford: Clarendon Press, 1970), 150 n. 2. These scholars anachro-

nistically assume that Rabbinic academies existed in every Jewish community in late antiquity.

83. That is, the term "study-house" (*bet midrash*) is attested in (other) Palestinian traditions, where it refers to a small school. The Stammaim, who reworked the sources, think of the *bet midrash* as an academy, consistent with the descriptions found in late Bavli narratives.

Chapter 2. *Dialectics*

1. Cf. the story of R. Yohanan and Ilfa, bTa 21a. Ilfa proves his abilities by demonstrating his knowledge of *baraitot*. So dialectics is not the only possible way to demonstrate excellence in Torah.

2. See bBM 84b, cited below, and see bYom 78a, bHag 14a, bAZ 31b.

3. On the significance of shame in the Bavli, see Chap. 4.

4. Cf. bHor 14a, tYad 2:16 and tSot 7:9 (= bHag 3a; yHag 1:1, 75d; ySot 3:4, 18d).

5. In the continuation of the story both sages are again relegated to the ground for fear of the evil eye. The equal treatment irks R. Eleazar b. R. Shimon.

6. The Palestinian parallels lack the addendum; see n. 12 and Gafni, "Yeshiva and Metivta," 29.

7. bMak 11b. Parallels at bBQ 92a and bSot 7b. Certain manuscripts of the parallels read "conform his tradition to the law" (*salqa shmayta aliba dehilkheta*) in place of "solve an objection." These versions reflect different evaluations of the types of academic ability.

8. On the heavenly academy, see Chap. 1, "Heavenly Visions and Dreams."

9. bSanh 106b, parallel at bHag 15b. The phrase "and not one was resolved" is missing in the mss. Some mss of bHag 15b read "three hundred problems." Different mss attribute the tradition to R. Ammi, R. Asi, R. Abahu or Abaye. This tradition uses slightly different terminology: "problems" (*bayei*) and "resolved" (*ifshit*). R. Ammi and R. Asi are Palestinians, but there is no parallel in the Yerushalmi.

10. This line, however, is not found in all mss. See *DQS*, ad loc.

11. The Yerushalmi's account of Rav Kahana's arrival in the Land of Israel is so different that it cannot be considered a parallel version (yBer 2:8, 5c).

12. For Shimon bar Yohai, see yShev 9:1, 38d; *GenR* 79:6 (941–45); *PRK* §11 (191–94). For R. Eleazar b. R. Shimon and Rabbi, see *PRK* 11:18–25 (194–200) and yShab 10:5, 12c, cited below. For Judah's posthumous ban, see *GenR* 97:8 (1216), *SifDeut* §348 (406–7).

13. yBik 3:3, 65c. In the Yerushalmi there is no plot against Rabban Shimon b. Gamaliel. See Rubenstein, *Talmudic Stories*, 194–95.

14. See Ofra Meir, *Rabbi Judah the Patriarch: Palestinian and Babylonian Portrait of a Leader* (Tel-Aviv: Hakibbutz Hameuhad, 1999), 35–36 and n. 23 (Hebrew).

15. There is a slight variation here. Where *Ruth Rabbah* reads *meir panim bahalakha* (literally, "enlightens a face in law"), the Bavli reads *mareh panim bahalakha* (literally, "shows a face in law.") The idioms probably mean the same thing, to prove one's legal claims conclusively.

16. yBer 4:1, 7c; bBer 27b. See Chap. 5, under "Lineage and the Academic Hierarchy" for the full text.

17. See Chap. 5, under "Lineage and the Academic Hierarchy," for synoptic presentation of the texts.

18. For yet another comparative example, see David Rosenthal's analysis of the accounts of Hillel and the Passover (yPes 6:1, 33a; bPes 66a), "Mesorot erets-yisraeliot vedarkan lebavel," *Cathedra* 92 (1999), 33–36. In the Yerushalmi the Jerusalemites reject Hillel's proofs based on scriptural exegesis and logical deduction. They accept his ruling only when he appeals to tradition, that he heard the law from his teachers. In the Bavli they accept his proofs and immediately appoint him Nasi.

19. A proximate tradition, ySanh 4:2, 22a, mentions "forty-nine ways of interpreting the Torah [to prove] purity, and forty-nine ways of interpreting the Torah for impurity." A similar tradition appears in *PRK* 4:2 (56), *LevR* 26:2 (589).

20. The Bavli contains two traditions: "R. Abahu said in the name of R. Yohanan: R. Meir had a student named Symmachos who articulated forty-eight reasons for impurity on every matter of impurity, and forty-eight reasons for purity on every matter of purity. It was taught: There was a distinguished student at Yavneh who would [prove] that a reptile was pure with 150 reasons" (bEruv 13b).

21. However, here too the Bavli differs. Where the Yerushalmi simply mentions the large number of responses, the Bavli adds that Yonatan b. Harkinas "raised objections and stymied" Akiba (bYev 16a). For other large numbers of traditions in Palestinian sources, see tSanh 11:5 = ySanh 7:14, 25d.

22. Friedman, "La'aggada hahistorit," 119 63.

23. See p. 20.

24. David Goodblatt, "The Story of the Plot Against R. Simeon B. Gamaliel II," *Zion* 49 (1984), 362–67 (Hebrew). See too Rubenstein, *Talmudic Stories*, 176–77, 206–11.

25. See Rubenstein, *Talmudic Stories*, 206–11.

26. Ibid., 121–36. I have also argued for a late dating of the story of R. Meir and R. Natan, pp. 194–211.

27. See n. 6, this chapter.

28. See Chap. 8, under "Dialectics."

29. bBM 86a. See Introduction, under "The Stammaitic Innovation," and Halivni, *Midrash, Mishna, and Gemara*, 67–68.

30. This is not to deny that the Stammaim were interested in determining practical law, usually by adjudicating between Amoraic opinions (see Kahane, "Intimation of Intention and Compulsion of Divorce," 230–62), but legal adjudication was not their focus.

31. As mentioned in the Introduction, the Tannaim and Amoraim engaged in dialectical argumentation but did not consider it worthy of preservation. They primarily transmitted the conclusions of their legal debates, the final rulings. For the Stammaim argumentation was not only a means to an end, but an end in its own right.

32. See Introduction, "The Stammaitic Innovation."

33. H. Yalon, "PLL, PLPL in Hebrew and Aramaic," *Tarbiz* 6 (1935), 223–24 (Hebrew).

34. See e.g. bHul 110a; yTer 4:3, 42d.

35. bKet 103b, bBM 85b. Lest I be accused of translating to serve my interests, I have adopted the Soncino translation here (*Kethuboth,* trans. Israel Slotki [London: Soncino Press, 1936], 662.) The Yerushalmi parallel, yMeg 4:1, 74d, does not mention *pilpul.*

36. bTem 16a, Soncino translation (*Temurah,* trans. Isidore Epstein [London: Soncino Press, 1948), 110. This midrash is based on Josh 15:17.

37. See Rosenthal, "Mesorot erets-yisraeliot," 30–36.

38. yHor 3:5, 48c. For this translation see Marcus Jastrow, *A Dictionary of the Targumim, the Talmud Babli and Yerushalmi and the Midrashic Literature* (reprint, New York: Jastrow Publishers, 1967), 959, 1184.

39. *hu hapilpelan.* The translation is uncertain.

40. Cited by Rosenthal, "Mesorot erets-yisraeliot," 31.

41. So Rashi, bHor 14a, s.v. *sinai.*

42. Rashi, bHor 14a, s.v. *vehad:* "One who is sharp and analytical (*mefulpal*) in his Torah, even though his [knowledge of] Mishna and *baraita* is not so systematic."

43. bBB 145b. The *baraita* ranks a "master of aggadot," then a "dialectician" (*baal pilpul*), then a "master of traditions" (*baal shmuot*), and concludes: "All depend on the owner of wheat."

44. See too yShab 1:2, 3b, where R. Shimon bar Yohai is described as "sharp." And see Hezser, *Social Structure,* 255–56.

45. Rashi, bBM 85a, s.v. *delo.* Cf. bPes 34b for another disparagement of Babylonian study.

46. On the attitude to the *am ha'arets,* see Chap. 7. Rami's behavior evidently encountered some dissent. Rava claimed that Rami died for treating R. Menashiah in this manner (bBer 47b).

47. These passages are collected by Rosenthal in "Mesorot erets-yisraeliot," 33.

48. The term *pasaq,* "sever," also refers to punctuating Scripture. Abaye's interpretation depends upon a reorganization of the syntax, a "severing" of the words

from their places. Rava also uses this phrase in bMen 74a, although there he seems to disagree with Abaye's interpretation, perhaps implying that it is a little too clever.

49. The same phrase appears in a similar story at bYev 122a.

50. bBer 59b. I assume *bnei mahoza* refers to sages who hail from Mahoza. It can also be understood as the people in general. See too the saying "One sharp pepper is better than a basketful of pumpkins," applied to an irrefutable proof: bYom 85b, bMeg 7a, bHag 10a.

51. bBer 36a, bShab 7a, and 25 other times in the Bavli. For this translation see Jastrow, *Dictionary,* 1564, 1607. Others translate "Big-tooth" from *shen,* "tooth."

52. See too bBM 38b. Rav Sheshet remarks that the sages from Pumbedita "draw an elephant through the eye of a needle," i.e., they resort to ingenious, though forced, arguments.

53. The only attestation of which I am aware appears in yNid 2:6, 50b, where R. Hanina is described as a man who "knows that his iron tools are sharp," i.e., who is an expert in law. (For this translation see Michael Sokoloff, *A Dictionary of Jewish Palestinian Aramaic of the Byzantine Period* [Ramat-Gan: Bar Ilan University Press, 1990], 445.) However, R. Hanina explains to two colleagues that he always judges in accord with teachings that he heard directly from his master. Hence his "sharpness" relates to breadth of knowledge and the faithful transmission of teachings, not to sophisticated reasoning.

54. "Enemies of scholars" is a euphemism for the scholars themselves.

55. bTa 7b. Parallel traditions: bBer 63b, bMak 10a. These traditions appear in different order in some mss. See Henry Malter, *The Treatise Ta'anit of the Babylonian Talmud* (New York: American Academy for Jewish Research, 1930), 21 (Hebrew).

56. See Hezser, *Social Structure,* 351–52, who considers study with a partner the norm in Palestine.

57. y'Ta 3:10, 66d.

58. *GenR* 69:2 (791).

59. In a story found at yShev 8:5, 38b, R. Yose bar Halafta tells R. Yehuda of Huzi that the reason he could not understand the law was that he "did not study with his colleagues."

Chapter 3. *Violence*

1. For apologetic attempts to smooth over the enmity between sages in an effort to portray them as courteous and gracious, see Ephraim Urbach, *The Sages: Their Concepts and Beliefs,* trans. I. Abrahams (Jerusalem: Magnes, 1979), 620–27, who cites many of the relevant sources.

2. yBer 2:9, 5d. The story is abbreviated in yBB 5:1, 15a.

3. This anecdote is preceded by a similar story involving different sages, in which

the students, R. Yohanan b. Beroka and R. Eleazar b. Hisma, do say "We are your disciples and we drink your waters" before informing their master. The Bavli's version of the story of R. Yose b. Durmaskit seems to have lacked this polite response. The redactors added R. Eliezer's brutal order to provide a sharp contrast to the similar anecdote about R. Yohanan b. Beroka and R. Eleazar b. Hisma. The *sugya* subsequently explains that R. Yohanan b. Beroka and R. Eleazar b. Hisma responded with such deference "on account of what happened," i.e., to avoid the sad fate of R. Yose b. Durmaskit. (The removal of an eye appears in a very different context in ySanh 6:6, 23c.)

4. Another insulting play on a name is found at bQid 25a.

5. yBB 5:5, 15a–b. See Catherine Hezser, *Form, Function and Historical Significance of the Rabbinic Story in Yerushalmi Neziqin* (Tübingen: J. C. B. Mohr, 1993), 174–77.

6. The tradition is attributed to R. Yohanan, but there is no parallel in Palestinian sources.

7. Rashi, bYev 84a, s.v. *shel,* comments: "They were knowledgeable and sharp, and they did not tolerate an unfamiliar cock among them."

8. The wood of olive trees tastes bitter. This tradition supplies the title of an article by Israel Ben-Shalom, " 'And I Took Unto me Two Staves: the One I Called Beauty and the Other I called Bands' (*Zach. 11:7*)," *Dor-Le-Dor: From the End of Biblical Times up to the Redaction of the Talmud. Studies in Honor of Joshua Efron,* ed. A. Oppenheimer and A. Kasher (Jerusalem: Bialik, 1995), 215–34 (Hebrew), which collects examples of hostile representations in the Bavli that do not appear in parallel Palestinian sources.

9. R. Oshayya and R. Yizhaq are Palestinians, although this tradition appears only in the Bavli. See too the previous passage where Rav Papa remarks that Palestinian scholars "cherish one another," and the Bavli brings two examples of their courteous behavior.

10. bNaz 49b = bQid 52b.

11. Rashi, bGit 29b, s.v. *qaphinhu.* The three rabbis "were embarrassed" when Rav Safra made his statement. See Chap. 4 on the significance of shame in the Bavli. That the Bavli presents two alternative versions of this event suggests that both have been influenced by the redactors.

12. bBM 59a–b; yMQ 3:1, 81c–d.

13. bRH 13a; bSanh 30b.

14. Cf. bSanh 68a, where R. Eliezer says to the sages who visit him upon his deathbed, "I would be surprised if these die a natural death."

15. For extensive treatment of this text, see Daniel Boyarin, *Unheroic Conduct: The Rise of Heterosexuality and the Invention of the Jewish Man* (Berkeley: University of California Press, 1997), 127–50. For evidence that this is a late source, see Friedman, "La'aggada hahistorit," 119–32.

16. This has been noted by Boyarin in *Unheroic Conduct,* 147–48.

17. R. Yohanan and Resh Laqish were Palestinians, but here they are fictional characters constructed by Babylonian storytellers.

18. See too the description of the deterioration of the relationship between Rav Huna and Rav Hisda, bBM 33a.

19. This is noted by Ben-Shalom, "And I Took Unto me Two Staves," 239–40. See Deut 25:11 and the Targums there; Sokoloff, *Dictionary,* 359; Jastrow, *Dictionary,* 928; Jacob Levy, *Wörterbuch über die Talmudim und Midraschim* (Berlin: B. Harz, 1924), 3:247.

20. The same term is used by Resh Laqish in bSanh 108b. I have not found this term in the Yerushalmi, although the term "defeat" is occasionally used for victory in argumentation. See ySanh 7:11, 25c.

21. David Kraemer, *Stylistic Characteristics of Amoraic Literature* (Ph.D. diss., Jewish Theological Seminary, 1984), 94, 141.

22. Ibid.

23. See the sources in the next paragraph, and see *SifDeut* §321 (370); *GenR* 54:1 (576); *LevR* 30:1 (687).

24. Parallel in bSanh 111b. Although these two traditions are attributed to Palestinians, neither is paralleled in Palestinian sources.

25. bMak 11b. See p. 43.

26. bSanh 93b. See p. 45.

27. bShab 63a; Rashi, s.v. *bedivrei.*

28. S.v. *naasu.*

29. Cf. bBM 33b, where "scholars" (*talmidei hakhamim*) are said to hate sages who specialize in study of Mishna. See too bYom 22b–23a and bShab 63a, where scholars are said to take vengeance like snakes.

30. bBer 27b, s.v. *baalei.*

31. See Chap. 1, under "The Academic Setting."

32. In this case the violence is more pronounced in the Yerushalmi: "R. Yehoshua Onaya taught: Students of the House of Shammai stood below and were killing those of the House of Hillel. It was taught: Six of them went up and the rest stood upon them with swords and spears" (yShab 1:4, 3c). Here, however, the violence is real. It is not the verbal violence of argumentation. See too Hezser, *Social Structure,* 243–44.

33. Quintilian advises that a young lawyer prepare for court by writing out practice speeches, "training himself with the real weapons of his warfare, just as gladiators do"; X.v.20; trans. H. E. Butler (Cambridge, Mass: Harvard University Press, 1936), 125. Philostratus reports of the sophist Polemo: "[O]n seeing a gladiator dripping with sweat out of sheer terror of the life-and-death struggle before him, he remarked: 'You are in as great an agony as though you were going to declaim'"; Philo-

stratus, *The Lives of the Sophists,* §541, in Philostratus and Eunapius, *The Lives of the Sophists,* trans. W. C. Wright (London: William Heinemann, 1921), 129–31. See too Eunapius, *The Lives of the Philosophers,* §490, pp. 497–99 and §491, p. 503. And see Stanley F. Bonner, *Education in Ancient Rome* (Berkeley: University of California Press, 1977), 73, 324, 326.

34. For evidence that the redactors worked in an oral milieu, see Elman, "Orality and the Babylonian Talmud," 52–99, esp. 58–61. On rabbinic orality in general, see Saul Lieberman, "The Publication of the Mishnah," in *Hellenism in Jewish Palestine* (New York: Jewish Theological Seminary, 1950), 83–99; Birger Gerhardsson, *Memory and Manuscript: Oral Tradition and Written Transmission in Rabbinic Judaism and Early Christianity,* trans. E. J. Sharpe (Lund: Gleerup, and Copenhagen: Munksgaard, 1961); and Martin Jaffee's studies in n. 37.

35. In many cases the sages disagree over the "text" of a Mishna or *baraita,* yet they never appeal to a written copy to settle the issue. See Lieberman, "Publication of the Mishnah," 87.

36. Ibid., 87–88.

37. Martin S. Jaffee, "Writing and Rabbinic Oral Tradition: On Mishnaic Narrative, Lists and Mnemonics," *Journal of Jewish Thought and Philosophy* 4 (1994), 123–46; Jaffee, "How Much 'Orality' in Oral Torah? New Perspectives on the Composition and Transmission of Early Rabbinic Traditions," *Shofar* 10 (1992), 212–33; and see now Jaffee's new work, *Torah in the Mouth: Writing and Oral Tradition in Palestinian Judaism 200 BCE–400 CE* (New York: Oxford University Press, 2001).

38. Yaakov Elman, "Pervasive Orality in Talmudic Babylonia" (paper presented at the AAR/SBL convention, New Orleans, 1996); Brody, *Geonim,* 156–61.

39. Walter J. Ong, *Orality and Literacy: The Technologizing of the Word* (London: Routledge, 1982), 43–46.

40. For some examples, see Chap. 8, under "Violence and Shame."

41. Cited in yYev 1:6, 3a. See too tAh 18:18.

42. See too yKil 1:6, 27a.

43. For one possible example of physical violence attested in Palestinian sources, see ySheq 3:2, 47c (= ySheq 8:1, 51a = yShab 8:1, 11a). R. Bibi kicked (*ba'it*) R. Yizhaq b. Kahana when the latter asked him a question. However, the story continues with R. Zeriqa asking R. Bibi why he kicked someone simply for asking a question, and R. Bibi explaining, "I had no sense in me." So this case appears to have been an aberration. In addition, the term *ba'it* sometimes means, "to disdain, to be contemptuous of," so perhaps R. Bibi expressed disdain for R. Yizhaq and did not strike him. See Sokoloff, *Dictionary,* 107. See too yHor 2:5, 46d: when R. Shimon b. R. Yose bar Laqonia misunderstood a question asked by R. Yohanan, believing it to be obvious, he "picked up a stone to throw at him." However, after R. Yohanan clarified his question, the two of them set out together to find an answer. The Bavli version of this en-

counter, bShevu 18b, is predictably more violent. Here the sage actually throws a clod of earth at his interlocutor. See too bPes 62b where R. Yohanan throws a clod at R. Simlai for asking to learn a certain topic in too brief a time span.

44. See Elman, "Orality and the Babylonian Talmud," 71–73. See too Y. Elman and I. Gershoni, "Introduction," and Paul Mandel, "Between Byzantium and Islam: The Transmission of a Jewish Book in the Byzantine and Early Islamic Periods," both published in *Transmitting Jewish Traditions: Orality, Textuality, and Cultural Diffusion*, ed. Y. Elman and I. Gershoni (New Haven: Yale University Press, 2000), 9–11 and 97–98.

45. See Mary Boyce, *Zoroastrians: Their Religious Beliefs and Practices* (London: Routledge & Kegan Paul, 1979), 134–38.

46. See Chap. 2, under "*Pilpul.*"

47. See e.g. yTa 4:8, 69b, where engaging in the "wars of Torah" simply means devotion to Torah study. To the best of my knowledge, only in one instance does the Yerushalmi compare rabbinic debate to war. In yPes 6:3, 33b, which comments on the unusually sharp debate between R. Eliezer and R. Akiba in mPes 6:2 (see above), R. Yehoshua cites Jgs 9:38 to R. Eliezer, "There is the army you sneered at; now go out and fight it." In other words, R. Eliezer must now "fight" with R. Akiba's sharp responses to his position. But this pales in comparison to the violence depicted in the Bavli's reworking of the story.

48. The Yerushalmi contains sharp and caustic remarks, but they are generally not described or thematized as violent. See e.g. R. Zeira's sarcastic response, yQid 3:9, 64b. And see tBer 5:2, cited in yPes 10:1, 37b; tHag 2:12, cited in yBes 2:5, 61c. I am aware of only one instance in which "defeat" is used of legal debate between sages; yKet 3:9. 27d. Even there, however, Rav claims that although R. Yaakov b. Abba "defeated" him in debate (*din*), the law (*halakha*) follows his own opinion!

49. Parallels at yYev 1:6, 3b; ySot 3:4, 19a.

50. The entire tradition appears in Hebrew, attributed to R. Abba in the name of Shmuel. However, in light of the Yerushalmi parallel, both the question and answer would appear to be a Stammaitic addition.

51. The famous story of the encounters between Hillel, Shammai, and the converts teaches the same lesson, though not in the context of legal debate (bShab 31a). When the prospective convert made unreasonable demands, Shammai "rebuked him and dismissed him with a reproach" and "drove him away with the builder's cubit that was in his hand." The explicit didactic point is that "one should always be a gentle man (*anvetan*) like Hillel and never be an impatient man (*qapdan*) like Shammai." See too n. 8 of this chapter.

52. A proximate tradition, attributed to Rav Mattena, states: "If one makes himself like the wilderness, upon which everyone treads, then his learning will be preserved" (bEruv 54a).

53. bSuk 29b; bHul 89a; bMeg 31a; bBer 16b; bNid 20b; bShab 30b–31a; yShab 1:3, 3c; yTa 3:10, 66d; yPe 1:1, 16b.

Chapter 4. *Shame*

1. The purpose of intercalating the year was to decide whether to add a leap-month (Second Adar) so that the festivals would fall in the proper seasons.

2. The story is brought in the context of a Talmudic discussion of the laws of intercalation. It follows the ruling found in the preceding *baraita* that the intercalation may only be conducted by those sages explicitly invited for that purpose. While the primary function of the story is to exemplify that law, it simultaneously teaches a lesson about ideal rabbinic character.

3. See Introduction, under "The Stammaitic Innovation," and Friedman, *Pereq ha'isha rabba babavli*, 301–2.

4. The *sugya* at bSanh 11a continues with stories of other rabbis and biblical figures who, like Samuel the Little, implicated themselves in the wrongdoing so as not to shame the true offenders. This is clearly an important aspect of the Bavli's ethical vision.

5. That is, the fates of Jews are not determined by the stars (horoscopes).

6. An "unusual death" is a premature or accidental death. Even the most righteous eventually die. The point is that they do not die prematurely ("an unusual death") nor do they live merely a normal lifespan ("death itself") but enjoy extreme longevity.

7. Rashi, bShab 156b, s.v. *betarti*.

8. Although it is sometimes cynically remarked that a "well-known" story is a story with which one happens to be familiar, in this case I think it is justified to describe the story as "well-known," at least in modern times. Almost every book of modern theology mentions the story, and there are now review articles summarizing scholarly treatments: Izhaq England, "Majority Decision vs. Individual Truth: The Interpretations of the 'Oven of Achnai' Aggadah," *Tradition* 15 (1975), 137–52 ("The 'Oven of Akhnai': Various Interpretations of an Aggada," *Annual of the Institute for Research in Jewish Law 1* [1974], 45–57 [Hebrew]); Suzanne Last Stone, "In Pursuit of the Counter-Text: The Turn to the Jewish Legal Model in Contemporary American Legal Theory," *Harvard Law Review* 106 (1993), 813–94.

9. For comprehensive analysis of the story, see Ari Elon, *Hasimbolizatsia shel markivei ha'alila basipur hatalmudi* (Master's thesis, Hebrew University, 1982), and Rubenstein, *Talmudic Stories*, 34–63.

10. The oven is made of alternating sections of clay and sand, thus resembling the coils of a snake (*akhna*).

11. The Mishna gives the examples of reminding a penitent of his former sins, mentioning to a proselyte the ways of his ancestors, and asking the price of an object when one has no intention to buy (disappointing the shopkeeper).

12. yMQ 3:1, 81c–d.

13. See the previous note.

14. Rubenstein, *Talmudic Stories,* 51–60. The traditions that precede the sugya mentioned above are attributed to Amoraim (mostly Babylonian Amoraim) and appear to be authentic Amoraic traditions. Note that these traditions mention shame in general, not shame in an academic context. In this respect they more closely resemble Palestinian sources on shame (see below) than Stammaitic traditions, which warn against shame within the academic setting.

15. Modern scholars, by contrast, focus on the first half of the Bavli and issues of rabbinic interpretive authority—most contemporary readings ignore the tragic turn in the second half, as well as the redactional context.

16. Chap. 1, under "The Academic Setting."

17. This is the reading in ms M.

18. Rashi, bHul 6a, s.v. *ve'im.* See too bMQ 16b, the episode of Zutra b. Tuvia.

19. See Rashi, bBM 20a, s.v. *mar* and s.v. *umar.*

20. For detailed discussion, see Rubenstein, *Talmudic Stories,* 176–211.

21. The portrayal of the Nasi as the head of the academy is an anachronism. The story projects the Babylonian reality onto the Tannaitic setting.

22. On Honi, see also Chap. 2, under "Study-Partners."

23. See the classic essay of Julian Pitt-Rivers, "Honour and Social Status," *Honour and Shame: The Values of Mediterranean Society,* ed. John G. Peristiany (1966; Chicago: University of Chicago Press, 1974), 27: "Public opinion forms therefore a tribunal before which the claims to honour are brought, 'the court of reputation' as it has been called, and against its judgements there is no redress. For this reason it is said that public ridicule kills."

24. See p. 18.

25. See too bYev 62b: "R. Akiba had 12,000 pairs of students . . . and they all died at the same time because they did not treat each other with honor."

26. The text is cited according to ms M and the parallel at bBM 59a. The midrash is attributed to Rava.

27. See bBM 33a for another example in which a rabbi interprets a question from his disciple as a covert personal attack and feels ashamed.

28. See Chap. 3, under "The Violence of Debate."

29. bBQ 117a; see p. 39. Note again the deterrent against difficult questions.

30. Ms M reads, "that you neither be shamed nor feel ashamed [yourself]."

31. See Chap. 3, under "Orality and Violence."

32. See John G. Peristiany, ed., *Honour and Shame: The Values of Mediterranean Society* (Chicago: University of Chicago Press, 1974 [1966]); David D. Gilmore, *Honor and Shame and the Unity of the Mediterranean* (Washington, D.C.: American Anthropological Association, 1987); David A. deSilva, "The Wisdom of Ben Sira:

Honor, Shame and Cultural Values of a Minority Culture," *Catholic Biblical Quarterly* 58 (1996), 433–55; Joseph Plevnick, "Honor / Shame," *Biblical Social Values and Their Meaning*, ed. J. Pilch and B. Malina (Peabody, Mass.: Hendrickson Publishers, 1993), 95–103.

33. See yPe 8:9, 21b; yHor 3:4, 48a; yKet 4:8, 28d; yBQ 8:6, 6c; yHag 2:2, 77d. The Mishna lists *boshet* (shame) as one of the damages paid in cases of personal injury (mBQ 8:1; mKet 3:4). mBQ 8:6 tells a story of a man who shamed a woman by exposing her hair in public and received a steep fine. See too mSot 1:6; ySot 3:8, 19b. Sin also brought shame upon the transgressor; tSot 4:2; yShab 9:3, 12a.

34. See e.g. yQid 1:6, 61b.

35. yPe 8:9, 21b; ySanh 6:3, 23c.

36. *LamR* 4:2, ed. Buber, 71b–72a. Geniza fragments are published in Zvi Rabinowitz, *Ginzei midrash* (Tel-Aviv: Rosenberg School for Jewish Studies, 1976), 153–54.

37. The closest source I can find is yNed 10:10, 42b. R. Hiyya b. Abba plans on leaving the Land of Israel to earn a living and seeks a letter of introduction from R. Yudan Nesia. Two versions of the letter are given. According to one, R. Yudan wrote, "Behold, we send you a great man, who is not ashamed to say, 'I have not heard [the answer].'" But clearly this is neither an academic setting nor similar to the Bavli sources cited above. The term *b'ish* in ySheq 3:2, 47c (= ySheq 8:1, 51a = yShab 8:1, 11a) should be translated "displeasing" not "ashamed" (Sokoloff, *Dictionary*, 83.) R. Eliezer was "displeased" that R. Simon did not answer him, not ashamed.

38. bBQ 117a, bBM 59a–b, bHor 13b–14a, bYev 105b, bTa 23a.

39. bBM 84a, bBM 84b.

Chapter 5. *Lineage and Rabbinic Leadership*

1. R. Hiyya's lineage was therefore inferior, hence it was not fitting that Rabbi's son marry into that family. Rabbi's final remark does not appear in all mss. See *DQS,* ad loc.

2. See Shulamit Valler, *Woman and Womanhood in the Stories of the Babylonian Talmud,* trans. Betty Rozen (Atlanta: Scholars Press, 1999), 65.

3. On the importance of lineage in Babylonia see Lewi Freund, "Über Genealogien und Familienreinheit in biblischer und talmudischer Zeit," *Festschrift Adolf Schwarz,* ed. S. Krauss (Berlin: R. Löwit, 1917), 175–92; Raphael Yankelevitch, "Mishqalo shel hayihus hamishpahti behevra hayehudit be'erets-yisrael bitequfat hamishna," *Uma vetoldoteha,* ed. M. Stern (Jerusalem: Shazar Institute, 1983), 156–62; Gafni, *The Jews of Babylonia,* 121–25; idem, "Expressions and Types of 'Local Patriotism' among the Jews of Babylonia," *Irano-Judaica II,* ed. S. Shaked and A. Netzer (Jerusalem: Yad Izhaq Ben-Zvi, 1990), 63–72; Kalmin, *The Sage in Jewish Society,* 115–33; idem, "Genealogy

and Polemics," *HUCA* 67 (1996), 77–94; Michael Satlow, *Jewish Marriage in Antiquity* (Princeton: Princeton University Press, 2001), 142–61.

4. See Deut 24:1 and mGit 9:10.

5. For this etymology, see Levy, *Wörterbuch,* 1:451–52, s.v. *hagan.* This usage seems clear from bQid 70a: "Whoever marries a woman who is not fit (*hogenet*) for him — Elijah binds him and the Holy One lashes him. And it was taught: Concerning all of them Elijah writes and the Holy One signs, 'Woe to him who invalidates (*posel*) his seed, and blemishes (*pogem*) his family.'" A partner who is "not fit" is equated with "invalid" and "blemished" offspring. This points to more than a character flaw. See too bBB 120a; bKet 28b; yQid 1:5, 60c.

6. See Levy, *Wörterbuch,* 1:452; *GenR* 48:9 (486).

7. Thus bQid 70b suggests that priests of arrogant character have tainted pedigree. Similarly, bQid 71b advises that a peaceful disposition indicates pure pedigree.

8. Chap. 1, under "The Academic Setting."

9. The High Priest had to remain awake throughout the night of Yom Kippur. Priests and sages read to him from the lesser-known books of the Bible to keep him attentive.

10. The Mishna itself need not be read this way. Zecharia could have been a Pharisee or sage who (in the rabbinic imagination) directed the priests. But the storyteller seems to have considered him a priest, as the phrase "served in the temple" usually refers to worship.

11. See Aharon Hyman, *Toledot tannaim ve'amoraim* (London, 1910; reprint, Jerusalem, 1964), 732, 781, 949.

12. See, however, the story in yQid 3:4, 64a, where R. Yose b. Kefar and R. Dosetai b. R. Yannai go to Babylonia to collect money.

13. See Yankelevitch, "Mishqalo shel hayihus," 152–54.

14. A *mamzer* is the product of an adulterous or incestuous relationship, and may not marry a Jew of "untainted lineage."

15. The Palestinian version of this source again points to differences between the two rabbinic cultures (yKet 2:10, 26d). In the Yerushalmi the ceremony takes place when a man either sells his ancestral field or marries a woman who is not fitting for him. Upon breaking the casks, the relatives say, "So-and-so is cut off from his family." The Yerushalmi adds that if he buys the land back or divorces the woman the relatives say, "So-and-so has returned to his ancestral field / family." In this context the "woman who is not fitting" probably means a woman from a different clan or tribe. The source reflects the ancient prejudice that both land and marriages should be kept within the tribe or family unit. No mention is made of descendants. The point is to "cut off" or stigmatize the culprit, rather than his offspring, as in the Bavli. For the Yerushalmi divorce resolves the problem. The Bavli does not mention divorce, as dis-

solution will not help in cases where the union has produced children, who will carry the taint forever. See Satlow, *Jewish Marriage in Antiquity,* 152–53.

16. bQid 71b–72a.

17. Ibid. See Gafni, "Expressions and Types of 'Local Patriotism,'" 63–72.

18. bQid 70b. The Bavli attributes this tradition to R. Hama b. Hanina, a Palestinian, but it is not found in the Yerushalmi and reflects Bavli values.

19. See Yankelevitch, "Mishqalo shel hayihus," 156–62.

20. Many of the early sages were of priestly descent; see Seth Schwartz, *Josephus and Judaean Politics* (Leiden: Brill, 1990), 100–105; Hezser, *Social Structure,* 70–71.

21. See e.g. the story of R. Berakhia, yQid 3:12, 64c. On the other hand, *GenR* 37:7 (349) suggests that "we no longer know our pedigrees."

22. I am grateful to Michael Satlow for this insight.

23. See Gafni, *The Jews of Babylonia,* 126–29; Kalmin, *The Sage in Jewish Society,* 115–33; Ehsan Yarshater, "Introduction," and "Iranian National History," *The Cambridge History of Iran,* xxxvii–xlii and 393–411; Arthur Christenson, "Sassanid Persia," *The Cambridge Ancient History,* vol. 12, ed. S. A. Cook et al. (Cambridge: Cambridge University Press, 1956), 114–18.

24. E. Benveniste, "Les Classes Sociales dans la Tradition Avestique," *Journal Asiatique* 121 (1932), 117–34.

25. Yarshater, "Iranian National History," 397–98.

26. Yarshater, "Introduction," xl.

27. Yarshater, "Iranian National History," 406.

28. Similar polemics may be attested in rabbinic sources. In bQid 70a–b, Shmuel, who claimed priestly lineage, impugns the ancestry of other priests claiming Hasmonean descent. See Geoffrey Herman, *Hakohanim bebavel bitequfat hatalmud* (Master's thesis, Hebrew University, 1998), 115–18, and Kalmin, *The Sage in Jewish Society,* 134–47.

29. In 212 C.E. Roman citizenship was granted to all freeborn inhabitants of the empire. This edict mainly codified a process of expansion of citizenship that had been progressing for some time. See William V. Harris, "On the Applicability of the Concept of Class in Roman History," *Forms of Control and Subordination in Antiquity,* ed. T. Yuge and M. Doi (Leiden: Brill, 1988), 598–610; R. Macmullen, *Roman Social Relations, 50 B.C. to A.D. 284* (New Haven: Yale University Press, 1974), 88–120.

30. The clearest explicit engagement with this question appears in *ARNA* §3 (7b–8a): "For the House of Shammai say: One should only teach [a student] who is wise and humble and of noble lineage (*ben avot*) and rich. But the House of Hillel say: Let him teach every one." Unfortunately, the date and provenance of *Avot derabbi natan* are in doubt. See too *ARNA* §40 (64a). In "Torah Study for All or for the Elite Alone," *Synagogues in Antiquity,* ed. A. Kasher et al. (Jerusalem: Yad Izhaq Ben-Zvi, 1987), 105 (Hebrew), Israel Ben-Shalom considers these traditions to be post-

Talmudic pseudepigraphs. See there p. 97 n. 2 for references to scholars who accepted the historicity of the traditions and on that basis made claims concerning aristocratic tendencies among the sages.

31. I. Sonne, "The Paintings of the Dura Synagogue," *HUCA* 20 (1947), 272 n. 22. Dura-Europos, located on the Euphrates, on the border of the Roman and Persian empires, had been possessed alternately by Parthians and Romans until its destruction in 256 C.E. For detailed discussion of Iranian themes in the paintings, see Bernard Goldman, "The Iranian Element in the Dura Synagogue Murals," *Irano-Judaica IV,* ed. S. Shaked and A. Netzer (Jerusalem: Yad Izhaq Ben-Zvi, 1999), 298–310.

32. See Reuven Kimmelman, "The Conflict between the Priestly Oligarchy and the Sages in the Talmudic Period," *Zion* 48 (1983), 135–48 (Hebrew).

33. Herman, *Hakohanim bebavel.*

34. Ibid., 85–92.

35. Ibid., 89–90. See too bPes 49a on sages marrying into priestly families. The attributions there may be suspect. See Stephen G. Wald, *BT Pesahim III: Critical Edition with Comprehensive Commentary* (New York: Jewish Theological Seminary, 2000), 215–20.

36. Rav Hisda was a priest; Rav Papa and Rav Yeimar married daughters of priests.

37. Rabba bar Nahmani, Abaye, Rav Kahana, and Rav Aha b. Rabba were priests. Rav Yehuda and Rava were nonpriests who married daughters of priests.

38. On the rise of academies, see Chap. 1. The focus on these sages of course simultaneously informs us of the values of the Geonim: they claimed for their predecessors sages with priestly lineage.

39. bGit 59b. Herman, *Hakokanim bebavel,* 92–93.

40. Ginzberg, *Geonica,* 10–20; Avraham Grossman, "From Father to Son: The Inheritance of the Spiritual Leadership of the Jewish Communities in the Early Middle Ages," *Zion* 50 (1985), 199–201 (Hebrew). See too the list of the succession of Geonim in Brody, *Geonim,* 344–45. Brody indicates which Geonim claimed priestly and Levitical descent.

41. Several of the other putative heads of academies claimed Davidic lineage: Rav, Rav Huna, and Rav Nahman. See Herman, *Hakohanim bebavel,* 91.

42. bMen 53a, cited in Herman, *Hakohanim bebavel,* 91. See the following note for textual comments. While R. Preda is apparently Palestinian, this story appears only in the Bavli and reflects Babylonian values.

43. However, some manuscripts read, "If he is the offspring of nobility and a scholar, *that is well*" (*yae*) in place of "that is even better" (*yae veyae*). I think this reading resulted from a scribal omission of the repeated word and it should be seen as a corruption. If authentic, this textual tradition may imply that distinguished pedigree confers no advantage. Whether one is simply a scholar or a scholar with pedigree, "that is well." For this interpretation, see Urbach, *Sages,* 639. The different textual

traditions themselves may reflect different perspectives on the value of lineage relative to Torah.

44. The translation follows Gafni, "Expressions and Types of 'Local Patriotism,'" 68–69.

45. Pum Nahara was close to Harpanya (= Neharphanya). See ibid., 68; Oppenheimer, *Babylonia Judaica*, 368–71 and n. 2.

46. See Chap. 4, under "Shame and the Late Babylonian Academy." For discussion of the Babylonian coloring of the story, see Goodblatt, "The Story of the Plot," 349–74. For comprehensive analysis see Rubenstein, *Talmudic Stories*, 176–212.

47. Elsewhere I have suggested that the Nasi in this story may represent the Exilarch or his appointee, who functioned as the head of the academy, at least nominally. In later times Exilarchs appointed Geonim and occasionally served as Geonim / heads of the academy themselves. See Rubenstein, *Talmudic Stories*, 206–11.

48. See Nathan b. Yehiel of Rome (citing Sherira Gaon), *Sefer arukh hashalem*, ed. A. Kohut (Vienna, 1878–92), 7:127; Jacob Neusner, *A History of the Jews in Babylonia* (Leiden: Brill, 1965–70; reprint, Chico, Calif.: Scholars Press, 1984), 1:74–79; Shaul Shaked, "Items of Dress and Other Objects in Common Use: Iranian Loanwords in Jewish Babylonian Aramaic," *Irano-Judaica III*, eds. S. Shaked and A. Netzer (Jerusalem: Yad Izhaq Ben-Zvi, 1994), 110–11.

49. "Precedes" pertains to the allocation of scarce resources, such as provision of sustenance and clothing, return of lost objects, redemption from captivity, and prevention of degradation.

50. The term "rule" (*malakh*) is the typical term used by late Talmudic and Geonic sources for the authority of the head of the academy (*rosh yeshiva*). It is applied anachronistically to the third generation Amoraim Rabbah and Rav Yosef in this passage. As we have argued in Chap. 1, academies did not develop until the post-Amoraic era. From the context, it appears that the "head" speaks first at a small gathering of sages. See Neusner, *A History of the Jews in Babylonia*, 4:93–97; Goodblatt, *Rabbinic Instruction*, 249; Hezser, *Social Structure*, 286–87.

51. On the late dating, see Rubenstein, *Talmudic Stories*, 176–77, 195–211.

52. For discussion see Ofra Meir, "The Story of Rabbi's Death: A Study of Modes of Traditions' Redaction," *Jerusalem Studies in Hebrew Literature* 12 (1990), 147–77 (Hebrew); Cohen, "Patriarchs and Scholarchs," 74–85; Martin Jacobs, *Die Institution des Jüdischen Patriarchen* (Tübingen: J. C. B. Mohr, 1995), 70–77.

53. yKet 12:3, 34d. The parallel in yKil 9:4, 32a contains minor differences that are not germane to our purposes.

54. yTa 4:2, 68a.

55. See G. Alon, "Those Appointed for Money," *Jews, Judaism and the Classical World*, trans. I. Abrahams (Jerusalem: Magnes, 1977), 374–435; Hezser, *Social Structure*, 425–28.

56. At most there is an implication, based on Rabbi's instruction to his son, that his son would take his place.

57. See Goodblatt, "The Story of the Plot," 368.

58. R. Levi was lame; bSuk 53a, bTa 25a. R. Shimon means that he may have possessed such outstanding qualities that he deserved the top position were it not for a specific directive. Thus, it was indeed "necessary to state this."

59. Ms M reads "tradition of wisdom" (*mesoret hokhma*); ms Vatican reads "traditions of wisdom." On the meaning of this phrase see Cohen, "Patriarchs and Scholarchs," 80 and n. 56.

60. "High-handedly" translates *beramim*. Some text witnesses read "with blood" (*bedamim*).

61. See e.g. Yosef Hazan, *Responsa Heqrei lev, Yoreh deah,* part 3, #100: "It is well known that the Nasi was the head of the academy."

62. See Chap. 1.

63. For this interpretation see Goodblatt, "The Story of the Plot," 362–67, and the references in n. 46.

64. The discussion also objects, "Was not R. Hiyya there?," i.e., Why did Rabbi appoint R. Hanina b. Hama to an important position when R. Hiyya, a superior scholar, was alive? This objection assumes that the "Head" is an office.

65. See n. 49 of this chapter.

66. Goodblatt, "The Story of the Plot," 370 and n. 73. Cf. Brody, *Geonim,* 49.

67. The term Levi uses, *tsrikha lemeimar* ("Was it necessary to state this?") appears thirty-one times in the Bavli, all in the Stammaitic stratum. (Twenty-six are unambiguously Stammaitic; the other five appear in what are most likely Stammaitic extensions of briefer Amoraic dicta. Four of these gloss statements of Rava [bYev 70a, bYev 88b, Naz 63b, Nid 51a], and one glosses a statement of Rav Ashi [bMQ 7a]. So even if these cases are authentically Amoraic, the earliest attestation is the fourth generation Amora Rava, three generations after Levi.) This term is part of the dialectical portion of the *sugya,* usually following a question framed by *hokhi dami* or *i leima,* which characterizes the Stammaitic stratum. Levi is mentioned in the proximate discussion and was probably "borrowed" here. Furthermore Levi and R. Shimon b. Rabbi study together in bAZ 19a and are mentioned together in bKet 8a, so the two are an attested unit. In bYev 9a Rabbi Yehuda HaNasi says of Levi, "It seems that he (Levi) has no brains in his skull." That Rabbi's son insults Levi replicates this motif. Their interchange cannot be taken as evidence that the story comprises an authentic *baraita* known to early Amoraim.

68. On pseudo-*baraitot* see Rubenstein, *Talmudic Stories,* 261–62; and Friedman, "Uncovering Literary Dependencies."

69. On the distance between the Bavli's depiction of R. Yehuda HaNasi and the Yerushalmi's, see Ofra Meir's conclusion to her comprehensive study, *Rabbi Judah*

the Patriarch, 338–46. This reading may also help explain the historical puzzle of Gamaliel. On the basis of this source historians generally argue that Gamaliel followed R. Yehuda HaNasi as patriarch; see e.g. Lee Levine, "The Jewish Patriarch (Nasi) in Third Century Palestine," *Aufstieg und Niedergang der Römischen Welt* II.19.2 (Berlin: de Gruyter, 1979), 686. Because few Palestinian sources mention him, historians assume that he did not occupy the office for long. It may be that Gamaliel did not become patriarch in reality, that the construction of his patriarchate is based on a Bavli fiction. Clearly this topic requires detailed attention.

70. Cohen, "Patriarchs and Scholarchs," 57–86.

71. Ibid., 66–68.

72. Ibid., 79–80; see too Chap. 1, under "The Christian Academy at Nisibis." According to Cohen, the final instruction ("Conduct your patriarchate high-handedly, and cast bile upon the students") is a part of, or the introduction to, the protocols.

73. Ibid., 68: "The headship of schools was the concern of scholarchs exclusively, while widows and funerals were not."

74. In the third and fourth centuries the patriarch in Palestine became progressively more estranged from the rabbinic movement. R. Yehuda HaNasi was a central rabbinic figure, probably the redactor of the Mishna. His descendants were less involved with the sages, and their traditions are hardly cited in Yerushalmi. The story of the death of R. Yehuda HaNasi perhaps reflects more on his descendants, the contemporary patriarchs, than on the historical R. Yehudah HaNasi.

75. Cohen, "Patriarchs and Scholarchs," 84–85.

76. R. Hanina b. Hama's appointment, which lacks a hereditary aspect, is probably retained from the Yerushalmi tradition mentioned above (yTa 4:2, 68a). The Bavli added or invented the appointment of his sons but retained, in a modified form, the appointment of R. Hanina b. Hama. That R. Hanina was of priestly descent may have added to his stature in the eyes of the Bavli (bBekh 51b).

77. On the inheritance of offices in earlier times see G. Alon, "The Sons of the Sages," *Jews, Judaism and the Classical World,* trans. I. Abrahams (Jerusalem: Magnes, 1977), 442–43. See too I. Gafni, "The Rod and the Scepter: On New Types of Leadership in the Age of the Talmud," *Kehuna umelukha,* ed. I. Gafni and G. Metzkin (Jerusalem: Zalman Shazar Center, 1987), 84–85. *SifDeut* §162 (212–13) states that not only should a king be succeeded by his son, but all "public officials" (*parnesei yisrael*) should be succeeded by their sons. However, this directive does not really pertain to rabbinic offices. See too Moshe Beer, "The Sons of Moses in Rabbinic Legend," *Bar Ilan Annual* 13 (1976), 149–57 (Hebrew); "The Sons of Eli in Rabbinic Legend," *Bar Ilan Annual* 14–15 (1977), 79–87 (Hebrew); and "Torah and Derekh Eretz," *Bar Ilan Annual* 2 (1964), 141–42 (Hebrew). And see Hezser, *Social Structure,* 267–69.

78. Cf. Gafni, "Expressions and Types of 'Local Patriotism,'" 69.

79. See p. 46.

80. The meaning of "they cannot punish him" is not completely clear. Apparently R. Eleazar's ancestral merit will provide a sort of supernatural protection lest others try to harm him.

81. Ms M reads, "Will you arise and lead (*namlikh*)?" The term *malakh,* to "rule" or "lead" is used for the head of the academy. See n. 49 and Gafni, "Yeshiva and Metivta," 32–34.

82. This point has been noted by Devorah Steinmetz, "Must the Patriarch Know *'Uqtzin?* The *Nasi* as Scholar in Babylonian *Aggada,*" *AJSR* 23 (1998), 179; Hayyim Shapira, "The Deposition of Rabban Gamaliel: Between History and Legend," *Zion* 64 (1999), 15–17, 30–31; and Moshe Beer, *The Babylonian Exilarchate* (Tel-Aviv: Devir, 1970), 40 and n. 26 (Hebrew).

83. See Shapira, "The Deposition of Rabban Gamaliel," 31: "While the Yerushalmi understands the patriarchate as a political institution, the Bavli sees the Nasi as the head of the academy."

84. I follow the standard account of the rise of the patriarchate, which attributes the office's power primarily to its status within the Roman bureaucracy. The most thorough treatment is David Goodblatt's, *The Monarchic Principle* (Tübingen: Mohr, 1994). Recently this account has been challenged by Seth Schwartz in "The Patriarchs and the Diaspora," *JJS* 50 (1999), 209–22, and *Imperialism and Jewish Society* (Princeton: Princeton University Press, 2001), 110–30. Based on the nature of Roman provincial government and renewed scrutiny of rabbinic sources, Schwartz argues, "It is thus overwhelmingly unlikely that the Roman state was responsible for creating and maintaining the office of the patriarchate" (210). In Schwartz's view, "individual patriarchs were powerful not because they occupied the patriarchal office, but because as individuals they painstakingly acquired authority, which they held at first only informally, mainly as powerful patrons, and which only gradually, mainly in the fourth century, came to be institutionalized." For a similar view see Hezser, *Social Structure,* 411–14. These views also are consistent with my position that the patriarch / Nasi as depicted in Palestinian rabbinic sources is not the chief rabbinic officer or leader of a rabbinic school. See too Goodblatt's response, "Patriarchs, Romans and (Modern) Scholars: A Response to Seth Schwartz," *JJS* 51 (2000), 313–18.

85. Actually the Yerushalmi does not state explicitly that they appointed R. Eleazar b. Azariah as Nasi, but only that they appointed him "to the assembly." See Goodblatt, *Monarchic Principle,* 252–53; Shapira, "The Deposition of Rabban Gamaliel," 5–14.

86. See Chap. 1, under "The Academic Setting," on the significance of this shift.

87. See Steinmetz, "Must the Patriarch Know *'Uqtzin?*," 170.

88. The demand for wealth is part of the image of nobility. In *Tosefta Ki-fshuta: A Comprehensive Commentary on the Tosefta* (New York: Jewish Theological Seminary, 1955–88), 8:761–62, Saul Lieberman, commenting to tSot 15:3, "the crown of the sages is their wealth," notes that portrayals of wealthy sages are more common in the

Bavli than the Yerushalmi. He also observes that the Tannaim depicted as wealthy in the Bavli are all priests.

89. Actually the story of the attempted deposition of Rabban Shimon b. Gamaliel is based on a very brief Palestinian anecdote found in yBik 3:3, 65c, but in this case the reworking is so substantial as to essentially comprise a free composition.

90. Translation from Brody, *Geonim,* 51, based on the original Arabic. Cf. Goodblatt, *Rabbinic Instruction,* 161–62.

91. Ginzberg, *Geonica,* 1:14, speaks of the "quasi-hereditary character of his office."

92. See Grossman, "From Father to Son," 201–2.

93. Salo Baron, *A Social and Religious History of the Jews* (New York: Columbia University Press, 1952–76), 5:21.

94. I am by no means claiming that the cultural dynamics were identical. Lineage and the cultural significance of genealogies functioned differently in Islamic and Sasanian societies. See Grossman, "From Father to Son," 189–220, and Arnold Franklin, *Shoots of David: Members of the Exilarchal Dynasty in the Middle Ages* (Ph.D. diss., Princeton University, 2001.)

Chapter 6. *Wives*

1. bGit 57; bBer 63b.

2. See I. Gafni, "The Institution of Marriage in Rabbinic Times," *The Jewish Family: Metaphor and Memory,* ed. David C. Kraemer (New York: Oxford University Press, 1989), 20–21; Boyarin, *Carnal Israel,* 139–42.

3. In bQid 29b Rav Huna states, "If a man reaches the age of twenty and has not married a woman — all his days are sinful." See too bYev 61b and 63a. Babylonian rabbis seemed to have esteemed marriage even more than their Palestinian colleagues. See Gafni, "The Institution of Marriage," 20–22; Satlow, *Jewish Marriage in Antiquity,* 3–41. On Ben Azai, a sage who never married, see below.

4. bYev 61b: "Rav Nahman said Shmuel said: Even if a man has many children, it is forbidden for him to remain without a wife, as it says, *It is not good for man to be alone (Gen 2:18).*"

5. See Chap. 1, under "Esteem of Torah."

6. Cf. Rashi and Tosafot to bQid 29b, s.v. *ha.* While their analysis of the source differs, they agree that Babylonian sages generally studied at a distance from home, whereas Palestinian sages were not required to travel to the same extent.

7. See bEruv 54b: "*You riders on tawny she-asses (Jgs 5:10)* — these are scholars who travel from city to city and province to province to study Torah." On travel in search of schooling throughout the Greco-Roman world of late antiquity, see Robert A. Kaster, *Guardians of Language: The Grammarian and Society in Late Antiquity* (Berkeley: University of California Press, 1988), 126–29.

8. Satlow, *Jewish Marriage in Antiquity*, 31, emphasis in original.

9. Yonah Fraenkel, *Iyyunim be'olamo haruhani shel sipur ha'aggada* (Tel-Aviv: Hakibbutz Hameuhad, 1981), 99–115; Boyarin, *Carnal Israel*, 142–56; Valler, *Woman and Womanhood*, 51–72. See too Satlow, *Jewish Marriage in Antiquity*, 31–32. My reading of this text differs to some extent from all three. Neither Fraenkel nor Boyarin reads the entire set of seven stories, so our projects differ fundamentally, for only by examining the whole *sugya* and the interrelationship of its parts can we attempt to understand the intentions of the redactors. Fraenkel in any case analyzes the Palestinian version of the story of R. Hananiah b. Hakhinai found in *Leviticus Rabbah* (story 4 below), while Boyarin bases his analysis mostly on the version of the story of R. Akiba found in bNed 50a (story 6). (Boyarin's statement "At this point in the text of the Babylonian Talmud, the story of Rabbi Akiva and his romance with Rachel is produced" [p. 150] is slightly misleading, for he skips over stories 3–5 and thus loses the context, which I discuss below.) I share with Valler a focus on the entire textual complex but disagree with her grouping of the stories into dyads (1–2, 3–4, 5–6) and with her conclusion that the "solution is based on partnership and understanding between husband and wife" (p. 53). Valler minimizes the force of the final story, which suggests that there is no solution (see her extremely brief analysis, pp. 75–76), as does the *sugya* taken as a whole. And while Valler might be correct that the optimal arrangement is a "spiritual closeness and a common purpose that continues over time despite the physical distance between marriage partners" (p. 76), the *sugya* suggests that this outcome is neither achievable in practice nor quite so simple

10. The Mishna, A1–A2, does not mention scholars specifically.

11. A pillar of fire is a sign of an extremely holy man.

12. Overturning beds is a mourning ritual. In a house of mourning the bed of the deceased, and sometimes all the beds, are overturned. Mourners customarily sit on the floor or on benches.

13. The story reflects the folk belief that something uttered cannot be retracted and may come to pass.

14. Thus the biblical law appears in the context of a second marriage: "If he marries another, he must not withhold from this one her food, clothing, or conjugal rights" (Exod 21:10).

15. Rashi, bKet 62a, s.v. *orha*. The Yerushalmi offers a similar limitation: yKet 5:6, 30a.

16. See n. 6, this chapter.

17. The Aramaic "at the cost of their lives" (*benafshayhu*) can also be translated "themselves," i.e., the rabbis themselves acted in accord with their ruling. I think the continuation of the passage makes clear that the first translation is the intended meaning.

18. Fraenkel, *Iyyunim*, 101.

19. There were in fact several sages named Rav Rahumei. The storyteller chose

this rabbi as a character because of the symbolic value of his name. On symbolic names see Shamma Friedman, *"Nomen est Omen:* Dicta of Talmudic Sages Which Echo the Author's Name," *These Are the Names,* vol. 2., ed. Aaron Demsky (Ramat-Gan: Bar Ilan University Press, 1999), 51–77 (Hebrew), with further references; Rubenstein, *Talmudic Stories,* 246–47.

20. See Fraenkel, *Iyyunim,* 102.

21. Ibid., 102–4; Boyarin, *Carnal Israel,* 149–50.

22. Fraenkel, *Iyyunim,* 102. Also Boyarin, *Carnal Israel,* 150.

23. I omit a scene not germane to this topic. The scene is quoted at the beginning of Chap. 7.

24. The first verse cited, from Exodus 15, proposes that the people and God be united ("married") when they reach the Holy Land and Mount Zion. In the second passage, just a few chapters later, God instructs the people to build the Tabernacle so that he may dwell among them while they journey through the Sinai desert. Thus God changed his mind, as it were, and made the "marriage" earlier.

25. According to mYev 6:6, a husband whose wife has not become pregnant for ten years must take measures so as to fulfill the commandment of procreation. He could either marry a second wife or divorce her and remarry.

26. They will say that he procreates with his second wife and keeps the first wife purely for his sexual pleasure.

27. Similar versions of this story appear in *GenR* 95 (1232) and *LevR* 21:8 (484–85).

28. Bisa, Hama, and Oshaya were all sages and apparently all lived long lives.

29. bQid 29b; see Boyarin, *Carnal Israel,* 138–40.

30. For suggestions on how the sages may have coped with this problem, possibly including recourse to "temporary wives," see Gafni, "The Institution of Marriage," 23–25; Boyarin, *Carnal Israel,* 145.

31. See Pinhas Mandel, "'Aggadot hahurban: bein bavel le'erets yisrael," *Israel-Diaspora Relations in the Second Temple and Talmudic Periods,* ed. I. Gafni et al. (Jerusalem: Zalman Shazar Center, forthcoming), 11–13.

32. "Twelve" is a stock number in the Talmud and need not be taken literally. Read "many years."

33. One who swears under mistaken assumptions may ask a sage to annul the oath, that is, to rule that the oath was not valid in the first place. Here R. Akiba annuls the oath because Ben Kalba Savua swore under the mistaken impression that his daughter was about to marry an ignorant shepherd. Had he known that she married a great sage (or a man who was to become a great sage), he would not have sworn.

34. tYev 8:7, bYev 63b. Boyarin, *Carnal Israel,* 154–55.

35. The word for "ewe," *rahel,* is the name given to R. Akiba's wife in *ARNA* §b (15a). See Boyarin, *Carnal Israel,* 150–53, for the symbolic resonances of the name.

36. This is developed by Boyarin, *Carnal Israel,* 151–56.

37. This is not to say that the miraculous stories are realistic. Rather, the portrayal of wives who will be disappointed and age, and of children who will not know their father, are realistic.

38. In this respect I part company with Boyarin, who, in *Carnal Israel,* says: "My reading of the textual complex surrounding rabbinic marriage has suggested that the major goal of the hegemonic rabbinic discourse was the securing of a self-abnegating role for Jewish wives," (166) and "There really is no tension, the text implies, between marriage and lust for learning; all you need is the right kind of wife" (154). We should also bear in mind that the intended audience of these stories was husbands, not wives. In medieval times the story may have served the purposes Boyarin articulates, once it became a part of Jewish folklore. But within the Talmudic *sugya* I think it serves a different function.

39. Jonathan Z. Smith, "The Bare Facts of Ritual," in *Imagining Religion* (Chicago: University of Chicago Press, 1982), 53–65. Satlow has applied Smith's theories to rabbinic sources concerning ideal age of marriage. See *Jewish Marriage in Antiquity,* 109–10.

40. Smith, "Bare Facts of Ritual", 63 (emphasis in the original).

41. Smith's interpretation is based on Siberian bear-hunting rituals, which arguably have little in common with rabbinic marriages.

42. For a similar interpretation see Satlow, *Jewish Marriage in Antiquity,* 34–38. Satlow sees the *sugya* as venting frustration against the institution of marriage: "The purpose of our sugya is not to solve the problem, but to gripe about it; to release the frustration of being caught between two poles in the controlled environment in which these texts were produced and read, the House of Study."

43. This is the thrust of Valler's reading: "The moral here, therefore, is that separation from home, whether forced or desired, is negative and brings disaster" (*Woman and Womanhood,* 75.)

44. yBik 3:3, 65c: "Yehuda b. Hiyya was accustomed to go up and ask after the welfare of R. Yannai his father-in-law every Sabbath eve. . . . Once he went up late. He [R. Yannai] said, 'It is not possible that Yehuda my son-in-law changed his routine.' He said, '[But] it is [also] not possible that sufferings should afflict that righteous body. It stands to reason that our Yehuda b. R. [Hiyya] is no more.'"

45. bNed 50a. This version places greater emphasis on the poverty endured by the sage and his family. At the beginning of the story R. Akiba picks straw from the hair of his wife as they sleep in a barn and wishes that he could buy her an expensive crown. Elijah then appears in the guise of a man asking them for straw for his wife who is giving birth. This prompts R. Akiba to observe that some people are even poorer than they are. Only at this point does his wife send him off to study. None of

these motifs appears in bKet 62b. In bNed 50a there is less emphasis on the issue of abandoning the wife and on the question of the sage's true love. So it appears that the redactors have tailored our version specifically for its context.

46. yShab 6:1, 7d; see Satlow, *Jewish Marriage in Antiquity*, 31–32.

47. *LevR* 21:8 (484–86). A similar version appears in *GenR* 95 (1232).

48. Boyarin, *Carnal Israel*, 156–58.

49. So Fraenkel, *Iyyunim*, 108 n. 12.

50. The manuscript evidence is far more ambiguous than Boyarin, *Carnal Israel*, 158 n. 39 suggests. That the phrase "this poor women . . ." is identical to the reading of the Bavli is not probative. Often medieval scribes changed the readings of the Palestinian midrashim to conform to the Bavli versions. So the formulation alone, not the content, may have been influenced by the Bavli.

51. Ofra Meir, "Hashpaat maase ha'arikha al hashqafat ha'olam shel sipurei ha'aggada," *Tura* 3 (1994), 67–84.

52. See n. 8 and Satlow, *Jewish Marriage in Antiquity*, 30–41.

53. For scholarship on this issue see Ari Elon, "The Torah as Love Goddess," *Essential Papers on the Talmud*, ed. Michael C. Chernick (New York: New York University Press, 1994), 463–77, and Boyarin, *Carnal Israel*, 65–66.

54. bBer 57a.

55. See Chap. 8, under "Wives."

56. See *DQS* ad loc. And see Satlow, *Jewish Marriage in Antiquity*, 357 n. 66.

57. bSanh 99b. There is no Palestinian parallel.

58. See Chap. 1, under "Esteem of Torah."

59. See Chap. 5, n. 79 for ms variants.

60. Some mss omit this question.

61. Ben-Shalom, "Torah Study for All," 108–9, notes the addition of the episode with the wife and observes that the storyteller believed that women opposed their husbands' studying in the academy.

62. In this case, however, she acts at her husband's behest.

63. *PRK* 11:23–24 (198–200).

64. This provides another example of the phenomenon discussed in Chap. 1, "The Academic Setting," where a study-house appears in the Bavli version of a story but is lacking in the Palestinian parallel.

Chapter 7. *Elitism*

1. Neh 10:32, Ezra 10:11 etc. In some cases the term refers to foreigners, i.e., non-Israelites. The phrase appears in many other biblical passages with a variety of meanings. See Aharon Oppenheimer, *The 'Am Ha-aretz*, trans. I. H. Levine (Leiden: Brill, 1977), 10–11, and the references cited there.

2. See tDem 2:5–3:17; tToh 8:1–9:6; Oppenheimer, *The 'Am Ha-Aretz*, 118–69.

3. Cf. mAvot 2:5: "an *am ha'arets* is not pious."

4. See yMS 4:6, 55c; yShab 12:3, 13c; and sources cited elsewhere in this chapter.

5. See n. 2, this chapter.

6. This *baraita* follows the citation of tAZ 3:10. It also appears in bSot 22a.

7. Wald, *Pesahim*, 211–39.

8. That the *sugya* is Babylonian, not Palestinian, was also recognized by Shaye J. D. Cohen, "The Place of the Rabbi in Jewish Society," *The Galilee in Late Antiquity*, ed. Lee Levine (Jerusalem and New York: Jewish Theological Seminary, 1992), 167. See too Satlow, *Jewish Marriage in Antiquity*, 154; Wald, *Pesahim*, 214. And see n. 68 of this chapter.

9. Wald, *Pesahim*, 230–32, 235–36, 238.

10. This *sugya* follows an Amoraic *sugya* that deals with marriages between Jews of priestly and nonpriestly descent.

11. Wald, *Pesahim*, 213–21.

12. Or, "prepare food in a state of purity with his utensils."

13. tDem 2:16–17; bAZ 39a; bBekh 30b. See too the *baraita* cited at bKet 66b.

14. tDem 2:15, tToh 9:11, tAZ 3:9–10; see Oppenheimer, *The 'Am Ha-Aretz*, 156–69.

15. Cf. *PRK* 27:9 (416).

16. So Rashi, bHul 92a, s.v. *alin*.

17. Some mss read, "If they did not need us for business, they would kill us." See Wald, *Pesahim*, 238, for discussion of the correct reading.

18. Note the discrepancy between tAZ 3:9, quoted above, in which R. Meir prohibits marriage to an *am ha'arets* because he does not eat foods in a state of purity, and D, the Stammaitic fiction, where R. Meir prohibits marriage because of the *am ha'arets*'s bestial character.

19. Wald, *Pesahim*, 233–34.

20. See bMen 103b, bHul 17a, etc.

21. See Jonathan Brumberg-Kraus, "Meat-Eating and Jewish Identity," *AJSR* 24 (1999), 243–45.

22. The application of the verse appears in an addition to the Bavli *baraita* at bBer 47b (cited above), which is probably a Stammaitic gloss. To the *baraita*'s definition of an *am ha'arets* as one who "has studied Scripture and Mishna but does attend upon the sages," bSot 22a first adds the category of "boor" as those who know Scripture but not Mishna, and then applies Jer 31:27 to one who knows neither Scripture nor Mishna.

23. See C. Reines, *Torah umusar* (Jerusalem: Rav Kook, 1954), 101–6; Oppenheimer, *The 'Am Ha-Aretz*, 237; Wald, *Pesahim*, 236–37.

24. Some mss read "R. Abba." This exegesis, a play on the orthographic identity of *im* (= with) and *am* (= people), hence "with the ass" read as "people [similar to]

an ass," is a commonplace: see bKet 111a, bQid 68a, bBQ 49a; *GenR* 56:2 (596); *LevR* 20:2 (448).

25. yBer 2:8, 5b; cited by Wald, *Pesahim*, 236. See too bYev 61a and bQid 22b: Rav Ashi said: A minor slave is as an animal and therefore can be acquired by "pulling" (*meshikha*).

26. bGit 38a, bAZ 22b.

27. A late medieval midrash correctly understood the thrust of the Bavli sources with the paraphrase: "An *am ha'arets* is equated to a gentile, 'Do not give your daughters to their sons or take their daughters for your sons (Deut 7:3).'" The application of the verse construes such unions as prohibited intermarriages. See "Pirqei rabenu haqadosh," 6:11, *Otsar midrashim*, ed. J. D. Eisenstein (New York: Eisenstein, 1915), 512.

28. See bSanh 57a, which forbids the murder of a gentile but does not legislate a penalty. Some rabbinic sources ask that God destroy the "nations of the world" who oppress Israel.

29. This view is not found in Palestinian sources but appears to be consistent with the perspective of Babylonian Amoraim. See too bBer 43b: a scholar "should not eat in the company of *amei ha'arets*."

30. See Reines, *Torah umusar*, 100–101; Oppenheimer, *The 'Am Ha-Aretz*, 179–80. And see the next note.

31. That I am not merely retrojecting modern sensibilities can be seen from apologetic Geonic traditions, which struggle to explain these traditions. See *OG, Pesahim*, pp. 67–70, and Chap. 8, under "The *am ha'arets*."

32. The Hebrew is *meshupa*. See Margulies's note to *LevR* 9:3 (176). Others translate it "meek, humble."

33. See Ritba to bBB 8a, s.v. *ve'amei*.

34. Cf. the tradition attributed to R. Eleazar in bSanh 92a denouncing the giving of bread to those who lack knowledge (*daat*), although the term *am ha'arets* is not used.

35. Wald, *Pesahim*, 234.

36. To bury an "abandoned corpse" (*met mitsvah*) is considered among the most important commandments.

37. He should have buried it where he found it.

38. A similar maxim appears in other rabbinic sources. mAvot 1:13 attributes to Hillel the maxim, "Whoever does not study is worthy of death." See too *ARNB* §27 (29a); *ARNA* §12 (28a).

39. See e.g. *Sifre* Numbers §115, ed. H. S. Horovitz (Leipzig, 1917; reprint, Jerusalem: Wahrmann, 1966), 128–29 = bMen 44a.

40. Another possible Palestinian source is a tradition attributed to R. Antigonos: "The garment of the wife of a *haver* takes precedence over the sustenance (or "life") of an *am ha'arets*" (yHor 3:4, 48a–b). This dictum appears in the discussion of the allocation of scarce resources. The point is that clothes should be provided for the wife

of a *haver*, to spare her from the shame of nakedness, before food is provided to an *am ha'arets*. The principle that a scholar takes precedence over an *am ha'arets* is established by mHor 3:8.

41. A slightly different version appears in bQid 33a: R. Yohanan used to rise before Aramaean (= gentile) elders, saying "how much troubles have passed over these." This version does not recognize the merits of an *am ha'arets*.

42. *LevR* 34:13 (801).

43. *GenR* 78:12 (932–33).

44. bShab 33b-34a. See Chap. 1, under "Esteem of Torah."

45. See Rubenstein, *Talmudic Stories*, 121–30.

46. See too Brumberg-Kraus, "Meat-Eating and Jewish Identity," 245.

47. bKet 111b–113a vs. yPeah 7:4, 20a–b. See Jeffrey L. Rubenstein, "Coping with the Virtues of the Land of Israel: An Analysis of Bavli Ketubot 110b–112a," *Israel-Diaspora Relations in the Second Temple and Talmudic Periods*, ed. Gafni et al. (Jerusalem: Zalman Shazar Institute: forthcoming) (Hebrew).

48. This solution appears to be a Stammaitic adaptation of a similar statement found at bSanh 99a and bBer 34b, which does not specify the *am ha'arets*. See too the tradition attributed to R. Eleazar at bSanh 92a concerning benefacting a sage.

49. Cf. bBM 33b, a tradition attributed to R. Yehuda b. R. Ilai, who insists that *amei ha'arets* have a share in the world to come.

50. bAZ 2a–3b. See Jeffrey L. Rubenstein, "An Eschatological Drama: Bavli Avodah Zarah 2a–3b," *AJSR* 21 (1996), 1–37, and *Talmudic Stories*, 212–42. The focus of that narrative is the exclusion of gentiles vis-à-vis Israel. But the cultural logic underpins the exclusion of the *am ha'arets* in bKet 111b.

51. See Chap. 6, under "The Erotic Torah."

52. Ibid.

53. See e.g. mAvot 1.12; tHor 2:7; *LevR* 3:6 (71); bBM 85b. In bSanh 96a R. Zeira attributes to the Tanna R. Yehuda b. Betera the statement: "Take heed of the sons of *amei ha'arets*, for Torah will go forth from them." The most restrictive Palestinian tradition known to me appears in yAZ 2:8, 41d, attributed to R. Shimon bar Yohai: "*These are the rules that you shall set* (tasim) *before them* (*Exod 21:1*). Just as a treasure (*sima*) is not revealed to all creatures, so you do not have permission to delve (*le-shaqea*) into words of Torah before men who are not worthy (*kesherim*)."

54. Cf. mAvot 2:12; *Midrash tannaim* to Deut 33:4, ed. David Hoffmann (Berlin: H. Itzkowski, 1909), 212–13; bNed 81a.

55. See too Chap. 6, under "The Erotic Torah."

56. For literature on this story see Meir, *Rabbi Judah*, 97–102, and the references there.

57. mAZ 2:5; tHul 2:24; *GenR* 10:7 (81), 34:15 (327), 62:2 (673), and especially 97:10 (1219): "the Nesiim of the House of Rabbi who teach Torah in public." See too

yAZ 3:13, 43c; *LevR* 24:3 (553); bEruv 54b. For additional sources, see A. Büchler, "Learning and Teaching in the Open Air in Palestine," *JQR* 4 (1913–14), 485–91; and Krauss, "Outdoor Teaching in Talmudic Times," 82–84; Hezser, *Social Structure*, 213.

58. See e.g. bShab 127a, bEruv 34b, bHor 12a. The articles mentioned in the previous note discuss Palestine, but many of the sources cited by the authors come from the Bavli and probably reflect Babylonian reality. Abaye and Rava are quoted several times as saying "I am like Ben Azai in the marketplace of Tiberias," although they refer to his intellectual abilities, not the locus of his study (bEruv 29a, bSot 45a).

59. The exegesis of Song 7:2 appears in bSuk 49b in a different context (cited in Chap. 6, under "The Erotic Torah"). The redactors may have adapted the exegesis to provide a reason for Rabbi's decree.

60. See Fraenkel, *Iyyunim*, 86–87.

61. See the analysis of Steinmetz, "Must the Patriarch Know *'Uqtzin?*," 163–90. Ben-Shalom, in "Torah Study for All," 106–13, recognized the uniquely Babylonian additions. Meir, *Rabbi Judah*, 362 n. 64, has noted the connection between this Bavli story and the story of Rabbi Yehudah HaNasi's ban on teaching in the marketplace.

62. See Steinmetz, "Must the Patriarch know *'Uqtzin?*," 173–76.

63. Scholars have noted that the locution, "But it is not so" (*velo hi*), often introduces late, redactional material. For references see Friedman, "Pereq ha'isha rabba babavli," 286 n. 14. The phrase "any student whose inside is not like his outside" was borrowed by the redactors from a statement of Rava at bYom 72b. See Ben-Shalom, "Torah Study for All," 113–15.

64. Fraenkel, *Iyyunim*, 66, has noted that this is the only source in all of rabbinic literature describing fees for entry to the study-house. So the fee should probably be seen as a fiction invented to teach the story's moral that no one can plead that poverty prevented study, as no one was as poor as Hillel. Still, it is possible that the guard reflects some real phenomenon. Ben-Shalom, "Torah Study for All," 114–15, refers to medieval traditions that explain that the Babylonian synagogues and academies were located at some distance from towns, hence watchmen were hired to stand guard at night. And see bBM 24a and Rashi, ad loc., s.v. *kenesiot*.

65. Goodblatt, "The Story of the Plot," 358–60, first pointed out that this is a Babylonian motif.

66. See Chap. 5, under "Lineage and the Academic Hierarchy." For evidence of the late date, see Rubenstein, *Talmudic Stories*, 194–97, 206–211. In the Yerushalmi's much briefer version of the story, R. Meir leaves of his own accord (yBik 3:3, 65c).

67. bBB 23b. mBB 2:6 rules that a pigeon found within fifty cubits of the cote belongs to the owner but beyond fifty cubits belongs to the finder. R. Yirmiah asked about a case in which the bird had one foot within fifty cubits and one without. bBB 165b relates that R. Yirmiah was readmitted.

68. Lee I. Levine, for example, in *The Rabbinic Class of Roman Palestine in Late An-*

tiquity (Jerusalem: Yad Izhak Ben-Zvi; New York: Jewish Theological Seminary, 1985), attempts to reach conclusions about social relations between sages and *amei ha'arets* based on these traditions, though he seems to be confused as to whether the traditions reflect the situation in Palestine or in Babylonia or both. See p. 112 n. 62 ("the degree of animosity and its intensity towards the *'am ha-aretz* were unique and reflect deep social and religious rifts") and p. 117 n. 93 ("Alternately, the fact that the Babylonian Talmud includes this material may indicate that animosity between the rabbis and certain segments of the population continued to be a problem in Babylonia.") And see Kalmin, *The Sage in Jewish Society*, 45–46. Kalmin too tends to consider these to be authentic Palestinian traditions (though he also notes the suspicious fact that they appear only in the Bavli), and he is therefore forced to explain why they contradict his own general conclusion that Palestinian sages have more cordial relations with nonsages than do the Babylonian sages.

69. In a tradition found at bBB 168a, Abaye recommends that a sage take an *am ha'arets* along with him when going to betroth a woman, lest another be substituted for the designated bride. (A sage is not used to looking at women and can be easily fooled.) Of course it is hard to make much of this tradition, but it is unlikely that an Amora would recommend depending on an *am ha'arets* were social relationships not common.

70. There may be a humorous aspect to these traditions. R. Eleazar's response to his students' entreaty to say "slaughter" instead of "stab"—that "the one (slaughtering) requires a blessing" and "the other (stabbing) does not require a blessing"—is probably meant to be funny, although I am aware of the problem of judging what would have been considered humorous in a distant culture.

Chapter 8. Conclusion

1. See Halivni, *Midrash, Mishnah, and Gemara*, 105–19, on aspects of the intellectual legacy of the Stammaim.

2. Brody, *Geonim*, 36–37.

3. Neubauer, *Mediaeval Jewish Chronicles*, 2:88; translation in part from Brody, *Geonim*, 61. On Nathan the Babylonian, see Chap 1.

4. Translation from Brody, *Geonim*, 55. Text published in Solomon Schechter, *Saadyana* (Cambridge: Deighton and Bell, 1903), 118.

5. Ephraim Urbach, *Baalei hatosafot*, 4th ed. (Tel-Aviv: Bialik, 1980), 22.

6. On parallels between the Tosafot and Talmudic dialectic see Haym Soloveitchik, "Rabad of Posquieres: A Programmatic Essay," *Studies in the History of Jewish Society in the Middle Ages and in the Modern Period*, ed. I. Etkes and Y. Salmon (Jerusalem: Magnes, 1980), 19. This is not to deny the influence of medieval intellectual trends, especially scholasticism, on the Tosafot. See Urbach, *Baalei hatosafot*, 17–21.

7. Soloveitchik, "Rabad of Posquieres," 19–20.

8. bBM 84a; see Chap. 2, under "Objections and Solutions."

9. On *pilpul* see Dov Rappel, *The Debate over the Pilpul* (Tel-Aviv: Devir, 1979) (Hebrew).

10. See Chap. 2, under *"Pilpul."*

11. Urbach, *Baalei hatosafot,* 25–26.

12. On the lack of information concerning the internal situation of academies, see M. Breuer, "Toldot hayeshiva ke'aspaklaria shel toldot yisrael," *Hinukh vehistoria,* ed. R. Feldhay and I. Etkes (Jerusalem: Shazar Center, 1999), 181–83. A number of descriptions are collected in Simha Assaf, *Meqorot letoldot hahinukh beyisrael* (Tel-Aviv: Devir, 1925–42). See too the sources collected by M. Breuer, "Toward the Investigation of the Typology of Western *Yeshivot* in the Middle Ages" (Hebrew), *Studies in the History of Jewish Society in the Middle Ages and in the Modern Period,* eds. I. Etkes and Y. Salmon (Jerusalem: Magnes, 1980), 44–46, many of which include violent imagery.

13. *Sefer hasidim* §752, ed. J. Wistinetzki (Berlin: Itzkowski, 1891), 191.

14. From his book *Maaseh ephod.* Cited in Simha Assaf, *Meqorot letoldot hahinukh beyisrael,* ed. Shmuel Glick ([1925–42]; New York: Jewish Theological Seminary, 2001), 2:94–95. Here Duran explains why many students no longer study Bible but focus all their time and energy on the Bavli.

15. R. Yaakov b. Yehezqel Zlatovi, *Shem Yaakov* (Frankfurt de Oder: Mikhel Gotshalk, 1716), 23; cited in Rappel, *The Debate over the Pilpul,* 24.

16. R. Zelig Margoliot, *Hiburei liqutim* (Venice, 1715), 2–3; cited in Rappel, *The Debate over the Pilpul,* 124.

17. The anecdotes are cited by R. Shmuel b. R. Moshe Haide (d. 1685) in his "Sifra ziquqin denura uviurin de'esha," a commentary to *Tanna devei eliyahu* (Warsaw, 1880; reprint, Jerusalem: A. Vider, 1969), *petihta,* p. 28. Haide repeatedly rebukes students for embarrassing others and for rejoicing when their fellow students falter. That a man who shames others will be punished by angels probably draws on Tractate Kallah 1:8.

18. bHor 13b–14a. See Chap. 4, under "Shame and the Late Babylonian Academy."

19. The text continues by quoting the Talmudic passage from bHul 6a, cited in Chap. 4, under "Shame and the Late Babylonian Academy."

20. Shmuel b. Moshe de Medina, *Responsa of MaHaRSHDaM, Hoshen mishpat* #361.

21. Aharon b. Joseph Sasson, *Responsa Torat emet,* #148.

22. Avraham b. Mordekhai Halevi (17th century), *Responsa Ginat veradim, Yoreh deah* #1:20.

23. Yehezqel Landau, *Responsa Noda bihuda, Even ha'ezer, Mahadura tinyana,* #27.

24. Yaakov Berab, *Responsa MaHaRI berav,* #59.

25. Levi ibn Haviv, *Responsa of MaHaRLBaH,* #1.

26. Moses b. Yosef of Trani, *Responsa of MaBiT,* part 1, #280.

27. Israel Isserlein, *Responsa Terumat hadeshen,* part 2, #138.

28. Cf. Ovadiah Yosef, *Responsa Yabia omer, Orah hayyim,* part 1, #1:12: "This is the meaning of [the Mishna], *Let your house be a meeting place for sages, and cover yourself* (mitabeq) *with the dust of their feet (Avot 1:4).* This [word] derives from the same root as, *And a man struggled* (vayeaveq) *with him (Gen 32:25),* which pertains to struggling in war, because it is a holy war. So too are we with respect to our holy rabbis, those who have died but whose souls are in the heavens, the famous authors whose books are with us: since their books are in our houses, our houses become a meeting place of sages, and we are enjoined, indeed we are given permission, to struggle and to fight with their words, and not to be partial in judgment, but only to love the truth."

29. *Divrei harivot,* ed. Dov Drakhman (New York: Rachlin, 1907).

30. Ibid., pp. 31–32. The translation is somewhat uncertain. See the editor's notes there and the Introduction, p. xxi.

31. Ibid., p. 47: "The customs of Spain that you mention — I have never seen them nor heard of them."

32. Cited in Chap. 3, under "The Violence of Debate." R. Avraham invokes as precedent the Bavli tradition from bQid 30b, cited in Chap. 3, "The Wars of Torah," that teachers and disciples who study Torah together start out as enemies but eventually become friends.

33. See Chap. 5, under "Dynastic Succession in the Geonic Era."

34. Grossman, "From Father to Son," 199–201; Franklin, *Shoots of David,* 25–26; 53–54.

35. *Iggeret rav sherira gaon,* ed. Lewin, 92.

36. Brody, *Geonim,* 102–103; Grossman, "From Father to Son," 191–93.

37. Grossman, "From Father to Son," 207–14. See too idem, "Yihus mishpaha umeqomo behevra hayehudit be'ashkenaz haqeduma," *Studies in the History of Jewish Society in the Middle Ages and in the Modern Period,* eds. I. Etkes and Y. Salmon (Jerusalem: Magnes, 1980), 7–41.

38. Grossman, "From Father to Son," 214–15.

39. *Mishneh torah,* Laws of Kings 1:7.

40. *Yore deah* 245:22.

41. bKet 103b; see Chap. 5, under "Lineage and the Academic Hierarchy."

42. For bKet 103b, see Isaac b. Sheshet, *Responsa of RIBaSH,* #271; Moses Isserles, *Responsa of RaMA,* #133; Yaakov b. Yekutiel Bardugo, *Responsa Shufrei deyaakov,* part 1, #48. For bBer 27b–28a, see Moses Sofer, *Responsa Hatam sofer,* part 5, #21; Malkiel Tenenbaum, *Responsa Divrei malkiel,* part 4, #82. For bHor 13b–14a, see Yosef Hazan, *Responsa Heqrei lev, Yoreh deah,* part 3, #100; Ovadiah Yosef, *Responsa Yabia omer,* part 4, *Yoreh deah* #18:5.

43. See Yaron Harel, "The Controversy over Rabbi Ephraim Laniado's Inheri-

tance of the Rabbinate in Aleppo," *Jewish History* 13 (1999), 83–101. The controversy involved other issues as well.

44. Raphael Shlomo Laniado, *Responsa Kise shlomo* (Jerusalem: Zuckerman, 1900), #1.

45. See Shaul Stampfer, "Inheritance of the Rabbinate in Eastern Europe in the Modern Period: Causes, Factors and Development over Time," *Jewish History* 13 (1999), 36: "Inheritance of rabbinical posts is almost taken for granted in contemporary orthodox or ultra-orthodox Jewish communities. This is true not only in hassidic groups, where inheritance is an integral element of the dynastic system, but in yeshivot and orthodox communities as well."

46. From his book *Divrei hayamim*. Cited in Assaf, *Meqorot letoldot hahinukh*, 2:189.

47. Jacob b. Moses Moellin, *Responsa of MaHaRIL hahadashot*, #187.

48. See Chap. 6. In bKet 62b the sages rule that a scholar may depart for "two or three years" without permission. Moellin attributes the eighteen months to a later rabbinic edict.

49. For the standard codes and some discussion, see Maimonides, *Mishneh torah*, Laws of Marriage 14:2; *Shulhan arukh* and *Tur, Even ha'ezer* §76.

50. Elliot Wolfson, "Female Imaging of the Torah: From Literary Metaphor to Religious Symbol," *Circle in the Square* (Albany: State University of New York Press, 1995), 1–28; idem, "Eunuchs Who Keep the Sabbath: Becoming Male and the Ascetic Ideal in Thirteenth-Century Jewish Mysticism," *Becoming Male in the Middle Ages*, ed. J. J. Cohen and B. Wheeler (New York: Garland Publishing, 1997), 151–85. See too Yehuda Liebes, *Studies in the Zohar*, trans. A. Schwartz et al. (Albany: State University of New York Press, 1993), 67–74.

51. *Zohar* 1:49b–50a, cited from Isaiah Tishby, *The Wisdom of the Zohar*, trans. D. Goldstein (Oxford: Oxford University Press, 1989), 1398. On this passage see Liebes, *Studies in the Zohar*, 15.

52. bKet 62b; see Chap. 6, under "Torah and Wives," section 2A.

53. Cf. *Zohar* 3:36a: "All those engaged in the [study of] Torah cleave to the Holy One, blessed be He, and are crowned in the crowns of Torah . . . how much the more so those who are engaged in the [study of] Torah also during the night . . . for they are joined to the *Shekhinah* and they are united as one." Translation from Wolfson, "Female Imaging of the Torah," 18.

54. *Zohar* 3:49b, cited by Wolfson, "Eunuchs who Keep the Sabbath," 160.

55. Wolfson, "Eunuchs who Keep the Sabbath," 160–61.

56. Ibid.

57. Moses Hayyim Ephraim of Sudlikov, *Degel mahaneh efrayim* 52a, cited in Wolfson, "Female Imaging of the Torah," 24. See too Moshe Idel, *Hasidism: Between Ecstasy and Magic* (Albany: State University of New York Press, 1995), 181.

58. See Wolfson, "Female Imaging of the Torah," 10, 23, 25.

59. Sherira's opinion appears in both responsa and citations of medieval jurists. See *OG, Pesahim,* Responsa, §168, pp. 67–68.

60. *Zohar* 3:125a. Translation from Tishby, *Wisdom of the Zohar,* 1151.

61. See too *Zohar* 2:119a, 3:153b, 3:277b.

62. *Zohar* 2:89b. Translation from Tishby, *Wisdom of the Zohar,* 1393.

63. Also at bPes 49b. An *am ha'arets* may neither give nor receive testimony, may neither be appointed a guardian for orphans nor a supervisor for charity funds, and may not be entrusted with a secret.

64. See too Jacob Neusner, *Judaism, the Classical Statement: The Evidence of the Bavli* (Chicago: University of Chicago Press, 1986). Neusner attributes the Bavli's success to certain literary aspects.

65. That is, the leading competitors for authority among rabbinite Jews. The Geonim waged a different battle for the authority of the oral tradition against the Karaites.

66. Pirqoy b. Baboy apparently was a student in the academy of Rav Yehudai Gaon, leader of the Sura academy from 757 to 761 C.E. See Shalom Spiegel, "Lefarashat hapolmos shel pirqoi ben baboi," *Harry Austryn Wolfson Jubilee Volume,* ed. S. Lieberman et al. (Jerusalem: American Academy for Jewish Research, 1965), 243–74; Brody, *Geonim,* 113.

67. This claim is found near the end of Alfasi's *Halakhot* of Tractate Eruvin. See too Jonathan HaKohen of Lunel (b. 1135) cited in *Shita mequbetset* to bBM 12b: "We do not concern ourselves with the Yerushalmi, because those very sages who edited the Bavli included therein the traditions (from the Yerushalmi) that are in accord with the law . . . and they left in the Yerushalmi that which they saw was not in accord with the law." See the sources collected in Isadore Twersky, *Rabad of Posquières* (Cambridge: Harvard University Press, 1962), 207–9.

68. This consensus recently has been challenged by Alyssa Gray, *A Talmud in Exile: The Influence of PT Avodah Zarah on the Formation of BT Avodah Zarah* (Ph.D. diss., Jewish Theological Seminary, 2001).

69. See C. Tchernowitz, *Toldot haposqim* (New York: Jubilee Committee, 1946), 1:141.

70. *Midrash Tanhuma, Noah,* §3 (New York and Berlin: Horev, 1926), 15a–b. Translation from Goodblatt, *Rabbinic Instruction,* 13–14.

71. bKet 111a: "Abaye said: We hold that Babylonia will not experience the travails of the messianic age."

72. I. Gafni has devoted several studies to this topic. See *Land, Center and Diaspora;* "Expressions and Types of 'Local Patriotism'"; and "Talmudic Babylonia and the Land of Israel: Between Subservience and Assertiveness," *Teuda* 12 (1996), 97–109.

73. bBer 63a; ySanh 1:2, 19a. See Chap. 1, under "The Academic Setting."

74. Gafni, *Land, Center and Diaspora,* 110.

75. This precedent is probably based on mYev 16:7: "R. Akiba said: When I went down to Nehardea to intercalate the year . . ."

76. See Brody, *Geonim,* 118–20.

77. See the discussion of this story in Chap. 1, where arguments for the late dating are summarized.

78. So Rashi, bBQ 117b, s.v. *aʾl dilchon.* See Sperber, "On the Unfortunate Adventures of Rav Kahana," 86. Sperber argues that the story is a Saboraic polemic against Palestinian tradition.

79. This tradition is (pseudepigraphically) imputed to Resh Laqish. It may be a Babylonian adaptation of *SifDeut* §48 (112), which explains why the Torah was given to all of Israel, not just to elders, prophets, priests, and Levites: "And so it says, *You stand this day, all of you, before the Lord, your God (Deut 29:9).* Had not this one stood up and established Torah in Israel, the Torah would have been forgotten. Had not Shafan in his time, Ezra in his time, R. Akiba in his time [established Torah in Israel], Torah would have been forgotten." Here the point is not that Babylonians preserved the Torah, but that various laymen did so.

‿∴‿

Selected Bibliography

Assaf, Simha. *Meqorot letoldot hahinukh beyisrael*. Edited by Shmuel Glick. New York: Jewish Theological Seminary, 2001.

Avot derabbi natan. Edited by Solomon Schechter. Vienna, 1887.

Ben-Shalom, Israel. "'And I Took Unto me Two Staves: the One I Called Beauty and the Other I called Bands' (*Zach. 11:7*)." In *Dor-Le-Dor: From the End of Biblical Times up to the Redaction of the Talmud. Studies in Honor of Joshua Efron*, edited by A. Oppenheimer and A. Kasher. Jerusalem: Bialik, 1995, 215–34 (Hebrew).

———. "Torah Study for All or for the Elite Alone." In *Synagogues in Antiquity*, edited by A. Kasher et al. Jerusalem: Yad Izhaq Ben-Zvi, 1987, 97–115 (Hebrew).

Boyarin, Daniel. *Carnal Israel: Reading Sex in Talmudic Culture*. Berkeley: University of California Press, 1993.

———. *Unheroic Conduct: The Rise of Heterosexuality and the Invention of the Jewish Man*. Berkeley: University of California Press, 1997.

Brock, Sebastian. "From Antagonism to Assimilation: Syriac Attitudes to Greek Learning." In *East of Byzantium: Syria and Armenia in the Formative Period*, edited by N. Garsoïan et al. Washington, D.C.: Dumbarton Oaks, 1982, 17–34.

Brody, Robert. *The Geonim of Babylonia and the Shaping of Medieval Jewish Culture*. New Haven: Yale University Press, 1998.

Brumberg-Kraus, Jonathan. "Meat-Eating and Jewish Identity." *AJSR* 24 (1999), 227–62.

Cohen, Shaye J. D. "Patriarchs and Scholarchs." *Proceedings of the American Academy for Jewish Research* 48 (1981), 57–86.

Diqduqei Sofrim: The Babylonian Talmud with Variant Readings. Tractates Yebamot, Ketubot, Nedarim, Sotah. Edited by Moshe Hershler and Avraham Liss. Jerusalem: Institute for the Complete Israeli Talmud, 1977–91.

Drijvers, H. J. W. "The School of Edessa." In *Centres of Learning: Learning and Lo-*

cation in Pre-Modern Europe and the Near East, edited by H. J. W. Drijvers and A. MacDonald. Leiden: Brill, 1995, 49–59.

Elman, Yaakov. "Orality and the Redaction of the Babylonian Talmud." *Oral Tradition* 14/1 (1999), 52–99.

Elman, Y., and Gershoni, I. "Introduction." In *Transmitting Jewish Traditions: Orality, Textuality, and Cultural Diffusion,* edited by Y. Elman and I. Gershoni. New Haven: Yale University Press, 2000, 1–25.

Fraenkel, Yonah. *Iyyunim be'olamo haruhani shel sipur ha'aggada.* Tel-Aviv: Hakibutz Hameuhad, 1981.

Friedman, Shamma. "La'aggada hahistorit batalmud habavli." In *Saul Lieberman Memorial Volume,* edited by Shamma Friedman. New York: Jewish Theological Seminary, 1993, 119–63.

———. "Pereq ha'isha rabba babavli." In *Mehqarim umeqorot,* edited by H. Dimitrovksi. New York: Jewish Theological Seminary, 1977, 277–441.

———. "Uncovering Literary Dependencies in the Talmudic Corpus." In *The Synoptic Problem in Rabbinic Literature,* edited by Shaye J. D. Cohen. Providence: Brown Judaica Series, 2000, 35–57.

Gafni, Isaiah. "Expressions and Types of 'Local Patriotism' among the Jews of Babylonia." *Irano-Judaica II,* edited by S. Shaked and A. Netzer. Jerusalem: Yad Izhaq Ben-Zvi, 1990, 63–72.

———. "The Institution of Marriage in Rabbinic Times." *The Jewish Family: Metaphor and Memory,* edited by David C. Kraemer. New York: Oxford University Press, 1989, 31–30.

———. *The Jews of Babylonia in the Talmudic Era: A Social and Cultural History.* Jerusalem: Shazar Center, 1990.

———. *Land, Center and Diaspora: Jewish Constructs of Antiquity.* Sheffield: Sheffield Academic Press, 1997.

———. "Nestorian Literature as a Source for the History of the Babylonian *Yeshivot.*" *Tarbiz* 51 (1981–82), 567–76 (Hebrew).

———. " 'Yeshiva' and 'Metivta.' " *Zion* 43 (1978), 12–37 (Hebrew).

Ginzberg, Louis. *Geonica.* New York: Jewish Theological Seminary, 1909.

Goodblatt, David. *The Monarchic Principle.* Tübingen: Mohr, 1994.

———. *Rabbinic Instruction in Sasanian Babylonia.* Leiden: Brill, 1975.

Grossman, Avraham. "From Father to Son: The Inheritance of the Spiritual Leadership of the Jewish Communities in the Early Middle Ages." *Zion* 50 (1985), 189–220 (Hebrew).

Halivni, David Weiss. *Meqorot umesorot.* 5 vols. Tel-Aviv: Devir, and Jerusalem: Jewish Theological Seminary, 1968–94.

———. *Midrash, Mishnah, and Gemara: The Jewish Predilection for Justified Law.* Cambridge: Harvard University Press, 1986.

Herman, Geoffrey. *Hakohanim bebavel bitequfat hatalmud.* Master's thesis, Hebrew University, 1998.

Hezser, Catherine. *Form, Function and Historical Significance of the Rabbinic Story in Yerushalmi Neziqin.* Tübingen: J. C. B. Mohr, 1993.

———. *The Social Structure of the Rabbinic Movement in Roman Palestine.* Tübingen: J. C. B. Mohr, 1997.

Iggeret rav sherira gaon. Edited by B. M. Lewin. Berlin, 1921.

Jacobs, Louis. *Structure and Form in the Babylonian Talmud.* Cambridge: Cambridge University Press, 1991.

Jastrow, Marcus. *A Dictionary of the Targumim, the Talmud Babli and Yerushalmi and the Midrashic Literature.* Reprint. New York: Jastrow Publishers, 1967.

Kalmin, Richard. *The Sage in Jewish Society of Late Antiquity.* London: Routledge, 1999.

Lamentations Rabba. Edition cited is *Midrash eicha rabba.* Edited by Salomon Buber. Vilna, 1899. Reprint, Hildesheim: Georg Olms, 1967.

Levy, Jacob. *Wörterbuch über die Talmudim und Midraschim.* Berlin: B. Harz, 1924.

Lieberman, Saul. *Tosefta Ki-fshuta: A Comprehensive Commentary on the Tosefta.* 11 vols. New York: Jewish Theological Seminary, 1955–88.

Liebes, Yehuda. *Studies in the Zohar.* Translated by A. Schwartz et al. Albany: State University of New York Press, 1993.

Meir, Ofra. *Rabbi Judah the Patriarch: Palestinian and Babylonian Portrait of a Leader.* Tel-Aviv: Hakibbutz Hameuhad, 1999 (Hebrew).

Midrash bereshit rabba. Edited by J. Theodor and H. Albeck. 3 vols. Berlin, 1912–36. Reprint, Jerusalem, 1965.

Midrash vayiqra rabba. Edited by Mordechai Margulies. Jerusalem, 1953–60. Reprint, New York: Jewish Theological Seminary, 1993.

Neubauer, Adolf, ed. *Mediaeval Jewish Chronicles and Chronological Notes.* Oxford: Clarendon Press, 1887–95.

Neusner, Jacob. *A History of the Jews in Babylonia.* 3rd ed. Leiden: Brill, 1965–70. Reprint, Chico, Calif.: Scholars Press, 1984.

Oppenheimer, Aharon. *The 'Am Ha-aretz.* Translated by I. H. Levine. Leiden: Brill, 1977.

———. *Babylonia Judaica in the Talmudic Period.* Wiesbaden: Ludwig Reichert, 1983.

Otsar hageonim. Thesaurus of the Gaonic Responsa and Commentaries following the order of Talmudic Tractates. Edited by B. M. Lewin. 13 vols. Haifa, 1928–43 (Hebrew).

Pesiqta derav kahana. Edited by Bernard Mandelbaum. New York: Jewish Theological Seminary, 1987.

Rabbinovicz, Raphaelo. *Diqduqei Sofrim: Variae Lectiones in Mischnam et in Talmud Babylonicum.* 12 vols. Reprint, New York, 1960.

Rappel, Dov. *The Debate over The Pilpul.* Tel-Aviv: Devir, 1979 (Hebrew).

Reines, Chaim. *Torah umusar.* Jersualem: Rav Kook, 1954.

Reinink, G. J. "'Edessa Grew Dim and Nisibis Shone Forth': The School of Nisibis at the Transition of the Sixth–Seventh Century." In *Centres of Learning: Learning and Location in Pre-Modern Europe and the Near East,* edited by H. J. W. Drijvers and A. MacDonald. Leiden: Brill, 1995, 77–78.

Rosenthal, David. "Mesorot erets-yisraeliot vedarkan lebavel." *Cathedra* 92 (1999), 30–36.

Rubenstein, Jeffrey L. *Talmudic Stories: Narrative Art, Composition, and Culture.* Baltimore: Johns Hopkins University Press, 1999.

Satlow, Michael. *Jewish Marriage in Antiquity.* Princeton: Princeton University Press, 2001.

Shapira, Hayyim. "The Deposition of Rabban Gamaliel—Between History and Legend." *Zion* 64 (1999), 5–38 (Hebrew).

Sifre to Deuteronomy. Edition cited is *Sifre devarim.* Edited by Louis Finkelstein. New York: Jewish Theological Seminary, 1983.

Sokoloff, Michael. *A Dictionary of Jewish Palestinian Aramaic of the Byzantine Period.* Ramat-Gan: Bar Ilan University Press, 1990.

Soloveitchik, Haym. "Rabad of Posquieres: A Programmatic Essay." In *Studies in the History of Jewish Society in the Middle Ages and in the Modern Period,* edited by I. Etkes and Y. Salmon. Jerusalem: Magnes, 1980, 7–41.

Sperber, Daniel. "On the Unfortunate Adventures of Rav Kahana: A Passage of Saboraic Polemic from Sasanian Persia." In *Irano-Judaica,* edited by S. Shaked. Jerusalem: Yad Izhaq Ben-Zvi, 1982, 83–100.

Steinmetz, Devora. "Must the Patriarch Know 'Uqtzin? The *Nasi* as Scholar in Babylonian *Aggada.*" *AJSR* 23 (1998), 163–90.

Sussmann, Yaakov. "Veshuv lirushalmi neziqin." In *Mehqerei talmud I,* edited by Y. Sussmann and D. Rosenthal. Jerusalem: Magnes, 1990, 55–134.

Tishby, Isaiah. *The Wisdom of the Zohar.* Translated by D. Goldstein. Oxford: Oxford University Press, 1989.

Urbach, Ephraim. *Baalei hatosafot.* 4th ed. Tel-Aviv: Bialik, 1980.

———. *The Sages: Their Concepts and Beliefs.* Translated by I. Abrahams. Jerusalem: Magnes, 1979.

Valler, Shulamit. *Woman and Womanhood in the Stories of the Babylonian Talmud.* Translated by Betty Rozen. Atlanta: Scholars Press, 1999.

Vööbus, Arthur. *History of the School of Nisibis.* Louvain: Secretariat du CorpuSCO, 1965.

———. *The Statutes of the School of Nisibis.* Stockholm: Estonian Theological Society in Exile, 1962.

Wald, Stephen G. *BT Pesahim III: Critical Edition with Comprehensive Commentary.* New York: Jewish Theological Seminary, 2000.

Wolfson, Elliot. "Eunuchs Who Keep the Sabbath: Becoming Male and the Ascetic Ideal in Thirteenth-Century Jewish Mysticism." In *Becoming Male in the Middle Ages,* edited by J. J. Cohen and B. Wheeler. New York: Garland Publishing, 1997, 151–85.

———. "Female Imaging of the Torah: From Literary Metaphor to Religious Symbol." In *Circle in the Square*. Albany: State University of New York Press, 1995, 1–28.

Yankelevitch, Raphael. "Mishqalo shel hayihus hamishpahti behevra hayehudit be'erets-yisrael bitequfat hamishna." In *Uma vetoldoteha,* edited by M. Stern. Jerusalem: Shazar Institute, 1983, 156–62.

Yarshater, Ehsan. "Introduction," and "Iranian National History." In *The Cambridge History of Iran*. Vol. 3, *The Seleucid, Parthian and Sasanian Periods,* edited by Ehsan Yarshater. Cambridge: Cambridge University Press, 1983, xvii–lxxv, 359–480.

General Index

Source Index